The Parents'
BOOK
OF FACTS

The Parents'

BOOK
OF FACTS

*Child Development
from Birth to Age Five*

Tom and Nancy Biracree

New York • Oxford

The Parents' Book of Facts: Child Develpment from Birth to Age Five

Copyright © 1989 by Tom Biracree and Nancy Biracree

Facts On File,® Inc.
460 Park Avenue South
New York, New York 10016

Library of Congress Cataloging-in-Publication Data

Biracree, Tom, 1947-
    The parents' book of facts: child development from birth
to age five / by Tom and Nancy Biracree.
        p.   cm.
    Includes index.
    ISBN 0-8160-1412-4
    1. Child development.   2. Infants (Newborn)   3. Infants.
4. Toddlers.   5. Preschool children.   I. Biracree, Nancy.
II. Title
HQ767.9.B55   1989
155.4—dc19

                                                            88-21177

British CIP data available on request

Jacket Design by Catherine Hyman
Composition typeset by Maxwell Photographics
Printed in the United States of America

10 9 8 7 6 5 4 3 2 1

CONTENTS

v

Authors' Note

Throughout this book, we've used masculine pronouns when writing about a child's development. We chose to use one gender for the sake of consistency and to avoid the awkwardness of such constructions as "he or she may begin to show a preference for his or her right or left hand . . ." Whenever masculine pronouns appear, the information provided applies equally to male and female children.

This book is dedicated to our son Ryan, and the other young children in our family: Erin, Lucy Star, and Katie. You inspired this book and make our lives richer every day.

Introduction

The Parents' Book of Facts is a comprehensive book of facts about how, why, and when children grow from birth to age 5. Its purpose is to provide parents and others who work with or care for young children with a complete description of a child's physical, intellectual, social, emotional, and moral development.

This book stems from our experience first as parents, then as the creators and administrators of a preschool program. As authors, one of our first responses to the prospect of becoming parents was to quickly assemble a library of over 100 books on the subject. These books could be divided into three types:

1. Child care books, which explained the details of caring for the everyday needs of infants and young children.
2. Medical books, which covered the nutrition and health care of infants and young children.
3. Parenting books, which presented advice on techniques of raising and educating young children.

Many of these books were interesting and useful. But as we became more and more fascinated by the complex process by which our son and the babies of our friends were developing, the more dissatisfied we were with the factual content of the parenting and child care books. They were filled with advice, anecdotal descriptions of children at various ages, and short lists of developmental milestones. However, we found ourselves looking through dozens of books to find the answers to such questions as exactly what can a 6-month-old see, and how does a 1-year-old's stream of sounds relate to his language development.

Our need for facts became more acute when our small play group blossomed into a formal preschool program for toddlers. In doing research to develop our program, we found several college- and graduate-level textbooks on the subject, but we couldn't find any child development book specifically aimed at parents and the burgeoning number of adults without college-level child development training who were working as care givers for young children in day care centers, preschool programs, in foster care, or in private homes. So we began the research that became the *Parents' Book of Facts*.

This book, the result of our extensive research, is a complete distillation of the essential facts of child development from birth to age five. We're certain that the book will allow you to enjoy and evaluate the development of your own children or children under your care, as well as giving you the solid knowledge to intelligently weigh the advice and opinions expressed in child rearing books and offered by child care professionals. Because this book also explains the major theories, issues, and even language used in developmental psychology, it also prepares the reader for advanced courses or readings in child development. We hope you find the book both useful and entertaining.

What Is Child Development?

Child development is the study of how, why, and when children grow and change over the long course of time between conception and adulthood. The goal of professionals in this field—who are called *developmental psychologists*—is to identify, describe, explain, and predict the physical, social, intellectual, emotional, and moral life course of children.

Why should parents, day care professionals, and other care givers have some knowledge of the major theories and issues of child development? One important and obvious reason is that the more they know about child growth and behavior, the better they'll be at guiding, directing, and encouraging a child's development. Although there are plenty of experts to consult—pediatricians, nurses, psychologists, teachers, school administrators, and the authors of the hundreds of books on parenting—a child's care givers are experts, too—experts on that specific child. The best care givers are those knowledgeable enough to sift through the often conflicting advice of professionals to take the best course of action for the child under their care.

A second and equally important reason to find out more about child development is that it makes raising and caring for a child more fun. Think about knowledge in relation to leisure activities—the more you know about baseball, the more you enjoy watching games; the more you know about ballet, the more you enjoy watching a performance. New parents, in particular, find that their child dominates almost all of their time. That time is a lot more fun if you're a "fan" of your own baby.

Finally, knowledge of child development allows detection or prevention of developmental problems. *Every* child encounters obstacles in the process of growing up, whether physical, emotional, intellectual, or social. The sooner the problems are detected, the easier they are to solve.

SOME IMPORTANT ISSUES IN CHILD DEVELOPMENT THEORIES

Raising children can be a difficult process, so it's understandable for parents and other care givers to seek out definitive "answers" to tough problems. Because all parents want their child to be a genius, to have lifelong good health, to stay away from the temptations of drugs, they are attracted to "experts" who peddle programs "guaranteed" to accomplish those goals.

Before following any advice, however, parents must distinguish between fact and opinion. A useful distinction is that a theory is an opinion that attempts to explain the facts. The best theories are based on the best facts. Unfortunately, some so-called child development experts have developed theories based on a few facts or limited research. The danger in these theories is that they make sense to the casual observer—just as the theory that the sun revolves around the earth made sense to countless generations who didn't have telescopes. Similarly, a child development program that showcases a few 2 year-olds-who can translate flash cards in Japanese can't demonstrate that it can turn every child into a genius without hard research that shows that such children do in fact grow up to have superior intelligence—and without research that shows the program has no detrimental effects on the emotional, social, and physical development of the children.

One purpose of this book is to provide parents and others who work with young children with as many facts as possible so they can choose for themselves which advice, opinions, and theories best apply to children under their care. In addition to facts, however, it's useful to have some background in the kinds of issues with which child development experts have been struggling for centuries:

1. "Nature versus nurture." This oldest of all controversies has to do with whether specific traits are due to heredity or the environment in which the child is raised. For example, arguments still rage about whether high (and low) intelligence is primarily a result of genetics, or whether parental influence and good schooling play a larger role. In recent decades, most experts have come to believe that both factors play a role in intelligence and temperament. Current research seems to hint that the environment plays a larger role in intelligence

than was previously thought, and that heredity plays a larger role in temperament.

2. "Continuous versus stepwise change." Some psychologists see development as a gradual, continuous sequence of events. Others see growth taking place in stops and starts. Under this theory, sometimes development takes place very rapidly and sometimes a child goes through an extended period of little or no growth.

3. "Maturation versus learning." Maturation signifies that certain events are brought about by genetically programmed growth and development. Learning indicates that changes are produced by outside influences. This issue is at the core of many controversies—for example, whether or not it's possible to teach an infant to walk before he's "ready" to walk.

4. "Inner directed versus outer directed." Some psychologists see young children as passively molded by what they experience. Others believe that children are motivated by something inside themselves to actively choose certain activities or experiences over others.

All these controversies are centuries old, and the debate on each continues today. In all likelihood, no definitive answer to every question about child development will be found. The process by which a human being matures from conception to adulthood is so complex that it's impossible to isolate all the variables for study. Our investigation of behavior is also limited by ethical issues and concern for privacy and human dignity, which prohibits placing children under constant observation or making them available for unlimited testing and experiments.

The fact that these controversies are ultimately unsolvable doesn't mean that the debate has no value. Indeed, passionate disagreement has always led to innovative research that continues to cast light on every side of every issue. For example, researchers who emphasize hereditary influences on human behavior continue to decipher the mysteries of genetic coding, while their counterparts who favor the "nurture" side of the controversy have been doing landmark research on the early environments of children who grew into exceptionally talented adults. Everyone interested in children has benefited from all these discoveries.

1
Your Newborn Baby

The Newborn's Appearance

Most first-time parents are shocked by the appearance of their newborn baby. Instead of the cherubic infant they've seen in so many pictures, they hold in their arms a misshapen little creature who looks as though he's been through a prize fight. Although parents may peer anxiously for signs of family resemblance, they find that their newborn looks a lot more like the other babies in the nursery than like Mom or Dad.

The reasons for this rather strange appearance are twofold: one, the trauma of squeezing down the birth canal, pummeled by the 30-pounds-per square inch force of contractions; two, the abrupt change from a cozy aquatic world to the very different environment outside the womb.

Below, we're going to take you on a tour of a newborn's body, describing what he'll look like, how his vital systems work, and how he senses the new world into which he's suddenly emerged. This knowledge is the starting point for one of the most fascinating of human experiences—observing the miraculous way in which an infant grows and develops.

SIZE

The average American newborn weighs 7 to 7.5 pounds, measures between 19 and 21 inches long, and has a head circumference of 13.7 inches. Newborn boys, on the average, are heavier and longer than girls, and firstborns tend to be smaller than subsequent children. For a normal baby, size at birth is not an indication of eventual adult size, but rather a function of heredity and the size of the mother.

Below is a table showing percentiles of weight, length, and head circumference for boys and girls at birth: For example, if a baby boy

1

WHAT YOU SHOULD KNOW ABOUT . . .

HOW MANY BABIES ARE BEING BORN

There are about 4 million babies born in the United States each year. About 2% of babies are multiple births (primarily twins).

The most American births ever recorded in one year was 4,300,000 in 1957—15% more babies than the 3,731,000 that entered the world in 1986. Those 1986 births averaged:

310,917	births a month
71,750	births a week
10,250	births a day
427	births an hour
7	births a minute

Of all babies born:

42%	were first babies
33%	were second babies
15%	were third babies
6%	were fourth babies
4%	were fifth or higher number babies

How many of these babies were twins or triplets? The natural occurrence of multiple births has been:

Twins	1 in 90 births
Triplets	1 in 9,000 births
Quadruplets	1 in 900,000 births
Quintuplets	1 in 85,000,000 births

---

weighs 8.0 pounds at birth, he's heavier than 75% of all baby boys; if a baby boy weighs 6.5 pounds at birth, he's heavier than 25% of all baby boys.

BOYS: Percentiles

	5%	10%	25%	50%	75%	90%	95%
Length (inches)	18.25	18.75	19.25	20.0	20.5	21.0	21.5
Weight (pounds)	5.5	6.25	6.5	7.25	8.0	8.5	9.25
Head Circum. (inches)	12.75	13.0	13.25	13.75	14.0	14.5	14.75

WHAT YOU SHOULD KNOW ABOUT . . .

WHO'S HAVING BABIES

It may surprise you to know that the median age of all mothers in 1986 was 25.9 years, less than 5 months older than the median age of mothers in 1960. Although there's been a great deal of publicity about women in their 30s having babies, the percentage of all babies born to women aged 30 and over was 26.2%, compared with 26.6% in 1960.

By age of the mother, the percentage of babies born was:

Under 18	6.7%	30-34	18.8%
18-24	35.7%	35-39	6.1%
25-29	31.3%	Over 40	1.4%

The major age difference between 1960 and the 1980s was that women—especially college-educated women—waited longer to have their first babies. The median age of women giving birth to first babies was 23.3, compared with 22.0 in 1960. The median age of women with four or more years of college at first birth, however, was 28.8 years in 1984. Forty-four percent of all mothers with four years of college or more had their first babies at age 30 or older, compared with just 11% of mothers with a high school diploma. Although women with at least one year of college made up only 40% of all women aged 30 to 44, they accounted for 71% of the first babies born to that age group.

Family income had the same relationship to age of childbirth as did education. Women aged 18 to 29 with incomes of $35,000 or more had the lowest childbirth rate of any income group, while women aged 30 to 44 with family incomes of $35,000 or more had the highest birth rate of any income group. Forty-two percent of first births to families with incomes over $35,000 were to women aged 30 to 44.

How many children were women having? By race, the expected lifetime births of married women 18 to 34 years old were:

Number of Children, By Race

Number of children	White (%)	Black (%)	Spanish Origin (%)
None	6.4	3.6	4.1
One	12.6	14.1	9.1
Two	49.8	46.1	40.2
Three	22.2	21.8	26.0
Four or more	9.0	14.5	20.5

The birth rate—that is, the number of babies born per 1,000 women aged 15 to 44—plummeted since its peak in the late 1950s. In 1985, the birth rate was 68.6, less than half the 1957 rate. Most of the drastic decline in childbearing took place between 1960 and 1970, with the rate virtually unchanged since 1975.

WHAT YOU SHOULD KNOW ABOUT . . .

WHERE AND HOW BABIES ARE BORN

In 1986, 3,693,000 babies were delivered by physicians in hospitals; 10,000 were delivered by physicians at the mother's home; and 28,000 were delivered by midwives or arrived with no professional assistance at all.

In 1986, 21.1% of all babies were delivered by cesarean section, compared with just 5.5% of all babies in 1970. The percentage of cesarean births rose with age of the mother, from a low of 16.5% of babies born to women under age 20 to a high of 28.7% of babies born to women age 35 and older. The National Center of Health Statistics projects that the percentage of cesarean deliveries could rise to 40% of all births by the year 2000.

While some experts believe that many cesarean deliveries were unnecessary, this increase may have been one reason that the deaths of women during delivery or as a result of postnatal complications dropped from 21.5 per 1,000 women in 1970 to 8.0 per 1,000 women in 1983. The death rate for infants in the first 28 days of life fell from 15.1 per 1,000 in 1970 to 7.3 per 1,000 in 1983.

GIRLS: Percentiles

	5%	10%	25%	50%	75%	90%	95%
Length (inches)	17.75	18.25	19.0	19.75	20.0	20.5	20.75
Weight (pounds)	5.25	5.75	6.5	7.0	7.75	8.0	8.5
Head Circum. (inches)	12.75	13.0	13.25	13.5	13.75	14.0	14.25

Low Birth Weight

Babies who weigh less than 5.5 pounds (2,500 grams) are considered low-birth-weight babies. Low birth weight occurs for one or both of the following reasons. The first is *prematurity*. The American Academy of Pediatrics designates as premature an infant who has developed in utero for less than 38 weeks. Between 5% and 10% of the babies born in the United States are premature, about 7% of white babies and 18% of nonwhite babies. The likelihood of complications and death are directly related to how premature the infant is: the death rate is one in ten for babies born earlier than 33 weeks and/or who weigh less than 4.5 pounds.

WHAT YOU SHOULD KNOW ABOUT . . .

WHEN BABIES ARE BORN

Because substantially more babies have been born in August and September than any other months, you'd think there must be something extraromantic about the Thanksgiving and Christmas holiday seasons. But studies show that a significant majority of parents want to have a baby in the springtime. Unfortunately, they underestimate the amount of time necessary to become pregnant. The result: proportionately, the fewest babies are actually born in April and May.

When you look at days of the week, most babies have been born on Tuesdays, followed by the other weekdays, with approximately the same number of births. Fifteen percent to 20% fewer babies have been born on weekends, primarily because doctors don't schedule cesarean sections or induced labor on the weekends.

The second reason for low birth weight is that a baby is *small for gestational age (SGA)*; that is, the baby is below the third percentile in weight, height, and head circumference even though the time in utero may have been normal. About 2% of babies born in the United States are SGA, and they account for 70% of all infant deaths.

The survival rate for low-birth-weight babies has risen greatly in recent years. Those rates are:

Birth Weight	% Surviving
4.4 - 5.5 lbs.	99
3.3 - 4.4 lbs.	94
2.2 - 3.3 lbs.	82
Below 2.2 lbs.	47

Although current research indicates that most premature infants will catch up developmentally to their peers by age 5 or 6, about one-third suffer from a mental or motor function handicap. Recent studies have also shown, however, that providing stimulation to low-birth-weight babies can minimize future developmental problems. The more these infants are held, cuddled, rocked, massaged, and talked to, the stronger and healthier they tend to become.

High Birth Weight

Babies born at full term who weigh over 8.8 pounds are considered *large for gestational age (LGA)*. These infants have an increased risk of trauma or injury during vaginal delivery, so a much higher percentage of mothers of LGA babies undergo cesarean sections.

SKIN

Skin Condition

The skin of a newborn is covered by a white, cheeselike substance called *vernix caseosa*. The vernix, which is made up of dead skin and oil from skin glands, forms about 3 months before birth to protect the developing glands and nerve cells on the skin. If the vernix is rubbed in or naturally absorbed, the newborn's skin is soft and smooth for twenty-four to forty-eight hours. Then the skin often becomes dry and flaky as the top layer of skin peels off. This process takes about a week.

Complexion

All newborns, even black babies, have a very ruddy complexion. The reason is that their blood contains about 20% more red blood cells and 50% to 70% more hemoglobin than that of a 3-month-old infant.

When a newborn gets slightly chilled, his skin becomes mottled or blotchy, and his hands and feet may turn slightly blue. Both are the result of an immature circulatory system and gradually become less intense as the baby ages.

Birthmarks

About 40% of babies are born with what's called a birthmark, or *hemangioma*, a cluster or growth of small blood vessels on or under the skin.

The most common is the *salmon patch*, salmon red specks or patches on the nape of the neck, across the bridge of the nose, or on the upper eyelid. Often called "stork bites," these marks usually disappear by the first birthday.

The *mongolian spot*, a bluish stain most commonly appearing on the lower back and buttocks, was found in a recent study on almost all Oriental and black babies, on half of Hispanic babies, and on 9% of white babies. This birthmark almost always disappears by age 2 or 3.

Port-wine stains are flat red or purplish marks ranging from patches less than an inch in diameter to large marks covering an arm, shoulder, or part of the face. These marks usually fade with age, but rarely disappear entirely.

About 10% of all babies—more frequently girls—develop *strawberry marks*. These bright red marks are seldom present at birth, but they soon grow rapidly, reaching peak size at 6 to 8 months of age. Later, the color changes from bright red to dark red, and the marks begin to shrink. One-third of all strawberry marks are gone by age 3, 70% disappear by age 6, and 90% are gone by age 9.

WHAT YOU SHOULD KNOW ABOUT . . .

BABY NAMES

According to the Facts On File Dictionary of First Names, the most common names given to babies in the 1980's are:

Boys		Girls	
White	*Nonwhite*	*White*	*Nonwhite*
Michael	Michael	Jennifer	Tiffany
Matthew	Christopher	Sarah	Crystal
Christopher	James	Jessica	Erica
Brian	Brandon	Amanda	Ebony
David	Anthony	Nicole	Latoya
Adam	Robert	Ashley	Candice
Andrew	Jason	Megan	Jennifer
Daniel	David	Melissa	Brandi
Jason	William	Katherine	Nicole
Joshua	Brian	Stephanie	Danielle

Fashion in selecting names changed most for girls—not a single girl's name on the recent list was on the list of most popular girls' names for 1950 (when Linda and Mary topped the list) or the 1925 list (when Mary and Barbara were on top). Boys' names on the 1950 list that are still popular are Michael and David. The name Robert headed the boys' list in both 1950 and 1925.

Popularity of names does vary by region of the country, however. The Gerber Products Company found that the most popular names by region were:

Region	*Most Popular* *Boy's Name*	*Most Popular* *Girl's Name*
Northeast	Matthew	Haley
Midwest	Ryan	Katherine
South	Robert	Jessica
West	Brandon	Nicole

Birth-Related Marks

A newborn baby may have bruises, redness, scrapes, and even sores caused by the intense pressure of being squeezed against the mother's bones on the trip down the birth canal and, possibly, by a doctor's forceps. The only birth-related marks that may last for some time are hard, purplish lumps that result from fat being squeezed between the baby's bones and the mother's bone. These lumps may persist for a month or more.

WHAT YOU SHOULD KNOW ABOUT . . .

INHERITIED PHYSICAL CHARACTERISTICS

As everyone learns in high school biology, all human beings develop accord-ing to instructions contained in the genes. Many of these instructions, such as those that determine the shapes of our hearts, the number of fingers on our hands, the operation of the kidneys, etc., are virtually identical from person to person. Some, however, such as those that determine hair color, eye color, and size of nose, do vary and are responsible for giving each of us a distinct physical appearance.

All genes are passed to each of us in pairs, one from each parent. In 1866, an Austrian monk named Gregor Mendel published a set of rules that determine how variable characteristics are inherited. Mendel found that certain characteristics could be described as either dominant or recessive; that is, when a gene for a dominant characteristic was passed along, it always prevailed over a gene for a recessive characteristic.

For example, long eyelashes are dominant and short eyelashes are recessive. Geneticists use a capital letter to express a dominant gene and a lowercase letter to express a recessive gene. Let's call the gene for long eyelashes E and the gene for short eyelashes e. A person will have long eyelashes if his or her genetic pair for that characteristic is either EE or Ee. He or she will have short eyelashes only if the pair is ee.

Genes are passed to offspring according to the laws of probability. It's obvious that if one parent has two dominant genes, EE, no offspring can have short eyelashes, even if the other parent has two recessive genes, ee. The reason is that every offspring will inherit one dominant gene, and have the gene pair Ee.

Two parents with long eyelashes can have a child with short eyelashes if both have a recessive gene. If they have four children, the laws of probability state that the genetic pairings of those children would be:

Parent Ee		*Parent* Ee	
Child EE	*Child* Ee	*Child* Ee	*Child* ee

In other words, only one child in four would be likely to have short eyelashes. However, it's possible that a recessive trait might not appear for two or more generations, simply because of chance. This is a little easier to understand if it's compared to tossing a coin, another activity governed by the laws of probability. Those laws state the probability is that, over the long run, an equal number of coins will come down heads and tails. However, in the short run, it's possible that ten heads in a row could appear. For the same reason, dark-haired parents and grandparents can be startled by a blond-haired baby.

In addition to chance, another factor that complicates predicting the physi-cal appearance of an offspring is that some characteristics are determined by a combination of several genes. Examples of such characteristics are eye color and skin color. Although certain general types of skin and eye color are dominant, differences in the exact combinations of several genes can produce many shades of skin and eye color within a family.

What are the major dominent and recessive characteristics? Many are listed below:

Dominant	Recessive

EYE CHARACTERISTICS

Brown, hazel or green	Blue
Astigmatism and farsightedness	Normal
Normal	Nearsightedness
Long lashes	Short lashes
Tendency to cataracts	Normal

NOSE CHARACTERISTICS

High convex bridge	Straight or convex bridge
Narrow bridge	Broad bridge
Straight tip	Upturned tip
Flaring nostrils	Narrow nostrils

EARS

Free earlobe	Attached earlobe

OTHER FACIAL TRAITS

Full lips	Thin lips
Normal chin	Recessive chin
Dimpled chin	Undimpled chin
Dimpled cheeks	Undimpled cheeks
High cheekbones	Normal cheekbones
Freckled	Nonfreckled

HAIR

Dark	Blonde
Nonred	Red
Kinky	Curly
Curly	Straight
Male baldness	Normal
Normal hair loss	Female baldness
White forelock	Normal
Premature grayness	Normal
Abundant hair on body	Sparse body hair
Heavy, bushy eyebrows	Normal eyebrows

HANDS, FINGERS, TOES

Index finger longer than ring finger (males)	Ring finger longer
Ring finger longer (females)	Index finger longer
Second toe longer than big toe	Big toe longer than second toe
Hypermobility of thumb	Normal
Right-handedness	Left-handedness

OTHER TRAITS

Dark skin color	Light skin color
A, B, AB blood groups	Group O blood
Tendency to varicose veins	Normal
Normal tongue control	Ability to roll tongue

Jaundice

At least half of all newborn babies exhibit what's called *physiologic jaundice*; that is, their skin and eyes start to turn yellow on the second or third day after birth. The culprit is a substance called *bilirubin*, which is a by-product of the breakdown of red blood cells. Normally, bilirubin is disposed of by the liver, which excretes it into the intestine.

When a baby is in the womb, the mother's liver takes care of his bilirubin level. After birth, the newborn's liver takes over, but in many cases it requires some time for this organ to begin processing at full efficiency. The result is a surplus of bilirubin in the blood, which produces the characteristic yellowing of jaundice.

For most babies, this jaundice is harmless and passes in a couple of days. Your doctor will carefully monitor the level of bilirubin in the blood, however, because extremely high amounts can cause brain damage. If the bilirubin count gets too high, he may have the baby placed under florescent light, which breaks down bilirubin.

Rashes

The external world is a far harsher environment than the womb, so it's natural that the skin of a newborn is very easily irritated. That irritation commonly produces rashes. Parents are often distressed by their newborn's blemished skin, but these rashes are normally harmless.

Perhaps the most common newborn rash is *toxic erythema* (erythema toxicum neonatorum) which is probably caused by the skin's inability to handle irritations. This rash, which begins as flat red spots that become raised as they turn yellow, normally disappears about 2 weeks after birth.

Another common rash, which normally appears on the face, consists of yellowish or pearly white bumps with no reddishness surrounding them. This conditions, known as *milia*, is caused by excessive oil from the vernix that covers the skin at birth.

A third common skin condition is *heat rash* or *prickly heat*. Heat rash normally consists of raised red spots that may be capped by a tiny blister. Heat rash is caused by pores blocked by excessive sweating. It's most common in the summer, but can occur at any time of the year if a newborn is dressed too warmly. The condition disappears when the skin is cooled.

A fourth common rash is *diaper rash*, which appears in the area of the body covered by the diaper. Diaper rash is caused by a combination of the chemicals in urine, bacteria in feces, and heat.

A final normal rash that affects newborns is the only one that's not related to the environment. This rash looks like teenage acne, and it's got the same cause—excessive levels of hormones in the body. It's most common in male newborns, and it disappears within 2 weeks after birth.

HAIR

Body Hair

During the latter part of the first trimester, the fetus begins to grow fine hair all over the body. This hair, called *lanugo*, may generously coat the face, neck, and shoulders of premature infants and, less commonly, may also be seen on full-term babies. This hair usually falls off within a couple weeks after birth.

Head of Hair

Parents hoping for a little blond offspring are often surprised to find their baby is born with a head of thick, black hair. The hair of newborns, however, soon falls out, either gradually or all at once. By about age 6 months, it's replaced by permanent hair that may be totally different in color and texture.

HEAD

At birth, you'll quickly notice two things about a baby's head. One is its size—the head of a newborn makes up about one-fourth of total body length, compared with one-eight of the total body length of adults.

The second, if the baby has been born vaginally, is its misshapen appearance. The reason is that the baby's head has been *molded* as it was squeezed down the birth canal and through the cervix. The result, in most cases, is a head that's narrowed, elongated, and pointed at the rear.

This molding can take place because the newborn's skull bones are separated by six areas of cartilage and tough connective tissue called *fontanelles*. These fontanelles allow the skull bones to shift under pressure. The shifting back to the unmolded shape begins shortly after birth and is usually completed within a week.

Premature babies, whose skull bones are softer than full-term babies, may show some elongation and narrowing of the head because they lie on their sides for long periods in the nursery. This molding, too, largely disappears with time.

Fontanelles

The largest of the fontanelles is a roughly diamond-shaped area at the top of the head. If it isn't covered by hair, you may be able to see it pulse with each heartbeat. This fontanelle is the last to *ossify*, or turn to bone, by 12 to 18 months after birth.

Bumps

No human skull is a perfect sphere, and a baby's head has natural bumps from the time it's formed. The most noticeable bump, in the center rear of the head, is often mistaken by parents for an injury.

FACE

Facial features can also be distorted by pressure inside the womb or during birth, most commonly the pushing of the baby's nose to one side or the other. The features will correct themselves in the days after birth.

One special feature common to all newborns is a pug nose. The bridge of the nose doesn't grow until later, so babies are born with a flat space above the nose that often makes them appear to be crosseyed.

Another thing you'll notice about a newborn's face is that it looks round, even pudgy. Fat pads under the cheeks prevent babies from having the haggard look of adults without teeth.

EYES

Eye Color

A newborn's pigmentation is immature, so almost all are born with blue or grey-blue eyes. If the baby's genes dictate another color—brown, green, etc.—the change will take place during the first year of life.

Appearance

A newborn's eyelids are usually swollen, and about half show red spots in the white of the eye. Both are a result of the pressures of the birth process and both will clear up in the first 2 or 3 weeks.

Tears

A newborn's immature tear-producing system provides moisture to lubricate and clean, but no tears while crying. Emotional tears start appearing between 3 and 12 weeks of age.

MOUTH

Almost all babies are born with small whitish cysts on their gums that are sometimes mistaken for teeth. These cysts disappear in the first 3 months. Only 1 in 1,500 babies is born with an erupted tooth.

NECK

Babies are born with such a short neck that it seems that they have none at all. Since an infant's neck muscles can't support that very large head, this shortness may be nature's way of minimizing the risk of serious damage.

CHEST

Babies have soft bones made up primarily of cartilage, which means their skeleton, including their rib cage, is very flexible. When a newborn takes a breath, a hollow appears in the middle of the chest, as if the whole rib cage were being sucked inward. When the baby exhales, the chest returns to normal. This hollow disappears as the bones of the body harden.

BREASTS

The breasts of both newborn boys and girls are commonly swollen, and may even produce a few drops of milk. The reason is increased hormonal activity in both the mother and infant immediately preceding birth. The swelling gradually diminishes in the weeks after birth.

ABDOMEN

Almost all infants look as if they were born with a pot belly. The reason is that their internal organs—especially the liver—are proportionately large and their abdominal muscles are too weak to hold in the organs.

GENITALIA

The genitalia of both male and female newborns are swollen by the trauma of birth, but this swelling subsides within a week to 10 days. Maternal hormones may enlarge the labia of female infants and produce a harmless vaginal discharge that also disappears a week to 10 days after birth.

LOWER BODY

An infant's lower body appears short and stubby because it makes up a third of his length, compared with half of the length of an adult's body.

FEET

Newborns have a pad of fat between the toe and heel that gives them flat feet. Exercise of the muscles of the foot, especially walking barefoot, gradually builds up a strong arch.

The Newborn's Senses

VISION

At birth, infant eyes are still growing, their retinal structure is incomplete, and their optic nerve is underdeveloped. But they can see, and, as recent research has shown, they have definite preferences in what they like to look at.

WHAT YOU SHOULD KNOW ABOUT . . .

THE NORMAL BABY

Every fertilized egg wages a battle to be born from the moment of conception. For every 100 such conceptions, only 31 live babies are born. Research has shown, however, that this process is a blessing, not a tragedy. Most of the 69 fertilized eggs that don't survive are severely abnormal, about half because of chromosomal deficiencies. Most of these pregnancies end in a spontaneous abortion, many so early that the miscarriage isn't even noticed.

The overwhelming majority of newborns are normal. The incidence of birth defects are approximately:

Type of defect	
Physical malformation	1 in 20 live births
Mental retardation	1 in 30 live births
Genetic disorder	1 in 100 live births
Chromosomal disorder	1 in 200 live births
Congenital deafness	1 in 1,000 live births
Congenital blindness	1 in 2,000 live births

First, newborns can detect brightness; that is, they can tell light from dark. Newborns can also follow a moving light and a moving object, though they track objects moving horizontally better than they do objects moving vertically. They prefer looking at curved lines, rather than straight lines, perhaps one reason babies seem to be born with a predisposition to stare at the human face.

The immaturity of the structure of the eye means that the newborn sees a somewhat blurry world. Their visual acuity has been estimated as 20/150 to 20/290. In adults, the lens of the eye changes shape to focus on objects of different distances; the lens of a newborn's eye doesn't change shape. The result is that the focus of a newborn is "preset" at 7 1/2 inches to 8 inches, or about the distance between the face of an infant cradled in his mother's arms and the mother's face.

Recent research has disproven the long-held belief that infants are color blind. Newborns can distinguish colors, but they have a distinct preference for strong primary colors, especially red and blue.

HEARING

At birth, amniotic fluid in the ear makes it hard for an infant to hear. A few hours later, when the fluid has drained, the newborn has about the same auditory acuity as an adult. Research has shown that in the first 24 hours of life, babies can discriminate between sounds of different tones and duration and can locate objects by sound. Other studies have shown that sensitivity to human speech has been genetically programmed in babies. In particular, babies respond to a female voice more vigorously than any other sound.

TASTE

Newborns can taste, showing a preference for sweet-tasting liquids and turning away from sour or bitter substances. Experts believe their palates are relatively insensitive to subtleties of taste. Since newborns don't get the chance to dine in many French restaurants, this insensitivity doesn't have much effect on their lives.

SMELL

The sense of smell is one of the earliest to be developed prenatally, and at birth babies can discriminate between a variety of odors. Smell is very important in early mother-child bonding. By the age of 1 week, a newborn can distinguish his mother's odor and tell the difference between her breast milk and that of other mothers.

TOUCH

Touch is perhaps the sense most important to infants at birth, as demonstrated by their need to be touched, stroked, cuddled, and swaddled. At birth, a baby's lips and face are the most sensitive to touch, and in succeeding days and weeks sensitivity extends first to the trunk of the body, then the legs and arms.

A newborn is relatively insensitive to a painful stimulus such as a pinprick until about a week after birth, with girl babies being more sensitive to pain than boys.

How a Newborn's Body Works

CIRCULATORY SYSTEM

One of the most amazing changes in an infant's body at birth takes place in routing blood through the heart. In adult bodies, the oxygen-depleted blood enters the right side of the heart, is pumped through the pulmonary arteries to the lungs to expel carbon dioxide and pick up oxygen, then goes back to the left side of the heart to be pumped through the body.

WHAT YOU SHOULD KNOW ABOUT . . .

EVALUATING THE NEWBORN

For obvious reasons, medical personnel in the delivery room are concerned with evaluating a newborn's medical condition right after birth. Dr. Virginia Apgar developed a standardized method of conducting such an evaluation, which is now known as the Apgar score.

The Apgar score is administered 1 minute and 5 minutes after birth. Infants are rated from zero to 2 on each of five important signs, with 10 being the top score and zero the lowest. The scoring system, with the vital signs, is:

Sign	0	1	2
Heart rate	Absent	Below 100	Over 100
Respiratory effort	Absent	Slow, irregular	Good, crying
Muscle tone	Limp	Some flexation of extremities	Active motion
Response to catheter in nose	No response	Grimace	Cough, sneeze
Color	Blue, pale	Body pink, Extremities blue	Completely pink

A score of 7 to 10 immediately after birth is the sign of a healthy baby, and 90% of newborns fall into this range. Newborns with scores of 4 to 6 may need assistance with breathing, and infants scoring lower than 4 require vigorous medical intervention to clear the lungs and airways so breathing can commence.

After the first day of life, a more comprehensive overall evaluation of the neurological condition and temperament of the newborn can be obtained through the Brazelton behavioral assessment scale, which was developed by T. Berry Brazelton, M.D., and published in 1973. Brazelton's scale evaluates the infant in four different ways:

1. *Interactive processes with the environment, such as orientation, alertness, and how easily the baby is consoled.*
2. *Motor processes, such as muscular tone, motor maturity, defensive reactions, hand-to-mouth activity, general activity level, and reflex behavior.*
3. *Processes related to control of physiologic state, such as habituation to a strong light, a rattle, a bell, and a pinprick, as well as self-quieting behavior.*
4. *Response to stress, including tremulousness, changes in skin color, and strength of startle response.*

The Brazelton scale is most useful for detecting neurological and behavioral problems, as well as acquainting parents with their baby's personality. The Brazelton scale can be administered up to six weeks after birth.

In the womb, however, the oxygen needs of the fetus are met by the mother through the umbilical cord, and the lungs don't function. So nature provides a shortcut from the right to the left side of the heart, a hole that physicians call a *shunt*. With the first breath after birth, the body sends a chemical message to the heart, and the shunt begins to close. Until this closure is completed, however, some blood "leaks." The result is that the infant's blood pressure may go up to compensate. The blood pressure may not stabilize until 7 to 10 days after birth, when the shunt is completely closed. When the blood pressure has stabilized, an average reading is 86/54, compared with an average adult reading of 120/65.

The newborn also has a much higher heart rate than an adult. The reason is that an infant has three times more body surface area for his weight than an adult. With more surface area to keep warm, infants burn fuel faster—a newborn burns about 25 calories a day per pound of body weight to keep warm, compared with about 11 calories a day per pound of body weight for an adult. To provide this increased fuel to the body, the heart of a newborn beats much faster than the heart of adult. The heart of a newborn normally beats between 130 and 160 times per minute (compared with 65 to 100 beats per minute for an adult). The heart of a newborn weighs about 84 ounces grams and is relatively larger for the size of his body than the heart of an adult.

RESPIRATORY SYSTEM

You'll notice a newborn breathes much faster than you do—30 to 50 times per minute, compared with 15 to 20 times per minute. One obvious reason is the same as for his faster heart rate—his body burns oxygen more quickly.

A second reason is that it takes a while for a newborn's lungs to work at peak efficiency. Until birth an infant's lungs are collapsed. When he starts to breath, more air tends to get trapped in the upper reaches of the respiratory tract. As a baby grows, proportionately more air reaches the lower lungs, and he has to breath less often.

Newborns also breathe only through their noses; they are unable to breath through their mouths for several weeks after birth. Some researchers believe the reason is that their tongues are too far back in their mouths to allow mouth breathing, while other experts believe newborns haven't developed the reflex that allows mouth breathing. In any case, newborns often sneeze and snort, especially in their sleep, to clear their nasal passages. Parents often mistake this sneezing for a cold.

A severe cold that blocks nasal passages could be very dangerous for a young infant. That may be one reason why natural immunity is passed from the mother to the newborn, reducing the chances of a devastating illness after birth. It's also the reason that newborns should never be exposed to anyone with a cold, even if that person is a relative who's "dying to see the baby." Unfortunately, even with natural immunity and precautions, newborns can get colds. Apart from congenital disorders, respiratory illnesses are the leading cause of hospitalization for young infants.

DIGESTIVE SYSTEM

A baby's digestive system—what goes in and what comes out—is one of a care giver's first major concerns. The most important thing to realize about that system is that at birth it's very much like the baby—it's small, brand-new, physically immature, and it responds best to very gentle handling.

Eating

The small size of the stomach is the major reason why 95% of babies at least occasionally vomit its entire contents. An 8-pound baby's stomach can hold 3 ounces of milk. If the baby takes in a volume of air along with the milk—and most babies do—the stomach will be overextended and everything will come up. The only way to get air out is by burping, which is recommended after every fluid ounce a newborn consumes.

Immaturity of the digestive system is the cause of spitting up, or *reflux*. The problem occurs at the point where the esophagus meets the stomach. When a baby swallows, the end of the esophagus should relax to let the food through, then tighten to prevent it from coming back up. The esophagus of the newborn, however, is immature, and the process occasionally doesn't work properly. The result—spitting up. The best solution for most infants is to keep them upright and handle them gently for twenty to thirty minutes after feeding.

A third problem related to the immaturity of the digestive system is associated with overproduction of gas. Almost every infant has occasional gas pains. In about one in five infants, the discomfort may be the primary cause of *colic*, long, daily bouts of unstoppable crying that can make parents' lives miserable for the first 3 months of their babies' lives.

Elimination

At birth, the lower intestine is filled with a thick, tar like substance called meconium. One study showed that 69% of newborns passed some of this material in the first 12 hours of life, and 94% had a bowel movement by 24 hours. The number of stools varies considerably in the first few days of life, with an average of five per day for both breast- and bottle-fed babies from the third to the sixth day. Traces of meconium may appear in the stools for the first week. After the first week, the average

---

WHAT YOU SHOULD KNOW ABOUT . . .

CIRCUMCISION

In a recent policy statement, the American Academy of Pediatrics stated that "there is no medical indication for routine circumcision of the newborn." In other words, the academy found no evidence that circumcision had any medical benefit. In particular, extensive research has failed to verify the long-held beliefs that circumcision reduces the risk of venereal disease or cancer in either the male or his sexual partners.

Still, an estimated 75% to 90% of male babies are circumcised in the few days following birth. The practice has ritual significance for those of the Jewish and Moslem faiths. The remaining justification for the rest of the procedures is that circumcision will allow the little boy to "look like Daddy" and the other kids.

---

number of stools per day is two to six for a breast-fed baby and one to three for a bottle-fed baby.

URINARY SYSTEM

At birth, 72% of a newborn's weight is water, compared with 60% of an adult's weight. Babies store up extra water in preparation for their entry into the world, probably to compensate for the fluid loss that results in the average newborn dropping 6% in weight after birth. By 1 month of age, the percentage of water in the baby's body will be down to 68%.

In addition to having more water weight, infants also lose four times as much fluid per day as an adult—20% of their total fluids, compared with 5% for adults. Over half this water is voided through urination. The newborn may not urinate for 12 to 24 hours after birth, then urine output increases rapidly from about 2 ounces per day to 10 to 14 ounces per day by the tenth day of life. Replacing this water is extremely important. An infant needs about 2.3 ounces of water per day per pound of body weight, compared with less than half an ounce per pound for an adult.

A newborn's kidneys are quite large in comparison to handle this volume, but they don't operate with the efficiency of adult kidneys for several months. The kidneys have difficulty processing too much protein, one reason why babies shouldn't be given cow's milk, which has three times as much protein as breast milk or formula. The immature kidneys also have trouble processing sodium, which means that salt in a baby's diet can lead to dangerous water retention.

CENTRAL NERVOUS SYSTEM

Full term babies are born during the most important period of brain growth, a span of time that runs from the start of the last trimester of pregnancy through the first 5 months of life. The brain of a newborn weighs about 12.25 ounces, one-quarter of its adult size, and in the first year of life it grows to 31 ounces, two-thirds of adult size. By the end of the first year, every brain cell the baby will ever have has been created.

Cell creation, however, is only the first stage in the development of a mature nervous system. The second stage is the growth of fibers called dendrites and axons that connect the cells with each other. Before nerve impulses can travel efficiently from cell to cell, the fibers have to be insulated, in the same way that an electrical wire must be insulated to prevent short circuits. The insulation is a fatty substance called *myelin*, and this third and final stage of nervous system development is called *myelinization*.

Myelinization begins before birth and continues at a rapid rate during the first 2 years of life. The pattern of myelinization determines the sequence of behavior performed by the infant. Babies can see, hear, taste, touch, and smell at birth because the pathways of sensation are myelinated in the brain before birth. Neurons controlling muscular activity are next and are myelinated from the head down and from the center of the body outward. That's why a baby can control his head long before he can stand.

Different parts of the brain also mature at different rates. The lower brain structures that control basic functions such as breathing, heart rate, and reflexes mature first. The cortex, the top part of the brain, which controls thinking, reasoning, and problem solving, matures later than the limbic system, the midbrain region responsible for emotion. That's why the behavior of young children is more often guided by emotion than logic.

REFLEXES

The normal full-term baby is born with about seventy reflex behaviors. Some of these are vital to survival—breathing, blinking, withdrawal from pain, sneezing, coughing, sucking. Some have little or no clear function.

Still others, which you may find interesting to test, have diagnostic significance for a pediatrician. These reflexes can be elicited by the second day after birth, if the infant isn't hungry, tired, overstimulated, or uncomfortable.

Below is a description of fifteen reflexes present at birth:

The Asymmetrical Tonic-Neck Reflex

Stimulation: Lay your baby on his back.

Reflex:
- Head rotates to one side
- Arm on that side is extended straight out like a fencer's, and leg on that side is also extended
- Arm and leg on opposite side flexed, with fist clenched

How long it lasts: 12 to 18 weeks.

Importance: The asymmetrical tonic-neck reflex produces a good position for breast feeding. It's also the first step in acquiring the ability to orient the head toward a visual target.

Moro's Reflex

Stimulation: Anything that startles the baby—sudden noises, his crib moving, being dropped or grabbed.

Reflex:
- Arms and legs extended
- Thumb and forefinger in a C shape, other fingers extended
- Back arched
- After a moment, arms brought to embrace postion

How long it lasts: 8 to 12 weeks.

Importance: The absence of this reflex has been associated with mental retardation, brain damage, and certain fractures. On the positive side, a strong reflex shows a high correlation with mental and motor proficiency at age 4.

The Neck Righting Reflex

Stimulation: Pull baby on his back and turn his head to one side.

Reflex: The baby responds by turning his shoulders, trunk, and pelvis in the same direction.

How long it lasts: 9 to 10 months.

Importance: Absence is an indication that a low-birth-weight baby is premature rather than small for his gestational age.

The Traction Response

Stimulation: Pull baby from his back to a sitting position.

Reflex: Baby will flex his arms and pull his trunk toward the upright position. His head will lag until about 4 months of age, when he can finally align it with his body.

How long it lasts: Becomes voluntary between 4 and 6 months.

Importance: If absent, or if the head continues to lag after 4 months, central nervous system impairment may be present.

The Tonic Labyrinthine Reflex

Stimulation: Place baby on his stomach, then turn him to his back.

Reflex: When he's on his stomach, his legs will be flexed; when he's on his back, his legs will be extended.

How long it lasts: 4 months.

Importance: Continuance of this reflex after 6 months has been associated with cerebral palsy.

The Positive Supporting Reaction

Stimulation: Hold baby upright, under his arms, and let the soles of his feet touch the floor, a table top, or other solid surface.

Reflex: Baby's hips and legs extend, and his ankles and knees will flex slightly to support his weight. When you lift him, his legs will usually cross because the muscles on the inside of his legs are stronger than those on the outside.

How long it lasts: May persist until voluntary standing occurs.

Importance: A motor dysfunction of the lower limbs may be present if a baby extends his legs totally, with no flex of the knees or ankles.

The Walking Reaction

Stimulation: Hold baby under his arms, his upper body tilted slightly forward, then tilt him so one bare foot is pressed against a solid surface.

Reflex: Baby will make steplike motions resembling well-coordinated walking.

How long it lasts: 2 to 3 months.

Importance: Neuromuscular complications may be present if this reaction doesn't disappear after 4 months.

The Placing Reaction

Stimulation: Hold your baby upright and have someone touch the top of his foot.

Reflex: He'll flex his leg at the knee and hip, as if attempting to place his foot on a surface that isn't there.

How long it lasts: 10 to 12 months.

Importance: Absence of this reaction is associated with spinal cord injury.

Galant's Reflex

Stimulation: Hold baby upright, turn his head to one side, and touch his back on that side.

Reflex: He'll turn his body toward the stimulation.

How long it lasts: 2 to 3 months.

Importance: Absence may indicate spinal cord problems.

The Plantar Grasp Reflex

Stimulation: Grab the heel of your baby's foot, with your thumb touching the sole.

Reflex: Baby will flex all his toes until you let go.

How long it lasts: 8 to 12 months.

Importance: Absence may indicate spinal cord damage.

The Withdrawal Reflex

Stimulation: Touch the sole of your baby's foot.

Reflex: He'll withdraw the foot by flexing his hip, knee, and ankle, and extending his toes.

How long it lasts: 3 to 4 months.

Importance: May be impaired in a baby born in a breech position. Poor or absent reflex may indicate nerve damage.

Babinski's Reflex

Stimulation: Stroke the bottom of baby's foot from the heel to the toe.

Reflex: His toes will fan out and his foot will turn in.

How long it lasts: 6 to 9 months.

Importance: Strength of the reflex is evidence of the maturity of the neuromuscular system.

The Crossed-Extensor Reflex

Stimulation: Lay baby on his back. Extend one leg, then touch the foot of that leg.

Reflex: Baby will flex the other leg, extend it, then draw it toward his stomach.

How long it lasts: 1 to 2 months.

Importance: Absence may indicate spinal cord or nerve damage.

The Rooting Reflex

Stimulation: Stroke baby's cheek lightly from the corner of his mouth toward his ear.

Reflex: He'll turn his head, mouth, and tongue toward the stimulus and begin sucking movements.

How long it lasts: 9 months.

Importance: Vital to a baby's ability to obtain nourishment. Absence indicates severe neurological problem.

WHAT YOU SHOULD KNOW ABOUT . . .

BABIES AND SMOKING

According to the U.S. Public Health Service and the American Academy of Pediatrics, "If someone in your household is smoking, then your baby is smoking, too."

The message: A parent who smokes can be a serious health threat to children, especially babies. Among the research findings compiled by the Centers for Disease Control are:

· *The children of mothers who smoke suffer twice as many lower respiratory illnesses than children of nonsmoking mothers—babies of mothers who smoke are at even more risk*
· *Children living in homes where three packs or more of cigarettes are consumed are much more prone to chronic middle ear disease, which can lead to deafness or to problems in school*
· *Children of smokers have more trouble breathing than children of nonsmokers, posing the threat of chronic lung disease in future years*
· *Spouses of smokers have shown between a 35% and 100% greater risk of lung cancer, and experts project a similar increased risk for children of smokers*

The Darwinian Reflex

Stimulation: Stroke the palm of baby's hand.

Reflex: Baby will make a very strong fist.

How long it lasts: 2 to 3 months.

Importance: Absence indicates neurological problems.

MUSCLES

At birth, an infant has all the muscle fibers he'll ever have. His muscles, however, are immature—the tissue contains largely water, and the muscle mass makes up 20% to 25% of body weight, compared with 40% of the body weight of an adult.

After birth, the muscles begin to grow and change in composition through a combination of exercise and hormonal action. Strength and stamina are added as water in muscle tissue is replaced by protein. The first muscles to develop are in the head and neck, thus head control is the first motor skill accomplished by a newborn.

WHAT YOU SHOULD KNOW ABOUT . . .

TWINS

About one in ninety women who give birth produce twins. About 80% of all twins are fraternal, or dizygotic, twins. The latter term refers to fraternal twins that are born from two separate eggs that are ovulated at the same time and are both fertilized. The double ovulation can sometimes be caused by fertility drugs. More commonly, the release of two eggs is a genetically determined, normal action of the woman's inherited menstrual cycle. That's why fraternal twins often run in families.

Although they're born at the same time, fraternal twins are no more alike genetically than brothers or sisters born at different times.

About one in every five sets of twins are identical, or monozygotic. The birth of identical twins results from one fertilized egg spontaneously duplicating and forming two embryos. These twins either share the same or very similar genes, which is why they look alike. Current evidence suggests that the birth of identical twins is coincidental rather than genetically determined.

Once in about every 80,000 births, the fertilized egg fails to separate after it duplicates, resulting in the birth of cojoined or Siamese twins. The name Siamese results from the fame of Chang and Eng, cojoined twins who were born in Siam (now Thailand) in 1811 and brought to Europe by a British merchant. They spent many years traveling the world under the management of P. T. Barnum. They married, had children, and died within hours of each other at age 63.

The study of both identical and fraternal twins has revealed a great deal of valuable information about the relationship between heredity and environment in the development of children. Traits that are very similar in identical twins but different in fraternal twins are likely to be genetically determined. Traits that are different in both identical and fraternal twins are more likely to be influenced by the environment in which the twins were raised.

BONES

The bones of a baby at birth are composed primarily of soft cartilage. This gives them the flexibility required to adapt to the confinement of the womb and survive the trip down the birth canal. In order for the infant's skeleton to support his weight so he can sit, crawl, stand, or walk, however, the bones must harden, or ossify.

The process of ossification begins with the long bones of the legs and arms before birth. The rate intensifies after birth, but it's not fully completed until about age 25.

The Newborn's Day

His sudden emergence into the world disorients a newborn, but by the third day he has adapted enough to begin establishing a distinct behavioral pattern in his day. Recent research has established that a baby will exhibit six distinct behavioral states during the day.

It's important for you to recognize these states for two reasons. The first is that a baby has different needs during different states. The more you know about a baby's pattern, the better you'll be able to time feedings, respond to the baby's vocalizations, and choose the right time to interact with the little fellow. Second, observing a baby's pattern over a period of time will provide an indication of the kind of temperament the baby will develop.

Of the six behavioral stages, three can be classified as sleep and three as stages of wakefulness.

SLEEP

Sleep dominates the life of a infant. Newborns will spend between 15 and 20 hours per day sleeping, with the average being 16.6 hours. This sleep will be broken up into an average of seven sleep periods a day, lasting 20 minutes to 5 hours.

The three behavioral stages of sleep are:

1. *Active Sleep:* Over the last two decades, sleep researchers have discovered that sleep is really a cycle of several stages that can be divided into two general categories. The first is active sleep, the most distinctive characteristic of which is rapid eye movements (REM). Other characteristics of REM sleep are irregular heart and breathing rates and facial and body movements.

   Active sleep emerges as a distinct pattern in the fetus at about 6 to 1/2 months, and this type dominates the sleep cycle of the infant during the last trimester in the womb and the first months of life. A full-term infant exhibits 50% to 60% active sleep, compared with 20% to 25% in an adult. Researchers theorize that increased brain activity during sleep may compensate for the relative inactivity forced on awake infants by their lack of motor skills. As motor skills develop, the percentage of REM sleep drops.

2. *Quiet Sleep.* Quiet sleep emerges in the fetus about a month after the appearance of active sleep. The characteristics of quiet or non-REM sleep are regular respiration and heart rates and no facial or body movements.

3. *Transitional State.* This state is characterized by drowsy or semidrowsy behavior.

WAKING

A newborn's longest periods of wakefulness reach two hours, but that time frame lengthens with every month of life. The three stages of waking are:

4. *Quiet Awake.* During this state, a baby's eyes are open and he's scanning the area around him, but his body is relatively inactive. This is the period in which the baby is most reponsive to external stimuli, and thus it's the best time for you to interact with him. You have to act quickly, however, since this is the shortest behavioral stage—no more than 10% of a baby's waking time.
5. *Active Awake.* The baby is awake, eyes open, but he's kicking, waving, and squirming. This makes him interesting to watch but difficult to interact with, because his movement interferes with his ability to concentrate on you.
6. *Fussing or Crying.* Crying is a newborn's sole method of communication. At birth, crying is stimulated only by internal stimuli such as hunger, but as the infant learns that crying can make an adult appear, crying becomes a deliberate method of producing contact with caregivers. Just as REM sleep decreases as a child's ability to move his body and limbs increases, the amount of crying decreases as motor and language capacities develop.

For generations, parents were told that going to their babies immediately when they cried could "spoil" the infant, encouraging them to cry more. Numerous recent research studies, however, have proved conclusively that the opposite is true—infants whose parents responded immediately cried dramatically less than infants whose parents were slower to react. Researchers theorize that babies whose care givers respond quickly feel more secure.

Although crying is a normal behavioral stage, it's important to find the most effective soothing techniques to shift a baby back to the quiet awake state. It seems that infants who spend the most time in the quiet awake state develop most quickly.

Research has shown that the most effective soothing technique is holding the baby to your shoulder—one study showed this quieted infants 77% of the time. In order of effectiveness, five other techniques were:

1. Moving the infant horizontally.
2. Moving the infant to a sitting position.
3. Holding the infant to your breast.
4. Holding the infant in an embrace.
5. Talking to the infant only.

WHAT YOU SHOULD KNOW ABOUT . . .

DEFINING AGE GROUPS

Physicians, child psychologists, educators, and others use specific terms that define the age of a child from conception to adulthood. Those terms are:

Prenatal period	
Ovum	*Conception to 14 days*
Embryo	*14 days to 9 weeks*
Fetus	*9 weeks to birth*
Premature infant	*Born earlier than 38 weeks after conception*
Newborn (neonate)	*First 4 weeks of life*
Infant	*First year of life*
Early childhood	*Age 1-6*
Toddler	*Age 1-3*
Preschooler	*Age 3-6*
Late childhood	*Age 6-10 or 12*
Adolescent	
Girls	*Age 10-18*
Boys	*Age 12-20*
Puberty (average)	
Girls	*Age 13*
Boys	*Age 15*

A Newborn's Temperament

Although all babies exhibit all six behavioral states, they differ widely in the amount of time they spend in each state, how rapidly they go from one state to another, how easily stimulation from parents can change their state, and how many changes from one state to another they go through in a day. In other words, every newborn has his own behavioral style—that is, every baby, from birth, has his own temperament.

That may come as a surprise, because for most of this century, child psychology was dominated by a school that believed that every infant was born a blank slate, on which behavior was "imprinted" by his family and society. The main result of this theory was a great deal of guilt, as parents shouldered blame if their babies proved "difficult" in any way.

Today, however, there's a growing awareness that, to a considerable degree, an infant's temperament is inborn, independent of later parental influence. It's very important for parents and other care givers to understand a baby's temperament, for several reasons. First, this knowledge sharpens parents' perceptions and observations of their infants. Second, it helps parents and other care givers to solve problems and anticipate the special needs of infants. Finally, it especially helps parents understand and deal with conflicts between their temperaments and the temperament of their baby.

Psychologists have developed a system of determining infant temperament that looks at nine different categories of behavior. These categories are:

1. *Activity level:* Assessment of the amount, frequency, and tempo of the baby's motor activity.
2. *Rhythmicity:* The regularity of various physical activities such as sleeping, eating, and bowel function.
3. *Approach or withdrawal:* An infant's first response to a new situation, such as a stranger or a new toy.
4. *Adaptability:* An infant's later response to the new situation. For example, picking up a new toy after initially refusing to touch it.
5. *Intensity of reaction:* How mild or intense a reaction—either positive or negative—a baby demonstrates.
6. *Threshold of response:* How strong a stimulus must be to get a response from the infant.
7. *Quality of mood:* The amount of time an infant is happy and friendly, as opposed to the amount of time he's crying or unfriendly.
8. *Distractibility:* How easily an infant is distracted in each behavioral state.
9. *Attention span and persistence:* The length of time an infant will spend pursuing an activity despite having difficulty with it.

One tool that helps parents assess their baby's temperament based on these nine categories is the Carey-McDevitt temperament questionnaire. This questionnaire, which can be completed by parents in twenty-five minutes and scored by a trained professional in fifteen minutes, fits the infant into one of five diagnostic "clusters," of which the three most important are:

1. *"Difficult":* Infants whose schedules lack regularity, who are very active, low in adaptability, intense, difficult to distract, withdrawing, and negative.

2. *"Easy"*: Infants whose schedules are very rhythmic, who are relatively inactive, adaptable, mild, easy to distract, and positive.
3. *"Slow to warm up"*: Infants who are inactive, withdrawing, adapt eventually but slowly, exhibit considerable negative behavior, but who have mild reactions.

The two other clusters are intermediate-difficult and intermediate-easy.

It's important for parents and care givers to realize that these clusters are not permanent labels, but simply indications of one portion of an infant's personality. A "difficult" infant whose parents understand his temperament and needs will become a far more emotionally healthy adult than an "easy" infant whose placidity may lead his parents and other care givers to actually neglect him.

Nourishing the Newborn

When a newborn feeds, more than his body is nourished, because feeding in infancy serves three very important functions. First and foremost, of course, feeding provides vital nutrients at the time of maximum growth—in the first year of life, a baby will triple his weight, increase his length 50%, double the size of his brain, and create every nerve cell he'll ever have. Second, feeding provides physical contact and social stimulation important to the emotional growth of an infant. Third, learning to feed encourages the development of muscle and coordination.

In recent years, researchers have proven conclusively that breast feeding best meets all three of these needs. Virtually all public health authorities and the American Academy of Pediatrics recommend breast feeding. As a result, the percentage of women breast feeding at birth has increased from 24.7% in 1971 to 62.5% in 1984, and the percentage of women breast feeding at 6 months has soared from 5.5% in 1971 to 27.5% in 1984. Those percentages increase dramatically for more educated women: 77.5% of college educated women breast-feed at birth and 40% are still breast feeding at 6 months.

For many parents, however, deciding whether or not to breast-feed and how long to breast-feed are complicated by the physical, emotional, social, and financial needs of the mother and/or pressure from relatives, friends, husband, and employer. The best way to make a choice is to weigh individual circumstances against the facts.

WHAT YOU SHOULD KNOW ABOUT . . .

ANALYZING COW'S MILK, HUMAN BREAST MILK, AND FORMULA

Percentage of Calories Supplied by

	Protein (%)	Fat (%)	Carbohydrate (%)
Breast milk	5	55	40
Formula	8	50	42
Whole cow's milk	20	50	30
2% low-fat cow's milk	25	35	40
Skim cow's milk	40	5	55

Approximate Calories per Ounce

Breast milk	20
Formula	20
Whole cow's milk	20
2% low-fat cow's milk	15
Skim cow's milk	11

Amount of Protein per Quart (in grams)

Breast milk	10 grms
Formula	14 grms
Whole cow's milk	32 grms
2% low-fat cow's milk	32 grms
Skim cow's milk	33 grms

Amount of Fat per Quart (in grams)

Breast milk	43 grms
Formula	34 grms
Whole cow's milk	36 grms
2% low-fat cow's milk	19 grms
Skim cow's milk	2 grms

BREAST FEEDING VERSUS BOTTLE FEEDING

What should you feed your newborn? Mother Nature's answer is breast milk, an elegantly crafted substance formulated by evolution over tens of thousands of years. For much of history, however, humankind has been searching for alternatives to breast milk for mothers unable or unwilling to breast-feed. Infant-feeding devices have been discovered that date back to Roman times. Over the centuries, substitutes for breast milk have included the milk of cows, goats, and other mammals combined with such substances as water, sugar, honey, ground wheat, barley, flour, bread, eggs, and even beer and wine.

Modern baby formula, developed by research into the composition of human breast milk, dates back to about 1915. Today, formulas based on cow's milk and on soybeans are widely considered acceptable and adequate for the feeding of infants. Whole cow's milk, widely used as recently as the 1970s, is strongly discouraged today by the American Academy of Pediatrics.

Why is breast milk best nutritionally? Below is a nutritional comparison between milk, formula, and cow's milk, followed by a discussion of what this means.

Composition Per 100 Milliliters

Nutrient	Breast Milk	Cow's Milk	Milk-based Formula	Soy-based Formula
Calories	77	65	67	67
Protein (g)	1.1	3.5	1.5	1.9
Fat (g)	4.0	3.5	3.8	3.9
Carbohydrate(g)	9.5	4.9	7.7	7.2
Vitamin A (IU)	240	140	212	212
Vitamin D (IU)	22	42	42	42
Vitamin E (IU)	2	0.4	2	2
Vitamin C (mg)	5	1	5.5	5.5
Thiamin (mg)	0.01	0.03	0.06	0.04
Riboflavin (mg)	0.04	0.17	0.09	0.06
Niacin (mg)	0.2	0.1	0.8	0.95
Pyridoxine (mcg)	10	64	40	40
Flacin (mcg)	5.2	5.5	7.5	7.5
Vitamin B-12 (mg)	0.3	4	0.1	0.2
Calcium (mg)	33	118	38	74
Phosphorus (mg)	14	93	37	53
Magnesium (mg)	2.3	1.3	4.6	5.9
Iron (mg)	0.1	Trace	0.15	1.27
Zinc (mg)	4	4	0.4	0.4
Copper (mg)	0.024	0.06	0.05	0.05
Iodine (mcg)	3.0	4.7	10	10

WHAT YOU SHOULD KNOW ABOUT . . .

SUGARS

Sugars are forms of carbohydrates, substances made of molecules combining carbon, hydrogen, and oxygen that provide the basic fuel burned by the body to produce energy. All carbohydrates are broken down by the digestive system into sugars so that they can be absorbed into the bloodstream.

Natural sugars can either be simple sugars (monosaccharides), which are directly absorbed into the bloodstream, or complex sugars (disaccharides), which have to be broken down by the digestive system. Sweetness is a quality of sugars that refers not only to their effect on the taste buds, but also the rapidity of their absorption into the bloodstream. The sweetest sugars are absorbed quickly, providing a burst of energy as the level of sugar in the blood soars. Following this burst, however, fatigue can set in as the blood sugar level plummets. For this reason, nutritionists recommend that a young child should have a diet with slowly absorbing (less sweet) sugars and complex carbohydrates, instead of sweet sugars.

Basic Types of Sugars

Sugar	Sweetness Index	Food Source
Glucose	74	Fruit, honey, corn syrup/sweeteners
Fructose	173	Fruit, honey, corn sweeteners
Galactose	32	Milk
Sucrose (table sugar)	100	Beet sugar, cane sugar
Lactose	16	Milk
Maltose	32	Cereal grains

Breast milk has twice the concentration of lactose as cow's milk, which makes breast milk ideal for an infant's needs. In contrast, glucose and sucrose are added to infant formula to increase the carbohydrate level.

Proteins

Proteins are the building blocks of human tissue. They're broken down into their constituent amino acids in the small intestine, absorbed into the bloodstream, then reconstituted into other proteins as the body grows.

Because babies grow so fast, you might think they'd be better off drinking cow's milk, which has three times the protein of breast milk. But the opposite is true, for two major reasons. First, 82% of the protein in cow's milk is casein proteins, which form a tough, hard curd that's very difficult for a baby's enzymes to digest. In fact, in older infants, cow's milk can cause bleeding in the stomach that may lead to anemia. The protein in breast milk, on the other hand, is primarily whey protein, which forms small, soft curds that are easily broken down and absorbed.

A second reason why cow's milk is not recommended for infants is that excess protein has to be excreted in urine, placing a dangerous strain on a baby's immature kidneys. Breast milk, on the other hand, has exactly the right amount of protein, and it's almost completely absorbed.

What about formula? Cow's-milk formulas are diluted to reduce the protein levels and heat-treated so that the proteins will form soft curds. However, because cow's milk was created to meet the nutritional needs of cows, not humans, the levels of amino acids don't meet human requirements as exactly as breast milk. As a result, a portion of the protein in formula is not absorbed and must be excreted through the kidneys.

One of the amino acids unique to cow's milk is beta-lactoglobulin, which causes allergic reactions in about 7% of babies. These allergic infants must be fed soy-based formulas.

Soy-based formulas contain all the necessary amino acids, but again, not in exactly the right amounts as those in breast milk. The protein in soy-based formulas is also incompletely absorbed, increasing the strain on the kidneys.

Fats

Fat is extremely important because it's a source of concentrated energy infants can hold easily in their small stomachs. Fat makes up only 3% to 4% of milk by weight, but it provides 40% of milk's calories.

Breast milk, cow's milk, and formulas contain about the same amount of fat, but the type of fat varies. Cow's milk contains primarily highly saturated butterfat, which is poorly absorbed by infants. The makers of formulas remove this butterfat and substitute various vegetable oils—coconut, corn, soybean, or safflower—that are more readily absorbed and lower the cholesterol levels in the infant. Still, about 20% of the fat in formulas goes unburned and is excreted.

Babies burn 95% to 98% of the fat in breast milk. Breast milk is high in cholesterol, but researchers theorize that this high level helps infants develop a mechanism to process cholesterol better as adults.

Carbohydrates

Breast milk contains about twice the carbohydrates of cow's milk. The predominate carbohydrate in milk is lactose, which is not a particularly sweet sugar and which is not absorbed directly into the bloodstream. Rather, it's broken down slowly, which provides a steady source of energy.

WHAT YOU SHOULD KNOW ABOUT . . .

COLIC

All babies cry, and most have occasional prolonged periods of crying that may last for an hour or more. About one in five babies, however, regularly cry intensely for four hours or more. This behavior is called colic.

Colic normally begins very suddenly. A baby's face turns red, his hands clench, his abdomen tenses and distends, and his legs draw up toward his stomach. No amount of soothing, cuddling, or other handling seems to help, and the infant cries until he's exhausted. Some relief may come if the baby passes feces or gas.

From his appearance, a colicky baby appears to be suffering from stomach or intestinal pain. The word colic comes from colon, and one common explanation for the condition is that it is caused either by air trapped in the intestines or an allergic reaction to milk or formula. Other explanations that have been offered include the belief that colic is a reaction to tension or stress and that colic is caused by an infant's frustration at his inability to interact with his environment.

The truth is that there is no scientific evidence that any of these explanations is correct. Although the condition appears to be related to digestion, a baby with colic is normally healthy and gains weight normally. Changes in formulas, feeding techniques, feeding equipment, or feeding patterns seldom have any effect. Research has failed to find a correlation between the likelihood of colic and any specific parenting style, parent personality, household stress, or other emotional conditions.

While there is no proof about what causes colic, however, there are medical conditions that can produce coliclike reactions. Among these are intestinal allergies, gastrointestinal infections, urinary tract infections, ear infections, hernias, a hair in the eye, and a number of other conditions. Any infant who cries for four or more hours, or who exhibits a regular coliclike pattern of behavior, should be thoroughly examined by a physician.

Colicky babies who've been found to be healthy suffer no lasting ill effects from the condition. However, colic can be devastating to the parents. Ignorant advice and comments from relatives, friends, and even unsympathetic physicians can often lead parents to blame themselves, and the guilt increases the already overwhelming stress and exhaustion. Parents sometimes develop strong feelings of anger, even hatred, toward their colicky babies, emotions that can continue even after the colic disappears.

Most experts begin counseling parents by assuring them that colic disappears naturally, usually by 3 months and almost always by 4 months. While the colic continues, parents are advised to take advantage of any help they can find, from friends, relatives, and paid baby-sitters. Finally, experts allay any concerns parents may have that attempts to comfort colicky babies may ''spoil'' them. Parents are told that any techniques that work are perfectly acceptable and will cause no psychological harm to the infant.

To match the carbohydrate content of breast milk, formula makers add sucrose, a sweeter sugar that is broken down and absorbed quickly, producing a peak in the sugar content of the baby's bloodstream. Some evidence links ingestion of sucrose by the infant with higher rates of diabetes in later life.

Vitamins

Breast milk meets the infant's vitamin requirements, with the possible exception of vitamin D. Many pediatricians prescribe a vitamin D supplement for babies of nursing mothers.

Cow's milk is also low in vitamin D, and both commercially available milk and infant formula contain supplemental amounts of this vitamin. Cow's milk is also low in vitamin C, which is added to formula.

Minerals

A baby is born with reserves of iron sufficient to last about 3 or 4 months. Both cow's milk and breast milk contain small amounts of iron, but the iron in breast milk is much more easily absorbed and meets a baby's requirements through infancy. Many pediatricians recommend switching bottle-fed babies to formulas with supplemental iron after they are 3 or 4 months of age.

Cows' milk contains a lot more calcium and phosphorus than breast milk, and eliminating these excess minerals can place a strain on the kidneys.

Immunization

A baby is born with an immature immune system. Without some protection against disease, a baby's chances of surviving the first few months of life would be very slim. That's why nature provides temporary immunity in the form of antibodies provided by the mother's body.

About half of the antibodies that provide the baby with some immunity in the first 6 months of life are passed through the placenta. But fully half must come through the mother's breast in colostrum, the rich milk excreted during the first 2 or 3 days after birth. The antibodies in colostrum protect the newborn against polio (if the mother has been vaccinated) as well as mumps, measles, chicken pox, influenza, and a wide variety of other respiratory and gastrointestinal diseases. Furthermore, recent research has shown that viruses acquired by the infant are often transferred to the mother's breast during nursing. The mother's body then makes antibodies to the virus and passes them back to the baby through the breast milk, resulting in milder illnesses.

The results of this added immunization are much lower rates of disease in breast-fed babies and dramatically lower rates of hospitalization during the first year of life.

WHAT YOU SHOULD KNOW ABOUT . . .

THE RECOMMENDED SCHEDULE OF IMMUNIZATION

With every month after birth, the infant's immune system becomes more and more capable of taking care of its own defense. Medical science has learned to provide immunity to certain dangerous diseases by developing vaccines, that is, forms of a virus that stimulate the body to form antibodies against a disease without actually contracting the disease.

The American Academy of Pediatrics has developed a schedule of vaccinations for young children. This schedule is based on a combination of the dangers presented by various diseases, the child's growing ability to create antibodies, and the child's ability to tolerate a possible reaction to the vaccine. The recommended schedule for the first 2 years of life is:

Schedule of Vaccinations

Age	Immunization
2 months	DPT (diphtheria, pertussis or whooping cough, tetanus) OPV (oral polio vaccine)
4 months	DPT (second dose) OPV (second dose)
6 months	DPT (third dose)
15 months	MMR (measles, mumps, rubella) DPT (fourth dose) OPV (third dose)
18-24 months	H. influenza type b (for bacterial infections, including meningitis, epiglottitis, and pneumonia)

How Breast Milk or Formula Is Digested

Breast milk contains unique substances that facilitate the growth of a type of intestinal bacteria that protects against many types of intestinal infections. Formula, on the other hand, facilitates growth of another type of bacteria that can cause such infections.

In addition, breast milk is naturally sterile, while formula must be carefully prepared and handled to avoid bacterial contamination.

Breast milk also has a natural laxative effect, which means that constipation in breast-fed babies is very rare.

Finally, breast-fed babies are less likely have colic, which has been linked to excessive intestinal gas, overfeeding, excessive carbohydrates in formula, and other digestive system conditions.

Obesity

Since breast-fed babies determine how much nutrition they take, they're seldom overfed. When bottle-fed babies are encouraged to "finish the bottle," however, they often end up overfed.

Overfeeding stresses the kidneys of infants, forcing them to process a high concentration of unused nutrients. It also encourages the creation of fat cells to store unused energy. Both these factors have been linked to obesity.

Jaw Development

A breast-fed baby has to suck harder than a bottle-fed baby, leading to better jaw development. Breast-fed babies also suck differently, pulling their tongues back to suck from the breast. Bottle-fed babies thrust their tongues forward to suck, and tongue thrusting can lead to malformation of the dental arch.

Flavor Preferences

Flavors from the mother's diet are passed to the breast-fed baby in breast milk. Recent studies indicate that these breast-fed babies may adjust to a solid food diet more easily than bottle-fed babies, and that their range of flavor preferences more closely approximates the range of flavor preferences of the mother.

Mother's Health

Breast-feeding releases in the mother a hormone called oxytocin, which helps the uterus contract more quickly and promotes healing after delivery. Since women who breast-feed are not given other hormones after birth to suppress lactation, they less frequently develop blood clots in the legs. Finally, the incidence of breast cancer in mothers who nurse for more than three months is lower than in women who've never breast-fed or who breast-fed for less than three months.

Ease of Feeding

Breast milk is free, always the right temperature, and always immediately available. Breast milk also doesn't stain clothing, as commercial formula does.

BOTTLE FEEDING

Although organizations such as the La Leche League argue that breast-feeding creates stronger mother-infant bonding, research shows that mothers who bottle-feed are equally capable of bonding with their newborns. Being a "good mother" is not dependent on the feeding method. Many parents feel more comfortable with bottle-feeding because:

WHAT YOU SHOULD KNOW ABOUT . . .

HOW INFANTS ARE FED

Below is a chart of the percentage of mothers who breast feed their children in the hospital and at 6 months, broken down by several characteristics:

	% Breast Feeding in Hospital	% Breast Feeding at 6 months
Race		
White	65.0%	28.6%
Black	33.3%	11.7%
Age of Mother		
Under 20	36.8%	10.2%
20-24	58.0%	19.7%
25-29	66.6%	30.6%
30-34	69.4%	39.1%
35-64	.7%	38.5%
Family Income		
Less than $7,000	36.6%	12.4%
$7,000-$14,999	54.5%	21.1%
$15,000-$24,999	64.8%	29.2%
$25,000 and over	71.8%	33.4%
Maternal Education		
Noncollege	50.7%	19.2%
College	77.5%	38.8%

1. Fathers and other family members can immediately become involved in feeding the baby.
2. The mother has more freedom, including the ability to obtain child care assistance and return to work.
3. The mother has no risk of sore nipples, painful breast engorgement, and other physical complaints associated with breast-feeding.
4. Babies don't have to be fed as often, because formula is digested more slowly than breast milk.

Nutritionally, commercial formula prepared in strict accordance with manufacturer's instructions is an acceptable food for newborns.

HOW MUCH A NEWBORN SHOULD CONSUME

After oxygen, water is the most essential substantance for your baby. As we learned above, the body of an infant is composed of a higher percentage of water than the body of an adult, and about five times as much of that fluid has to be replaced each day. That means that a newborn needs about 2-1/4 ounces of fluid for each pound of body weight per day, or about 18 ounces of fluid for an 8 pound baby.

We also learned above that infants burn more calories per pound than adults. Your newborn needs about 50 calories per pound of body weight, or about 400 calories for an 8 pound baby.

Milk or formula required. Both breast milk and formula contain about 20 calories per ounce. That means a newborn needs about 2-1/2 ounces of breast milk or formula per pound of body weight, or about 20 ounces for an 8 pound baby.

HOW OFTEN A BABY SHOULD BE FED

For decades, pediatricians dictated rigidly scheduling the feeding of newborns, but recent research proves that feeding babies on demand is much more preferable, for the following reasons:

1. The baby's physical needs for water and calories are promptly met.
2. The baby doesn't learn to associate prolonged crying and discomfort with feeding.
3. The baby doesn't develop poor eating practices, such as gulping the feedings.

Exactly how often your baby needs to be fed depends on how fast his stomach empties. By the end of the first week of life, your baby will be able to consume 2 to 3 ounces of breast milk or formula at a feeding, and will need to be fed 6-10 times per day. After the third week, his consumption should increase to 4-5 ounces at a feeding, and the number of feedings can be reduced to 5 to 7 per day.

2
Your Baby to Age Two

Physical Growth from Birth to Age Two

THE PRINCIPLES OF GROWTH

Newborn babies seem so tiny—on the first day of life, the average infant is about as long as the distance from your elbow to your fingertips. That baby, however, will grow astonishingly fast, tripling in weight and adding a foot in height in the first 12 months. It's fascinating to watch and record that incredible spurt, especially if you know what to look for.

Infants grow and develop physically according to certain principles. The most important by far of these is the *cephalocaudal* principle of growth. This means that all physical development begins with the head and proceeds downward. That's why, for example, the head makes up 50% of the length of an 8 week old fetus and 25% of the length of a newborn, compared with less than 20% of the length of an adult. It also means that infants first gain control of their neck muscles, then their arms, then their hands, then their legs.

The second important principle of growth is the *proximodistal* principle. This means that development takes place from the interior portion of the body outward. For example, an infant will be able to thrust an arm in the direction of a toy before he can control his hand and fingers well enough to pick up the toy.

The third important principle of growth is that all development takes place from the *general, unspecific* to the *controlled, specific*. For example, a young infant who sees a toy reacts with his whole body, grinning, wiggling, reaching. An older infant, although still excited about a toy, simply reaches to pick it up.

What does this mean to parents and care givers? It means that while individual growth rates vary, the pattern of a baby's growth and development is predictable. By keeping track of the milestones in that growth and development, you'll be far better able to anticipate such things as the kind of stimulation your baby needs, the kinds of toys you'll need to buy, and the increased safety measures you'll need to implement.

A BABY'S BODY PROPORTIONS

The principles of growth explained above result in a newborn's head and trunk being much larger proportionally than those of older children and adults. For example:

· At birth, a newborn's head and trunk make up about 65% of his length, compared with 50% of the length of an adult
· A newborn's trunk is longer than his legs
· A newborn's arms are so short they can't reach above his head (lift your own arms for comparison)
· Because his legs are so short, a newborn's sitting height averages 70% of his total height, compared with 57% for a 3 year old and about 50% for an adult
· In the first year of life, an infant's head is bigger around than his chest—at his first birthday, the average infant's head is about 80% of its adult circumference, while his chest measures only 50% of its adult circumference
· A newborn baby is wider in relationship to height (as measured by skeletal structure, not fat) than he will ever be in his life

HOW A BABY GROWS

The head of all infants grows very rapidly, especially in the first 6 months of life. In the first year, the average baby's head circumference increases 4.5 inches, compared with a growth of just 3.9 more inches from age 1 to adulthood.

From birth, the legs and arms of both boys and girls grow more rapidly than their trunks, a trend that continues until shortly before the onset of puberty. Boys are slightly larger at birth and grow more rapidly during the first 6 months. After the first 6 months, boys and girls grow at the same rate until puberty.

MEASURING GROWTH

At every checkup in the first 2 years of life, a baby will be weighed, then measured for his height, head circumference, and chest circumference. Most pediatricians will enter these measurements on a chart or graph that compares his measurements with the results of a survey of the measurements of several thousand babies the same age. Almost all the charts are based on studies conducted by or for the National Center for Health Statistics, a government agency that collects health information and vital statistics (births, deaths, marriages, etc.) for the entire population.

The first thing a doctor will probably tell parents from the chart is the height and weight percentiles into which a baby falls. If the doctor explains that a baby's weight is in the fiftieth percentile, that means that half of all babies surveyed weighed less at that age and half weighed more. If he's in the seventy-fifth percentile, that means that 75% of babies weighed less and 25% weighed more.

A pediatrician will also be looking for a pattern of growth. A pattern doesn't necessarily mean the baby will stay in the same percentiles. The relative growth rate of about a third of all babies gradually slows in the first 12 to 18 months, the rate of about a third of all babies gradually increases, and about a third of all babies maintain the same growth rate. A baby shows a normal pattern if his weight percentile drops from the seventy-fifth at birth to the fiftieth by 1 year of age, despite month-to-month ups and downs in between. However, a dramatic drop from the seventy-fifth percentile to the fiftieth in the course of a month or two might be a reason for concern.

DOES A BABY'S GROWTH PATTERN PREDICT HIS ADULT PHYSIQUE?

Few parents don't wonder if their tall, skinny baby is going to be a tall, skinny adult—or, on the other hand, if they have reason to worry that a chubby baby is going to have a weight problem.

Researchers classify people into three types by body proportion:

1. *Ectomorphs* are tall and thin.
2. *Endomorphs* are stocky and heavy.
3. *Mesomorphs* are relatively well proportioned, or "athletic looking."

As we've said above, most babies are born looking rather endomorphic. From birth, growth is controlled by a combination of genetics and environmental factors such as nutrition and exercise. Because growth patterns of most babies change in infancy, it's impossible to make accurate predictions about adult body type until after age 2—with one exception.

That exception is obesity. Research indicates that as many as 80% of infants who are more than 20% above the median weight for their relative height, weight, and skeletal structure become obese adults.

However, many babies who look "chubby" don't fall into this category. All babies in the first year of life have more body fat than older children—it's up to a pediatrician to determine what is normal chubbiness and what is obesity.

A BABY'S MEASUREMENTS

Weight
The National Center for Health Statistics' percentiles for weight in pounds are:

Boys

| | | Percentiles | |
Age	10th%	50th%	90th%
1 month	8.5	10.0	11.5
2 months	10.0	11.5	13.2
3 months	11.1	12.6	14.5
4 months	12.5	14.0	16.2
5 months	13.7	15.0	17.7
6 months	14.8	16.7	19.2
9 months	17.8	20.0	22.9
12 months	19.6	22.2	25.4
18 months	22.3	25.2	29.0
24 months	24.7	27.7	31.9

Girls

| | | Percentiles | |
Age	10th%	50th%	90th%
1 month	8.0	9.7	11.0
2 months	9.5	11.0	12.5
3 months	10.7	12.4	14.0
4 months	12.0	13.7	15.5
5 months	13.0	14.7	17.0
6 months	14.1	16.0	18.6
9 months	16.6	19.2	22.4
12 months	18.4	21.5	24.8
18 months	21.2	24.5	28.3
24 months	23.5	27.12	31.7

Most infants drop in weight immediately after birth, primarily because of fluid loss. Birth weight is usually regained by the 10th day, and after that newborns gain weight at the rate of about an ounce a day in the first 3 months. More specifically, the average weight gains per month are:

Weight Gain in the First Two Years

Age range	Average gain per month
0-1 month	1.4 pounds
1-3 months	1.7 pounds
3-6 months	1.3 pounds
6-9 months	1.0 pounds
9-12 months	0.7 pounds
12-18 months	0.5 pounds
18-24 months	0.4 pounds

The end result is that the average baby doubles his birth weight in 5 or 6 months and triples it in a year.

The weight gain is even more remarkable when you take a closer look at how a baby grows. The bodies of newborns are 72% water, compared with 64% of the weight of 1 year olds and 60% of adult weight. The ratio of protein to fat in a newborn's body is about 50-50, and muscles make up between 20% and 25% of the weight.

The percentage of fat increases dramatically in the first year of life, providing temperature regulation for the baby. Muscle weight also increases (muscles make up 33% of the weight of teenagers and 40% of the weight of adults).

Height

The National Center for Health Statistics percentiles for height (length) in inches are:

Boys

		Percentiles	
Age	10th%	50th%	90th%
1 month	20.2	21.2	22.2
2 months	21.5	22.5	23.5
3 months	22.8	23.8	24.7
4 months	23.7	24.7	25.7
5 months	24.5	25.5	26.5
6 months	25.2	26.1	27.3
9 months	27.0	28.0	29.2
12 months	28.5	29.6	30.7
18 months	31.0	32.2	33.5
24 months	33.1	34.4	35.9

Girls

Age	10th%	Percentiles 50th%	90th%
1 month	20.2	21.0	22.0
2 months	21.5	22.2	23.2
3 months	22.4	23.4	24.3
4 months	23.2	24.2	25.2
5 months	24.0	25.0	26.0
6 months	24.6	25.7	26.7
9 months	26.4	27.6	28.7
12 months	27.8	29.2	30.3
18 months	30.2	31.8	33.3
24 months	32.3	34.1	35.8

Height also increases most dramatically right after birth, with the rate of growth falling with age:

Relationship of Growth with Age

Age range	Average inches grown per month
0-1 month	1.5 in
1-3 months	1.2 in
3-6 months	0.8 in
6-9 months	0.6 in
9-12 months	0.5 in
12-18 months	0.4 in
18-24 months	0.4 in

Overall, the average baby grows about 10 inches in the first year of life and 5 inches in the second. However, this growth tends to occur in spurts, more so than gains in weight. If your infant is going to the doctor for monthly appointments, you may see virtually no gain one month, then 2 inches of growth in the next month.

Month-to-month changes in recorded height can also be due to measurement problems. The American Academy of Pediatrics recommends that height be measured in a reclining position during the first 3 years of life. Even then, holding a squirming child for exact measurements can be difficult.

Head Circumference
The average head circumference of American children is:

Age	Average circumference in inches
1 month	14.9
2 months	15.5
3 months	15.9
6 months	17.0
9 months	17.8
12 months	18.3
18 months	19.0
24 months	19.2

The dramatic slowing of brain growth after age 1 is easy to see in the above table. There are slight differences between the average head circumference of boys and girls, but the measurements seldom exceed one-half inch above or below the average.

Growth of the Head and Face

At birth a baby's skull is very large in comparison to his face, and to the rest of his skeleton. At birth, the ratio of the volume of the face to the volume of the rest of the head is 1 to 8.

The cranium, the nonfacial part of the skull, grows very rapidly in infancy to accommodate the rapid growth of the brain, reaching 90% of its adult size by age 2. Growth of the bones making up the face is faster than cranial growth after age 1. By age 2, the ratio of volume of face to cranium is 1 to 5, as compared with an adult ratio of 1 to 2. The size of the face at age 2 is only 70% of adult size.

Chest Circumference

The average chest circumference of American children is:

Age	Average circumference in inches
Birth	13.7
3 months	16.2
6 months	17.3
12 months	18.3
18 months	18.9
24 months	19.5

As we mentioned above, the arms and legs of a child grow faster than the trunk. Except for the first months of life, the fastest increase in chest circumference comes in the teenage years, when children begin to "fill out."

Bone Growth

The X rays of the body of a newborn baby would look much different than those of an adult—not only because of size, but because many bones haven't formed yet. Babies' soft connective tissue doesn't show up on X rays.

The process of turning soft tissue into hard bones, which is called ossification, begins at about the eighth or ninth week of fetal life and continues after birth until the end of the teenage years. The first 2 years of life are a time of particularly intense bone growth—a baby's body replaces 50% of its bone tissue each year, compared with 5% for an adult. In these first 2 years, the length of the major arm bones increases about 75% and the length of the major leg bones doubles.

If a pediatrician wants to make an accurate assessment of a baby's physical development, the best indicator to use is the baby's skeletal age—that is, the degree to which the bones have ossified. Skeletal age is a much better indicator of growth than any other measurement, including height and weight.

To determine skeletal age, the pediatrician will order X rays of the baby's hands and feet. Studies of thousands of infants have produced detailed schedules of the appearance of small bones in the hands and feet that, compared with the X rays of a specific baby, give an accurate reading of skeletal age.

THE PROCESS OF TEETHING

The appearance of the first tooth is one event most parents both eagerly await and dread. That first tooth is a sign that a baby is on the way to becoming a child. But the process of its emergence can cause irritation that disrupts the lives of parents and babies alike.

When Teeth Are Formed

A baby's twenty primary (first) teeth begin to form in the jaw in the fourth month of fetal life. About 1 in 1,500 babies is born with a tooth. For the vast majority, construction of the first teeth is completed in the first couple of months of life.

Although the order in which teeth emerge can vary, the most common order is:

1. Two front teeth (central incisors) on lower jaw.
2. Two front teeth (central incisors) on top jaw.
3. Two teeth on either of side of front teeth (lateral incisors) on top jaw.
4. Two lateral incisors on lower jaw.

5. Two first molars, top jaw.
6. Two first molars, lower jaws.
7. Two cuspids, lower jaw.
8. Two cuspids, top jaw.
9. Two second molars, lower jaw.
10. Two second molars, top jaw.

The age at which the primary teeth appear varies widely from child to child. The table below shows the age of emergence of the twenty primary teeth by percentiles:

Percentiles (with age in months)

Teeth	Min.	10%	30%	50%	70%	90%	100%
Lower central incisors	4	5	6	7.8	9	11	17
Upper central incisors	5	6	8	9.6	11	12	15
Upper lateral incisors	6	7	10	11.5	13	15	21
Lower lateral incisors	6	7	11	12.4	14	18	27
Upper first molars	8	10	13	15.1	16	20	28
Lower first molars	8	10	14	15.7	17	20	27
Lower cuspids	8	11	16	18.2	19	24	29
Upper cuspids	8	11	17	18.3	20	24	29
Lower second molars	8	13	24	26.0	28	31	34
Upper second molars	8	13	24	26.2	28	31	34

This table shows that the earliest a tooth will generally appear is in the fourth month. Half of all babies get their first tooth by their eighth-month birthday, and 90% have a tooth by age 1. The average baby has six to eight teeth by his first birthday, and sixteen teeth by age 18 months.

How Painful Is Teething?

There's a wide variance of opinion on the symptoms caused by teething. Some pediatricians maintain that the passage of teeth through the gums is no more painful than a hair growing through the scalp—personally, we'd like to lock up these pediatricians in a room with triplets who are getting their first molars. Other people, especially parents and even some physicians, attribute fever, diarrhea, and rashes to the teething process.

The consensus is that many babies experience gum discomfort because blood vessels are ruptured and tissue pushed aside when teeth emerge. That discomfort can make a baby cranky and possibly disrupt his eating and sleeping. The disruption of eating can produce a slight change in his bowel habits and movements.

The best way to relieve the discomfort is to give the baby something hard and cold to chew on, such as commercial teethers, wash clothes soaked in cold water, frozen bagels, etc. Some pediatricians also recommend administering acetaminophen for pain relief.

The overwhelming evidence is that teething doesn't cause fever, persistent diarrhea, vomiting, convulsions, earaches, or other signs of serious illness. If your baby experiences any of these symptoms, call your doctor at once.

What about Drooling?

Many parents associate drooling with teething, but a baby's salivary glands have nothing to do with the eruption of teeth. These glands grow very rapidly in the first 6 months of life, tripling their size. By about the fourth month, they produce significant amounts of saliva. Because a baby can't yet control the muscles of his mouth and face well enough to deal with all this moisture, he begins to drool. For babies who get teeth early, the appearance of the drooling with the teeth appears to connect the two. For the average baby, however, that first tooth won't appear until the end of his seventh month.

Changes in How a Baby's Body Works in the First Two Years of Life

THE BRAIN

The first year of life is an explosive period of brain growth. During this period, the brain nearly triples in size, going from 25% to nearly 70% of its adult weight. The weight of the baby's central nervous system is one-tenth the total weight at birth, compared with an adult's central nervous system that's only one-fiftieth of total weight.

During this growth, the brain has a ferocious need for oxygen received through the blood—the brain of an infant consumes a whopping 40% of the oxygen in the baby's bloodstream. Interruptions in this supply because of injury or illness can have serious permanent effects during this period.

To facilitate the passage of oxygen to the brain, the blood/brain barrier, the biological barrier that prevents most chemicals in the blood from reaching the brain, is more permeable, or open, to chemicals passing from the blood to the brain than at any other time in life. That's one reason why almost all over-the-counter medications caution against administering them to infants without a doctor's approval.

Brain growth in the first year is 50% of all brain growth after birth. In this first year, the most rapid growth is that of the cerebellum, the part of the brain that controls muscular activity and balance. Almost all growth of the cerebellum abruptly stops at about 12 months of age. That is why

WHAT YOU SHOULD KNOW ABOUT . . .

SUDDEN INFANT DEATH SYNDROME (SIDS)

When the first week of life is excluded, sudden infant death syndrome is the leading cause of death in infants, claiming 1 of every 350 babies, or 10,000 deaths per year. Typically, a seemingly healthy baby is put in his crib, then dies during sleep without a cry or any observable sign of distress. Invariably, the discovery of the infant's body the next morning causes intense and long-lasting emotional distress in the parents and other family members.

The most typical time for the syndrome to strike is 10 to 12 weeks after birth, with half of all victims under 3 months and 90% under 6 months of age. While SIDS has stricken families of all income groups in all areas of the country at all times of year, the following risk factors have been noted:

1. *Male infants are victims more often than female infants.*
2. *Slightly more deaths occur in the winter months, in parts of the country with cold winters.*
3. *Low-birth-weight and premature babies have a higher incidence of death.*
4. *Infants born to mothers under 20 years of age are slightly more at risk.*
5. *The incidence is highest among babies of American Indian ancestry, followed by blacks, Caucasians, and Orientals.*
6. *Babies are at greater risk if their mothers smoked during pregnancy and if their mothers received poor prenatal care.*
7. *A significant percentage of victims had or had just recovered from an upper respiratory tract infection at the time of their deaths, although the majority of victims appeared healthy.*

Despite the identification of these factors, the exact cause of SIDS is unknown. Experts generally agree that the victims die because they suddenly stop breathing, most likely as a result of some problem in the respiratory control center in the brain or the mechanisms of the respiratory system. Much attention has been centered on a condition known as apnea, in which an infant temporarily stops breathing during sleep. Apnea is common in infants, and has been shown to be a significant factor in ''near misses,'' babies who almost died. Unfortunately, only 5% of SIDS victims have had previous apnea episodes, so it hasn't been proven to be a reliable factor in identifying potential victims.

One very recent study has indicated that SIDS may be related to an abnormality of the blood's ability to carry oxygen. Oxygen is carried through the body by a blood protein called hemoglobin. The fetus produces an immature form of hemoglobin called hemoglobin F. After birth, hemoglobin F is replaced by hemoglobin A, the adult form. In checking the blood of fifty-nine victims of SIDS, researchers found an average of 47% hemoglobin F in the bodies of victims, compared with 19% in the blood of infants who weren't victims. Even if the immature hemoglobin doesn't prove to be the causative factor in SIDS, it may prove to be a predictive factor.

nutritional deficiencies in the first year of life can produce irreversible problems in muscle control and coordination.

Another 25% of postnatal brain growth takes place between ages 1 and 3, and another 15% between ages 3 and 7. Almost all of this growth involves the cerebrum, the largest part of the brain, which controls thought, language, and other mental functions.

THE SENSES AND PERCEPTUAL ABILITY

The Sense of Touch and Sensitivity to Pain

As we discussed in our description of the central nervous system of the newborn, the fibers connecting the nerve cells of a baby must be myelinated, or insulated, before they can carry messages to and from the brain. As this insulation process takes place, a baby becomes more sensitive to touch and pain. At the same time, a baby's skin has more receptors crowded closer together as he grows.

A newborn baby can't distinguish a touch from a pain very easily. Sensitivity develops gradually, and more slowly than muscle control, although it follows the general pattern of increasing from the head downward. For example, a baby gains the power to direct his arms and hands before his sense of touch and pain is developed enough to realize that the source of a pinprick is on his finger. A baby doesn't have the ability to locate accurately a source of irritation until he is between 7 and 9 months of age. It's between 12 and 16 months when your little one responds to pain by moving his hand to the place where it hurts and rubbing it.

Vision

As we explained when we introduced the newborn, a baby can see at birth. However, he has very poor visual acuity (as bad as 20/290), has trouble focusing on anything that isn't about 8 inches from his eyes, and has difficulty tracking moving objects.

As soon as 2 weeks after birth, a newborn begins to scan in all directions in search of interesting objects, including mobiles and other decorative items. From 3 to 14 weeks, he shows an increasing preference for complex patterns, bright colors, and strong contrast.

By age 4 to 6 months, an infant has nearly the visual acuity of an adult, and he can easily focus on objects at different distances. He also has begun to grasp the concept that an object is the same size when its distance from him varies, an idea called "visual size consistency." He has learned the connection between two-dimensional pictures of objects in a book and the actual three-dimensional object. Finally, he has acquired depth perception, along with the knowledge that crawling off a platform into the air is dangerous.

Testing the vision of infants and toddlers is difficult. Some signs of problems may be frequent rubbing of the eyes, shutting or covering an eye when playing or looking at a toy, tilting the head or thrusting it forward, holding an object very close for examination, or excessive redness or tears in the eye.

Hearing

A normal newborn can hear quite well at birth. In the first few days, he can distinguish the general direction from which a sound comes, and he can tell the difference between a real baby's cry and a simulated cry. Tests have shown that by 4 months of age, he can distinguish between sounds of slightly different frequencies about as well as an adult can.

Because the ability to hear normally is vital to language development, it is extremely important that any hearing problems are detected as early as possible, so that they can be treated or compensated for. Physicians use the following screening process to determine if a child's hearing is normal in the first 2 years of life:

Age	Behavior
0-2 months	Sound arouses baby from sleep
2-4 months	Child turns head when sound is heard
4-7 months	Child turns head in direction of sound
7-9 months	Child accurately locates a sound on the side and turns head inaccurately toward a sound from below
9-13 months	Child accurately locates a sound on either side or below
13-16 months	Child accurately locates sound to side and below, inaccurately turns head toward sound from above
16-21 months	Child accurately locates sounds from above, below, and side
21-24 months	Child accurately locates a sound from any angle

Some behavioral signs of hearing problems include:

1. Child doesn't pay attention or acts as if he doesn't understand.
2. Child exhibits frequent, excessively loud crying or screaming.
3. Child is hyperactive.
4. Child points, pulls, and uses gestures instead of using sounds.
5. Child exhibits balance problems or very late development of motor skills such as sitting or standing.
6. Child makes continuous, strange noises.
7. Child is excessively fearful of new situations.

The ability to perceive sounds doesn't mean that an infant understands and interprets what he hears. Interpretation depends on intellectual development. For example, a baby has to understand that he and his mother are separate persons before he completely identifies her voice with her body. The ability to listen with the accuracy and selectivity of an adult doesn't come until the child is about age 9 years of age.

Taste and Smell

A newborn can distinguish between basic tastes and strong smells. Acuity of these senses develops in relation to experience, but both senses are very difficult to test before a child can talk.

THE CIRCULATORY SYSTEM

The Heart

A baby's heart grows less quickly than the rest of the body after birth, only doubling its weight in the first year. But because of prenatal growth, it's still relatively large in relation to the chest cavity.

A baby's heart is located in almost the exact center of his chest. With the first breath the baby takes after birth, the heart begins to take over the task of oxygenating the blood through the lungs and pumping it to the body. Because the left ventricle of the heart, the "pump" that produces the force to push the blood through the body, is weakest at birth, a newborn's blood pressure is low. This low blood pressure is one of the reasons that a newborn baby's heart beats very quickly.

As a baby gets older, the left ventricle grows larger and stronger. Blood pressure increases and heart rate decreases. Below are tables of the average heart rate and average blood pressure for ages from birth to age 2. One note: the range of blood pressure and heart rate can vary widely for healthy infants, particularly because the examination can get babies excited, raising their readings dramatically. For example, the "normal" range of heart beats in a newborn can range from 70 beats a minute when asleep to 190 beats a minute when crying.

Average Heart Rate for Children at Rest

Age	Beats per Minute
Birth	140
1st month	130
1-6 months	130
6-12 months	115
1-2 years	110

Average Blood Pressure Readings

Age	Systolic/Diastolic
1 day	78/42
1 month	86/54
6 months	90/60
1 year	96/65
2 years	99/65

WHAT YOU SHOULD KNOW ABOUT . . .

BLOOD GROUPS

A major discovery that paved the way for safe blood transfusions was the identification of two substances on the surface of red blood cells that cause clumping of the blood in the presence of an antibody. These two substances were labeled A and B, and their discovery led to our modern system of blood grouping, the ABO blood group system.

In the ABO blood group system, there are four blood groups, A, B, AB, and O. The blood group is genetically determined by a gene from each parent, with A or B dominant over O, which represents the absence of both the A and B substances. There are six possible gene pairings, AA, AO, AB, BB, BO, and OO. Since O is recessive, AO is considered type A blood and BO is considered type B blood.

Relationship of Blood Group or Type to Transfusions

Blood Group	Can Donate To	Can Receive From
A	A, AB	A, O
B	B, AB	B, O
AB	AB	A, B, AB, O
O	A, B, AB, O	O

Since the O gene is recessive, it's the rarest blood group, and blood banks often suffer shortages of type O blood. Another substance on the surface of the red blood cell that affects both the transfusion of blood and pregnancy is the Rh factor. This factor is a protein first identified when the blood of a rhesus monkey was injected into a rabbit, causing the rabbit's blood to clump. The term Rh comes from rhesus.

Eighty-five percent of whites, 93% of blacks, and 99% of Asians are considered Rh positive, because they have this factor in their red blood cells. The absence of the protein, which is genetically recessive, leads to the designation Rh negative.

A serious medical problem can occur when an Rh-negative mother gives birth to an Rh-positive baby. The baby's blood cells pass through the placenta to the mother, giving rise to the formation of antibodies that can cause severe anemia and jaundice in the fetus. If the pregnancy is the woman's first, so few antibodies are produced that the infant seldom is affected. More problems can occur in later pregnancies. Today, such pregnancies are closely monitored. In some cases, transfusions of Rh-positive blood that "wash out" the antibodies have been given to the fetus in the womb.

Because infants have such large heads and trunks and short extremities, blood pressure readings from their arms and legs are virtually identical. As the limbs grow, however, and the distance the blood has to travel increases, leg blood pressure becomes lower than the blood pressure in the arms, which are closer to the heart. Your pediatrician may occasionally measure the difference, which is an indication of how well your child's circulatory system is working.

Heart Sounds

If you turn your bathroom faucet on just a little way, the relatively slow flow of the water is virtually silent. Turn the faucet up full blast, however, and the water gushes out with an audible hissing. The increased sound is a function of how fast the water is flowing.

A roughly similar situation exists in your baby's heart. An infant's heart rate is much faster than an adult's, especially when he's agitated. The fast flow produces vibrations that can be picked up by a doctor's stethoscope. These vibrations are called *heart murmurs.*

The word *murmur* strikes terror in the hearts of parents. In fact, murmurs can be detected in almost every child at some point in the first 7 years of life. In the vast majority of cases, these sounds are what doctors call "innocent heart murmurs." They are absolutely normal and harmless. Ninety percent of innocent heart murmurs disappear by age 14, and almost all of those that continue are also harmless for the rest of a person's life.

Unfortunately, the mention of a heart murmur has caused countless parents to panic needlessly—keeping their young children in the house, restricting play, even keeping them home from school. This overreaction can cause great physical and psychological harm to a child.

Another common activity of infant hearts that can cause parental panic is an occasional irregular heartbeat. However, an irregular heartbeat is so normal in young children that its absence—in other words, a totally regular heartbeat—is more likely to cause concern on the part of doctors.

The Blood

The average newborn baby has about 7 ounces of blood in his system, compared with about 6 quarts of blood for the average adult male and 4.5 quarts for the average adult female. The blood of a newborn is richer in red blood cells and hemoglobin than that of an adult. The primary reason seems to be that the blood of a newborn is designed to carry relatively more oxygen, because his lungs are not yet operating at full efficiency. As the lungs become more efficient, the red blood cell and hemoglobin counts go down.

WHAT YOU SHOULD KNOW ABOUT . . .

CONVERTING CENTIGRADE TO FAHRENHEIT

Some baby thermometers are calibrated in degrees centigrade rather than Fahrenheit. Here is a conversion table:

Conversion Table

Centigrade (C°)	to Fahrenheit (F°)	Centigrade (C°)	to Fahrenheit (F°)
36.3	97.3	38.7	101.7
36.4.	97.5	38.8	101.8
36.5	97.7	38.9	102.0
36.6	97.9	39.0	102.2
36.7	98.0	39.1	102.4
36.8	98.2	39.2	102.6
36.9	98.4	39.3	102.7
37.0	98.6	39.4	102.9
37.1	98.8	39.5	103.1
37.2	99.0	39.6	103.3
37.3	99.1	39.7	103.5
37.4	99.3	39.8	103.6
37.5	99.5	39.9	103.8
37.6	99.7	40.0	104.0
37.7	99.9	40.1	104.2
37.8	100.0	40.2	104.4
37.9	100.2	40.3	104.5
38.0	100.4	40.4	104.7
38.1	100.6	40.5	104.9
38.2	100.8	40.6	105.1
38.3	100.9	40.7	105.3
38.4	101.1	40.8	105.4
38.5	101.3	40.9	105.6
38.6	101.5	41.0	105.8

Temperature Regulation

Young babies have more surface area in proportion to their body weight than adults do and they've got very little body fat, so they lose body heat more quickly. Equally important, they lack the reflexes to shiver, an activity that generates heat that warms the entire body.

The ideal temperature for young infants is slightly higher than the ideal temperature for adults. The primary reason for this difference is that the body temperature of young children is higher. Infants commonly have normal rectal temperatures of over 100° Fahrenheit. A study of 18-month-olds found that their average rectal temperatures were 99.8° Fahrenheit, and half had readings of at least 100°. In comparison, the average rectal temperature of a 5-year-old was 98.6° and of a 11-year-old was 98.0°.

Too much heat, however, is also bad, because a young infant's sweat glands are immature. Severely overdressing an infant in the heat of summer can result in death.

The ability to compensate for changes in temperature increases rapidly, especially after the first 6 months. By about 18 to 24 months of age, a child usually has little difficulty maintaining body temperature under normal conditions.

THE RESPIRATORY SYSTEM

The growth rate of a baby's lungs parallel that of the rest of his body, with their weight doubling in the first 6 months and tripling in the first year. Because their hearts beat faster, babies breath more often than adults. The respiration rate of a newborn is 30 to 80 times a minute, compared with 20 to 40 times a minute for a 1-year-old, 20 to 30 times a minute for a 2-year-old, and 15 to 20 times a minute for an adult.

Children are stomach breathers for at least the first 5 years of life, with their diaphragms providing the force to expel air. Pauses in breathing, called apnea, are very common during the sleep of young infants, especially premature or small babies.

A Baby's Motor Development in the First Two Years of Life

Motor development is a fancy term for the process by which babies gradually gain control of their bodies. The process is a complicated one, but in 2 short years, children progress from immobile infants to perpetual motion machines who can walk, run, climb, and jump. The highlights of this development—shaking a rattle, sitting up, crawling, standing, and walking for the first time—are high on the list of parents' most cherished moments.

When a pediatrician evaluates a baby's motor development, he's likely to ask parents questions about three different kinds of behavior:

1. *Gross motor development* is the gradual control of the head, neck, trunk, arms, and legs that is required in sitting, crawling, walking, running, and other types of movement involving the large muscles of the body.
2. *Fine motor development* is the gradual control of the hands and fingers.
3. *Adaptive behavior* refers to the increasingly complex ways in which a young child makes use of his growing gross and fine motor skills. It includes such activities as swiping at a toy, finding the mouth with a rattle, stacking two blocks, or crawling off to find a missing toy.

THE PROCESS OF MOTOR DEVELOPMENT

The key word in understanding motor development is *control*. As any parent knows, every baby has some obvious physical skills at birth. Newborns can suck from a bottle, grab Dad's or Mom's finger, flex their legs, flail their arms, and act like they're swimming when they're placed on their stomachs. All these movements, however, are reflexes. They are totally involuntary—a newborn has no conscious ability to start them or stop them.

An infant achieves control of any part of his body in two separate steps. First, the muscles must have developed sufficiently for movement, the skeletal system must have become strong enough to support movement and weight, and, most important, the nervous system must have been myelinated so that messages from the brain can get through. This vital physical preparation for motor control is called *maturation*.

The second step is coordinating the muscle and joint movements necessary to carry out the motor activity. This step is a learning process, similar to an adult learning to hit a tennis ball. Infants have to practice new physical skills, and they're generally a lot more determined about it than adults. When a baby is reaching a new milestone, such as pulling himself to a standing position, he'll do it dozens, even hundreds, of times a day until he masters the action.

Research has shown that maturation is the most important step in a baby's motor development. This maturation proceeds in accordance with the general principles of infant growth we previously described, particularly the *cephalocaudal* (from head to toe) and *proximodistal* (from trunk to extremities). The pace at which maturation takes place is genetically determined. It cannot, and should not, be hurried by any kind of exercise, equipment, training, etc.

Research studies have shown that some training methods aimed at coordinating the movements necessary to achieve such gross motor skills as crawling and walking can slightly speed up the process. On the other hand, by restricting an infant's ability to practice physical skills—for example, by not giving a young infant any toys to practice reaching for and grabbing, or by confining an older baby in a crib, playpen, or infant seat for hours a day—parents can significantly retard motor development.

THE RATE OF MOTOR DEVELOPMENT

Later in this section, we'll describe the step-by-step progression by which babies achieve motor skills. The fact that this process is orderly, however, doesn't mean that it proceeds at anything like an even pace. Countless parents have been bewildered and frustrated when their baby has zipped through three steps in a month then makes absolutely no progress for another 2 or 3 months.

That pattern is totally normal. The development of children in any area proceeds in stops and starts, producing a pattern that's unique to each child. That's why any chart that indicates that a baby will reach a milestone in any given week, or even month, can't apply to all normal children.

What isn't normal is sudden, unexplained regression in motor skills—for example, when a baby who's been crawling all over the house becomes an awkward creeper again. There are circumstances that can explain such temporary regression, among them the birth of another child, a move to a new home, parental divorce or separation, a change from parental care to full-time day care, or any other abrupt change in the baby's life. If a baby regresses without such change, a pediatrician should be consulted.

EVALUATING MOTOR DEVELOPMENT

Many researchers have spent an enormous amount of time over the last half century observing and charting the motor development of young children. One result of this research is a well-defined sequence in which gross motor, fine motor, and adaptive behavior progresses. A second result, achieved by noting the age at which many children who developed into normal adults achieved certain motor skills, has been the determination of developmental "norms." A *norm* is an age range within which the vast majority of children acquire a given motor skill.

The first important thing to realize about these norms is that the only important date in determining them is the date of conception, not the date of birth. All norms are based on birth at full term. In the words of Dr. George Lowry of the University of California, "Premature birth does not confer any advantage on a child." On the average, an infant born 8 weeks prematurely will walk 8 weeks later than a full term infant born on the same day (given, of course, identical genetic imprinting.)

The second important fact about norms is that the normal age range for the acquisition of a motor skill widens with the complexity of that skill. Most young infants can turn their heads in both directions very close to the age of 16 weeks. On the other hand, a baby that walks at 9 months and a baby that walks at 13 months are both well within the norm for that skill.

The third fact about motor development norms is that they have no proven correlation to intelligence. There is absolutely no proof that a baby who walks at 9 months will be smarter than a baby who walks at 13 or 14 months. The predictions that can be made based on motor development have to do with later development of motor skills. Walking early in itself has little to do with later athletic ability. But a child who demonstrates unusually good physical coordination at age 2 is much more likely to be "gifted" physically in later years.

Finally, the most important reason that so much effort has been put into formulating motor development norms is their usefulness as a diagnostic tool for pediatricians, child psychologists, and others. If a child significantly lags behind the norms, that may indicate disease, physical handicaps, neurological problems, nutritional deficiencies, or even child abuse.

GROSS MOTOR DEVELOPMENT

The easiest way to understand how a baby gains control over his body is to break down development into some understandable sequences of behavior. Remember, while one child may reach a certain stage earlier than another or linger at a stage longer than another, every child's development follows the same pattern.

Head Control

Most newborns have no control over their head and neck muscles. If you put a newborn on his back, take his hands, and pull him to a sitting position, he'll likely demonstrate complete "head lag"—that is, his head will drop back as far as it can go. Because babies develop from the head down, head control comes early, in the following stages:

1. Lying on his stomach, a baby will lift his head up off the floor or mattress to a 45 degree angle.
   Average time achieved: 4 to 6 weeks.
   Normal range: 1 to 10 weeks.
2. Lying on his stomach, a baby will lift his head so high that his chest is also lifted.
   Average time achieved: 8 weeks.
   Normal range: 1 to 19 weeks.
3. When a baby is pulled to a sitting position from his back, head lag is apparent but not complete.
   Average time achieved: 6 to 10 weeks.
   Normal range: 4 to 20 weeks.
4. A baby can turn his head to both sides, and shows little or no head lag.
   Average time achieved: 16 to 20 weeks.
   Normal range: 8 to 24 weeks.
5. A baby can lift his head by himself when he's on his back.
   Average time achieved: 24 to 28 weeks.
   Normal range: 16 to 40 weeks.

Sitting

Sitting upright unsupported requires not only head control, but control of the back muscles as well. Getting to a sitting postion requires an infant to develop arm strength, some lower body strength, some physical coordination, and balance. That's why some experts refer to sitting unsupported as the "halfway" step between birth and walking.

If a newborn is put into a sitting position, he'll double over completely, his head nearly touching his feet and his back uniformly rounded. The steps in sitting are:

1. Baby can sit, if he is well supported, against a cushion or seat back for about ten minutes. His back is still somewhat rounded and his head tends to bob forward.
    Average time achieved: 8 to 12 weeks.
    Normal range: 4 to 24 weeks.
2. Baby can sit, if he is well supported, for thirty minutes, with back nearly straight and head steady.
    Average time achieved: 16 to 20 weeks.
    Normal Range: 12 to 32 weeks.
3. Baby can sit unsupported, with his weight resting forward on his hands.
    Average time achieved: 26 to 30 weeks.
    Normal range: 20 to 40 weeks.
4. Baby can sit unsupported for long periods of time, with his hands free for playing.
    Average time achieved: 36 to 42 weeks.
    Normal range: 24 to 52 weeks.
5. Baby can push himself into a sitting position.
    Average time achieved: 28 to 42 weeks.
    Normal range: 22 to 50 weeks.

You'll notice that the age when a baby can push himself into a sitting position is much more variable than the age for sitting unsupported. Some infants learn early, after "accidently" finding themselves in a sitting position when they're rolling over or trying to creep or crawl, even though they may have trouble staying in a sitting position for more than a moment or two. Other infants don't master the skill until they've been sitting up well for a month or two.

Rolling Over and Crawling

One of the big steps in gross motor development is a baby's acquisition of the ability to move from one place to another. This movement, or *locomotion*, requires first gaining control of the trunk of the body, which, along with momentum supplied by the arms and legs, allows a baby to roll over. Next comes forward motion, first by creeping (moving along with the body still touching the ground), then crawling (moving on hands and knees).

Babies are born with a reflex that produces crawling or swimming movements when they're on their stomach. But they're not strong enough to move anywhere. Soon the reflex disappears, and the sequence of behaviors leading to controlled crawling begins. That sequence is:

1. Baby can roll from his side to his back.
   Average time achieved: 8 to 10 weeks
   Normal range: 4 to 12 weeks
2. Baby kicks his legs when he's lying on his back, and the motion allows him to roll from his back to his side.
   Average time achieved: 10 to 14 weeks.
   Normal range: 8 to 16 weeks.
3. Baby pushes with his hands and flexes his knees when he's on his stomach, accomplishing a roll from stomach to back.
   Average time achieved: 14 to 28 weeks.
   Normal range: 14 to 28 weeks.
4. Baby can turn his head and shoulder, curve his back, and supply momentum with legs and arms to roll from back to stomach. (Note: Some babies who've practiced rolling from back to side can roll from back to stomach before they can roll from stomach to back.)
   Average time achieved: 14 to 30 weeks.
   Normal range: 14 to 30 weeks.
5. Baby gets his stomach up off the ground in at crawling position. He may rock back and forth, or flop forward, but does not actually crawl. He may be able to move across the room through some combination of rolling, flopping, and swiveling on his stomach.
   Average time achieved 24 to 30 weeks.
   Normal range: 20 to 36 weeks.
6. Baby starts to make progress by creeping and/or crawling, although the first progress may be backward.
   Average time achieved: 28 to 36 weeks.
   Normal range: 24 to 44 weeks.
7. Baby crawls well.
   Average time achieved: 32 to 48 weeks.
   Normal range: 28 to 52 weeks.

Standing and Walking

In the first year of life, a baby is really designed better for traveling on all fours than for walking erect. Compared with adults or older children, his shoulders are hunched, his neck short, his rib cage rounded, and his bone mass is very high compared with his muscle mass. By the second year of life, this begins to change rapidly, as muscle mass increases at twice the rate of bone mass, as the rib cage becomes flatter, as the neck lengthens, and as the shoulders become more square.

The urge to become upright, however, is very, very strong in babies, which is why they work extremely hard to accomplish the significant task of getting up on two feet and moving around. If we had to duplicate a baby's efforts of laboriously getting to his feet, toddling a few steps, falling down, then getting up again, most adults would quit after an hour, much less continue for weeks and months at a time.

The range of "normal" achievements in standing and walking is broader than that of other motor skills. Encouragement and opportunity to practice can quicken the pace of development somewhat. On the other hand, babies can easily be discouraged by parents who are overly fearful of falls and other physical mishaps.

Infants are born with a reflex that causes a walking-type movement of the feet when they're held upright. For the first 3 months of life, however, infants lack the lower body strength and muscular control to support any of their weight when standing. From that point, the steps to mastery of walking are:

1. The baby's control of his posture improves, and he gains strength in his lower body and legs. Gradually, he begins to support more and more of his weight when held in a standing position. At the same time, he pushes down on his toes, straightening his knees in the process. Eventually, he can support almost all his weight, and the rhythmic leg strengthening becomes bouncing.
   Average time achieved: 18 to 30 weeks.

2. When erect, the baby starts straightening one leg at a time. The bouncing or jumping looks more like dancing.
   Average time achieved: 24 to 36 weeks.

3. The baby pulls himself up on furniture, sides of crib and/or playpen, window sills, etc. He supports his own weight while standing, but at first may have little idea how to get down, leading to the need to be "rescued."
   Average time achieved: 26 to 52 weeks.

4. The baby starts walking around the room, holding on to the furniture. This is called "cruising."
   Average time achieved: 28 to 54 weeks.

5. The baby walks with two hands held, then with one hand held.
   Average time achieved: 28 to 60 weeks.

6. The baby takes his first steps on his own, but falls frequently.
   Average time achieved: 36 to 64 weeks.
7. The baby can get to a standing position without pulling himself up
   on anything.
   Average time achieved: 48 to 70 months.
8. Baby walks well on his own, seldom falling. At the same time, he
   takes a few steps walking sideways and backwards.
   Average time achieved: 52 to 78 weeks.

Other Gross Motor Skills

RUNNING   When you walk, you have one foot on the ground at
all times. When you run, both feet leave the ground for an instant
between strides. At some point between 18 and 24 months, most
toddlers progress from fast walking to running. By age 2, toddlers can
usually run fairly well in a straight line. However, they usually can't
swerve or change course quickly while running, and they have trouble
coming to a quick, smooth stop. Since they don't get very far off the
ground, they're likely to drag a foot and fall frequently, especially on a
lawn, the edge of a carpet, or other uneven surface.

NEGOTIATING STAIRS   A baby usually begins crawling up the
stairs on his hands and knees sometime after his first birthday. These
babies have to be watched so they don't try crawling headfirst down the
stairs. Most younger babies begin descending by crawling down
backward. A bit later, many parents teach toddlers to descend the stairs
on their bottoms, bumping down a step at a time while holding on to a
bannister.

When a baby begins to walk fairly well—getting across a room without
falling—he can start walking up and down stairs holding on to an adult's
hands. Unlike adults, who alternate feet as they climb or descend the
stairs, toddlers climb or descend by bringing both feet on each step before
proceeding to the next. By the second half of the second year, toddlers
begin to practice ascending and descending stairs by holding on to the
bannister with one hand. By their second birthday, a majority of toddlers
are fairly accomplished at this technique.

CLIMBING   Climbing is an important exercise for toddlers. It
strengthens muscles, improves physical coordination, and builds physical confidence, as well as providing a lot of enjoyment. Unfortunately, it
also leads to a lot of slips and falls.

Most babies begin to show an interest in climbing between 14 and 18
months of age. Some restrict their efforts to getting onto and off of their
parents' beds, couches, and chairs. Others become obsessed with the
activity, attacking bookcases, tables, counters, windowsills, and any

other objects that get in their path. These acrobats tend to be the earliest babies to try—and succeed—to climb out of their cribs.

One way to keep your baby in one piece and keep your household orderly is to buy a well-made baby slide that is set up in a safe place. Outdoor play equipment, either in your backyard or at a playground designed for toddlers, is another great outlet.

KICKING A BALL Kicking a ball with some force requires· momentarily balancing the body on one foot. Most toddlers can't manage that skill before their second birthday. But after age 18 months, most start to understand the concept of propelling a ball with their foot. By age 2, most can kick a ball forward by placing most of their weight on one foot and shuffling the other one forward.

THROWING Throwing a ball with accuracy and distance is a complicated skill that children don't completely master until their school years. Early in the second year, however, most babies begin throwing a ball underhanded from a standing position. Because they throw with a "stiff arm"—elbow straight—they have no control over direction and little force behind the throw. By 24 months, most babies have gradually learned to bend their elbows, and the balls go a little farther.

FINE AND ADAPTIVE MOTOR DEVELOPMENT

Fine motor development is the increasing ability of an infant to use his hands. In discussing the way this development proceeds, we're going to combine it with adaptive behavior, which is the way an infant uses his improving fine motor ability to manipulate objects and in other ways interact with the world around him. For example, it makes sense to explain the development of a baby's ability to reach out and grasp an object in conjunction with an explanation of what he does with it once it's in his hands. In other words, adaptive behavior is the practical result of fine motor development, in the same way that going to the supermarket in a car is the practical result of learning to drive.

Most parents are more interested in their baby's gross motor development than they are in the way he uses his hands and fingers. That interest is natural, because the former achievements are so obvious. No wonder more parents rush to the phone when a baby takes his first steps than when he masters a prehensile grip.

However, recent research has shown that fine motor development plays a crucial role in a baby's ability to understand and mentally organize the sensory input from the world around him. For this reason, fine and adaptive motor development play a more significant role in developing and predicting intelligence than does gross motor development.

By understanding the process by which a child explores the world around him, parents can provide the appropriate kinds and variety of stimulation. As we'll explain in more detail below, the key word here is *variety.* A baby who's learning to reach for, grab, and manipulate objects is creating a mental "story" to explain his environment. A baby who's given limited stimulation is like an author trying to write a book using a dozen words—the story will be short, incomplete, and boring, and the process of writing it will be frustrating. Just as an author can write a more complex, richer, more interesting story with a larger vocabulary, a baby's grasp of his environment is more complex, richer, and more interesting if he's given more and different kinds of appropriate stimulation.

What do we mean by "appropriate"? We mean stimulation a baby can make use of at a given stage of development. To use an extreme example, it's foolish to give a computer to an 8 month old baby, just as it's equally foolish to ask a fifth grader to write a story using technical terms out of a college physics textbook.

The Stages of Fine Motor Development

MEETING THE WORLD A newborn baby has very little control over his body, including his hands. His hands are closed most of the time, and he's born with a reflex that clenches his fists when his palm is touched. If you put a light rattle in a newborn's hand, he'll grab it. But he's got no idea that he's holding an object. He can't pay any special attention to it, and it will fall out of his hand when the hand muscles relax.

A newborn does have use of his senses, however, including vision. Although his vision is far from 20/20, he can focus on objects that are the right distance from his face (about 7 inches). Because motor control proceeds from the head downward, one of the first motor skills he develops is using his eye muscles, then his neck muscles, to visually locate and track objects. A newborn's gazing is mostly unfocused. But if infants are given interesting things to look at—for example, toys or pieces of colored paper hanging 7 to 9 inches above their faces—they'll soon begin to focus on the objects and even track their movement until they disappear from infants' rather narrow focus range. By 6 to 8 weeks of age, some infants who've been exposed to visual stimulation become physically excited when they see something colorful and interesting, by moving their legs and arms. In as little as 2 more weeks, they may even begin to take an awkward swipe at the object with one or both hands. Any contact, however, is strictly accidental, and the baby lacks the ability to grab anything he touches.

MEETING THE HANDS By about 8 weeks, a baby's clench (darwinian) reflex starts to fade, and his hands are mostly open. At approximately the same time, he also discovers his hands. He probably doesn't realize that his hands are part of his body—rather, they're just very fascinating objects he's suddenly discovered. He'll start playing with his hands, touching fingers, pulling at fingers, using the fingers to pull at his blankets or clothing.

At first, all the play will be by touch. When a baby plays with his hands where he can see them, that's an accident. By about 12 weeks, however, he can deliberately bring his hands into his vision field. He'll also start exploring his hands with his mouth by sucking on his fingers, his knuckles, etc.

GRABBING OBJECTS Around the time a baby can watch his hands while he plays with them, he begins to take an interest in other objects in his environment. If an object is lying on a flat surface, he'll make an attempt to sweep the object toward him with his entire arm, a movement called corralling. If an object is dangling above him, he'll make increasingly concentrated efforts to touch, then grab it.

Somewhere between 2 1/2 months and 4 1/2 months, a baby will start glancing between his hand and the object to gauge the distance, as if measuring the gap. About a month later, he'll begin to progressively correct the movement of his hand as it slowly approaches the object, then finally achieve the touch. This is the foundation of what we call *hand-eye coordination*.

Hand-eye coordination, like any other physical skill, improves more quickly with practice. Unfortunately, parents often severely limit their baby's practice time. One reason is that it's time consuming and tedious to hold an object within a baby's reach for long periods. This tedium can be eliminated by purchasing "toy bars," which allow parents to hang a wide variety of objects over a baby who's in an infant seat, in a crib, in a playpen, or on the floor. (See the section on "Toys" below.)

Parents who do spend time playing with their babies often make the mistake of misreading their baby's behavior. To an adult, the process of reaching and missing seems intensely frustrating. Believing that they're eliminating frustration, parents tend to hand a rattle to a baby immediately, or after one or two futile swipes.

But swiping and missing time after time is what a baby wants and needs to do. Being handed toys bores and frustrates most babies. It also delays the development of hand-eye coordination.

With enough practice directing their hands toward an object, the average baby will be able to grab an object within reach without looking at his hand by about 4 to 5 months of age. This skill, which is called "top-level" reaching, is as major a milestone in fine motor development as sitting up is in gross motor development.

MANIPULATING OBJECTS By about 3 months of age, a baby will consciously grab an object that he's offered. However, he's only able to hold the object (a rattle, e.g.) in his palm, with his fingers and thumb wrapped around the rattle on the same side. If you pick up a rattle in the same way (called a "palmer" grip), you'll see that it's difficult to do much more manipulation than shaking your hand or dropping the rattle, which is all a baby can do with it himself at age 3 months. And the dropping of an object at this age is involuntary, not deliberate.

Before he's about 6 months old, a baby reaches and grabs as if they were one motion. When he swipes at an object, his hand automatically closes, even if he misses. That's why he'll pull Mom's hair or Dad's eyeglasses so often. He'll also reach and grasp at a ray of sunlight or a reflection as if it were a tangible object.

Before a baby becomes more discriminating at what he grabs, he has to begin to learn about the properties of the physical objects he sees. The first step, which begins at 4 or 5 months, is to bring everything to his mouth. As with swiping, the importance of this mouthing is often misunderstood by parents. Some, believing it's unsafe and unsanitary, try to eliminate it. Some, believing the reason for it is teething, limit to a few teethers the objects they allow their baby to mouth. Still others keep a pacifier in their baby's mouth much of the time.

Without the chance to put things in his mouth, a baby can't easily learn such concepts as hard and soft, rough and smooth, light and heavy. At about 6 months of age, a baby who's had the chance to do a lot of mouthing expands his manipulation of objects to shaking, banging, turning, and dropping.

The result of this experimentation is that a baby begins to understand the difference between objects that can be grabbed, such as a rattle, and things that can't, such as a bright picture in a book. Instead of automatically grabbing when he reaches, he begins to touch with an open hand before he decides to grab. By about 8 to 9 months of age, he'll gain the ability to poke and prod with his index finger, rather than simply with his entire hand.

Also by 8 to 10 months, he'll begin to hold objects in his fingers instead of in his palm. At first, all his fingers will push against his thumb. Gradually, by 12 to 15 months of age, a baby will achieve what's called a "pincer grip," the ability to hold an object between the index finger and the thumb.

The ability to hold objects in his fingers gives a baby many more ways to manipulate them. It also makes it easier to pass an object from hand to hand. And holding an object in the fingers not only makes it easier to deliberately drop an object but also to drop it accurately.

USING OBJECTS AS TOOLS By age 1, a baby has achieved enough accuracy to drop an object into a receptacle—for example, dropping a ball into a bowl or a rattle into a box. This is one example of what experts call using an object as a "tool." In other words, at some point in the last 3 months of his first year, a baby's interest begins to include not only what objects *are*, but how they can be *used*.

One early step in using objects is comparing one to another. In the last 3 months of his first year, a baby will begin to hold an object in each hand, turning them as he shifts his gaze from one to the other. Then he'll start to compare their physical properties by banging them together, putting them in his mouth, and dropping them to see what kind of noise they make when they land.

By about 1 year of age, a baby who's holding two blocks will attempt to put one on top of another, an important developmental activity that child psychologists label *stacking*. The first attempts usually fail because he can't release the top block gently enough to keep it from falling off. Most babies can stack two small blocks by age 15 months and three blocks by age 18 months. They also love to experiment with stacking almost anything else they can get their hands on, such as cubes, shoe boxes, pots and pans, empty cottage cheese or yogurt containers, and a wide variety of toys.

Another kind of adaptive behavior that occupies 1-year-olds for hours is called *emptying and gathering*. This consists of assembling a collection of objects, placing them in a box, bowl, pan, or other container, dumping the objects on the floor, then starting all over again. By age 15 to 18 months, a baby's coordination and finger control improve to the point where he can drop a small object into a fairly small opening, such as the neck of a bottle. He'll also begin to fit objects into slightly larger openings—for example, trying to drop a cube into a square opening, a cylinder into a round opening, etc.

A third kind of adaptive behavior is called *nesting*. One example is fitting paper cups inside one another. Toy manufacturers sell a variety of progressively smaller cubes or cups that encourage nesting.

A fourth kind of adaptive behavior is manipulating objects with the fingers. Babies learn to push levers, twist dials, pull strings, and turn the pages of books. By age 2, young children who've had a lot of opportunity to develop dexterity can string large beads on a shoelace.

The importance of all four kinds of behavior go far beyond the development of fine motor skills. All normal babies have an enormous curiosity about the world around them, an innate love of exploration. Numerous research studies have shown that children who retain that curiosity and love of learning tend to perform very well in school. These studies have also shown that these superior performers tended to have parents and care givers who provided them as infants with a wide variety of objects to inspect and manipulate.

Second, manipulating objects is crucial to the development of many important concepts about the physical world, such as up and down, in and out, top and bottom, empty and full, heavy and light, small and large, etc. That's why adaptive behavior and language acquisition go hand in hand.

A Baby's Intellectual Growth in the First Two Years of Life

WHAT IS INTELLECTUAL GROWTH?

Intellectual, or cognitive, growth is the acquisition of the ability to think—that is, the ability to understand information received from the senses, to remember, to solve problems, to distinguish illusion from reality, to make decisions, and to anticipate the future. It also includes the ability to communicate thoughts, primarily through written and spoken language, but also through art, music, gestures, and other body movements.

THE AMAZING NEWBORN—A REVOLUTION THROUGH RESEARCH

In the past three decades, infant research has brought about a revolutionary change in our perception of the cognitive capabilities of a newborn baby. An anecdote that illustrates this change was related by psychologist Jerome Bruner, whose research at Harvard produced dramatic increases in our knowledge of infant perception, thinking, and education. In the late 1960s, a prominent pediatrician visited Bruner's infant research facility. During his tour, he saw a demonstration of one procedure, in which a 6-week-old baby learned to bring a blurred picture into focus by sucking on a pacifier. The visitor watched for a while, then angrily exclaimed, "That's ridiculous! Babies of that age can't see!"

For most of mankind's history, newborns were believed to be not only blind, but also deaf. Since they were supposedly unable to perceive anything, they were described in a 1935 textbook as a "picture of psychological incompetence," and their minds were described by William James as "one great blooming, buzzing confusion."

Beginning in the 1950s, however, pioneer researchers began to prove that all five senses were active from the moment of birth. At the same time, intense observations of infant behavior by the famed psychologist Jean Piaget revealed strong evidence of a logical sequence of cognitive development that also began at the moment of birth. Subsequent studies have proven that newborns are capable of perception, communication, imitation, and learning. Research has also begun to flesh out a complex, logical sequence of cognitive growth that begins at birth and continues through the preschool years.

RESEARCH INTO COGNITION

Research on the intellectual development of young children has been conducted basically in three ways. The first, pioneered by Jean Piaget, is based on direct observation of children in the course of their daily lives. Piaget and others observed everything a child did and they attempted to build a theory incorporating the entire structure and growth of a child's overall ability to think and reason.

The second method, used by the famous American behaviorist B. F. Skinner and others, was based on laboratory experiments with children. Since experiments were focused on specific learning situations, these scientists tended to concentrate on how children received, processed, and stored information, rather than on an overall theory of intellectual growth.

The third and oldest method of investigating intellectual development of children is mental measurement; that is, devising tests, such as IQ tests, to determine what a child knows at a specific age. Psychologists interested in mental measurement have little interest in general theories of how and why a child knows what he knows.

We're going to take a look at both structural and information-processing research as it applies to the first 2 years of life. Mental measurement tests aren't really applicable in the first 2 years of life because they depend on language skills. So in this section, we will discuss in detail the very important subject of language acquisition.

PIAGET'S THEORY OF COGNITIVE DEVELOPMENT

Jean Piaget, who died in 1980 at the age of 84, was by far the most important and influential figure in modern child-development research. His first position as a psychologist was working for Théophile Simon, who with Alfred Binet developed what became the Stanford-Binet Intelligence scale, our modern IQ test. Soon, however, Piaget became more interested in how children of different ages formed answers to questions than what those answers were. He soon began unstructured observation of children, including his own three. Decades later, his monumental theory of cognitive development, published in 1952, tried to explain how a child learned about the characteristics and functions of objects and people around him, how he learned to group objects to identify similarities and differences, how he understood what caused changes in objects and events, and how he formed expectations of objects and events.

Piaget believed that children weren't just passive receivers of information, but rather played an active role in organizing that information. Piaget used the term *schema* to refer to a basic unit of thought, either an object or experience. For example, an infant schema might be sucking anything that touches his lips. Piaget called the process of integrating and coordinating schemata (plural of schema) *organization*. A child's organization, or mental image of the world, was constantly being modified by two processes, assimilation and adaptation. Assimilation was the incorporation of new information into the existing organization—for example, learning that a rubber nipple could be sucked as well as a mother's nipple. Adaptation was changing the organization to fit new information—for example, realizing that a rattle could be dropped as well as shaken.

In his famous theory, Piaget suggested that intellectual growth proceeded through a series of developmental stages. He believed that all children went through the stages in the same order, although not all at exactly the same age. The changes in each stage were gradual and continuous, but the attainments in earlier stages were necessary before the later stages could be accomplished.

Piaget's first stage, which lasted from birth to about age 2, he called the *sensorimotor stage*.

The Sensorimotor Stage: Birth to Twenty-four Months

The sensorimotor stage is the time of life when a young child forms his knowledge of the world through his growing command of his senses and his motor skills. The most important achievements of this period are:

1. The ability to integrate information from the senses. For example, when an infant first sees a bell and hears a tinkling sound, he doesn't immediately associate the sound with the object. Later, he learns that he can see, hear, and even touch the same object.
2. The capacity to recognize that objects and people exist even when they can't be seen, heard, touched, smelled, or tasted. This extremely important ability is called *object permanence*.
3. The ability to imitate the behavior of others, even when they are not in the room.
4. A sense of time that includes the concepts of before and after, not just immediate experience.
5. The ability to conceive of goals and to plan and carry out behavior to achieve those goals.

These achievements of the sensorimotor stage are accomplished in six substages. Although Piaget defined these substages and labeled them by age, he cautioned that the pace of progress was gradual, not abrupt, and that rate of advancement varied considerably from child to child.

The six substages of the sensorimotor stage are:

STAGE ONE: USING REFLEXES—BIRTH TO ONE MONTH At birth, almost all the behavior of an infant is governed by reflexes. An example is the reflex to suck when the lips are touched. During this stage, an infant becomes more efficient in using his reflexes. For example, he may discriminate between sucking his mother's nipple, which produces food, and sucking an object that doesn't. He sucks more aggressively on the mother's nipple and may not suck at all on another object.

STAGE TWO: PRIMARY CIRCULAR REACTIONS—ONE TO FOUR MONTHS During this stage, reflex behavior is gradually replaced by more deliberate actions. For example, a baby who wants to suck on his fingers gains the ability to deliberately bring his hand to his mouth instead of having to wait until his hand reaches his mouth accidently. A baby's activity is focused on repeating actions that bring him pleasure, which is why Piaget labeled them *circular*. Almost all these actions focus on his own body, hence the label *primary*.

Piaget believed that the tendency to repeat actions that bring pleasure was the first proof of the development of memory. Memory, however, is very limited as yet. A baby in this stage has no sense of object permanence. If an object drops is removed from sight, he'll stare at the space where it was briefly, then forget all about it.

This stage also marks the beginning of imitation. The first step is called pseudoimitation; that is, the adult initiates the imitation, not the baby. For example, the baby will make a cooing sound, which the adult imitates. Then the baby imitates the adult. At this stage, babies haven't yet learned to discriminate between themselves and the world around them. Experts believe that when a baby hears an adult imitate his sound or when he hears another baby cry, he assumes that he made the noise and continues the activity on that assumption.

STAGE THREE: SECONDARY CIRCULAR REACTIONS—FOUR TO EIGHT MONTHS At this stage, a baby still concentrates on making pleasurable activities last, but these activities are increasingly concentrated on external objects, people, and events, rather than on his own body. This first introduction to cause and effect involves noticing the pleasurable results of some random action, such as banging a spoon on a tray, then deliberately repeating the action.

Instead of merely staring at the space previously occupied by an object, a baby will now follow it until it disappears. If it's totally hidden, he'll abandon the search. But he learns to recognize objects from partial images, and he'll reach for an object that's only partially visible.

In this stage babies deliberately imitate actions and sounds made by others, as long as they're not too complex.

STAGE FOUR: COORDINATION OF MEANS AND ENDS—EIGHT TO

TWELVE MONTHS During this stage, a baby becomes more goal directed, and learns to separate the means from the end. For example, during the previous stage, reaching for and grabbing a rattle was one continuous activity. If Mom held up a hand between her baby's hand and the rattle, he'd become confused and stop. In this stage, he'll just push Mom's hand out of the way, then continue reaching.

The reason a baby is more goal oriented is that he's attained the understanding that objects and people are permanent objects apart from himself, and that they continue to exist even when not in his sight. One manifestation of this understanding is separation anxiety, crying when Mom or another primary care giver isn't in the room, and stranger anxiety, crying when a stranger approaches.

A baby will now search for a hidden object if he sees it being hidden. However, if the object is moved from one hiding place to another, he'll only search in the first location, because his memory isn't yet good enough to recall a sequence of events.

During this stage, a baby's ability to imitate continues to improve, especially his ability to immediately imitate brand new sounds and actions.

STAGE FIVE: TERTIARY CIRCULAR REACTIONS—TWELVE TO EIGHTEEN MONTHS During this stage, a child becomes a miniscientist, learning about the world around him through endless exploration and trial and error. If he's given a round peg, he'll try it in every hole of a shape sorter until he discovers where it fits. If banging a pot with a spoon is fun, a baby will experiment with banging everything he can find. Since a baby usually walks during this stage, his house becomes his laboratory, with everything that's in reach becoming a target of his experiments.

Children also learn to use adults as resources during this stage. If they want to get into a toy box or drawer they can't open, they'll go get Mom or Dad to help.

Object permanence also advances, to the point where a child can remember changes in hiding places that he sees. If he doesn't find the object in the first hiding place, he'll move on to the second. However, he won't continue the search if he hasn't been able to see the objects moved from one hiding place to another.

Imitation during this stage is much more accurate, especially verbal imitation. A child also begins to imitate a series of actions, or rituals, when his memory is triggered by an object. For example, if he sees the teddy bear he takes to bed, he may lie down on the floor and imitate going to sleep.

STAGE SIX: INVENTING NEW MEANS THROUGH MENTAL COMBINATIONS—EIGHTEEN TO TWENTY-FOUR MONTHS In this culmination of the sensorimotor stage, a child finally begins to think, to form, store in memory, and recall mental images of the world. For example, when given a round peg and a shape sorter, he'll study the peg and the holes, mentally determining the proper hole before placing the peg, instead of experimenting physically through trial and error. His understanding of cause and effect has advanced to the point at which he may move a glass of milk out of the way before reaching for another object on the table, rather than knocking it over while reaching.

The ability to form mental images and remember also extends to object permanence. If a ball disappears during play, a child doesn't have to see where it went to search for it. Rather, he'll look in likely places where balls have been found before, such as under couches and behind doors.

A child also begins to imitate actions he's seen in the past. For example, a child who sees another toddler crying in the barber chair may begin to cry if he's taken to the barber. He may also begin to imitate things he's seen on television.

By about age 2, a child has progressed from being almost totally controlled by reflexes to being a thinker capable of imagining, planning, and carrying out relatively complex activities. Piaget emphasized, however, that the mental images upon which these activities are based are "pictures" of the real world, formed through the senses and motor activity. A child is not yet capable of forming thoughts based on abstract concepts. That advancement requires the acquisition of language.

LEARNING AND MEMORY

Learning is the acquisition of knowledge, skills, or behaviors through experience. Learning is a lifelong process that involves first accumulating experience, then storing it in memory for later processing. Anything we know or do that isn't innate has to be learned.

Piaget believed that behavior resulted from a person actively processing and modifying input from the environment. That's why his research technique consisted of passively observing the entire range of children's everyday activities. This research provided an invaluable overall look at the intellectual growth of children, but it didn't provide a detailed look at the process by which children learn specific facts or behaviors.

That kind of research has been conducted by the behaviorists, psychologists who believe that the environment, not the child, is the active force in shaping all behavior. These psychologists, the most famous of whom is B. F. Skinner, have done most of their research in the laboratory, where they can carefully control the environment and study the response it elicits.

The behaviorists' research has resulted in their identifying several different ways in which children learn. Unlike Piaget, who believed the ways in which children learn change as they mature, the behaviorists believe that babies learn in exactly the same ways as adults. These ways include:

Habituation

Habituation is the process by which a child becomes used to a particular sensation or experience over time. Habituation allows the mind to filter routine stimuli from new or important stimuli. For example, a young baby soon learns to differentiate between the ticking of a clock and his mother's voice.

Habituation becomes more rapid with age, allowing older children to learn more quickly. Studies have shown that among children of the same age, those who habituate more rapidly tend to have higher IQs and perform better on learning tests.

Classical Conditioning

The famous example of classical conditioning was Pavlov's dog, who was conditioned to drool when a light was flashed just before food was presented. Similarly, a baby may come to associate the sight of a nurse with the pain of an injection, and may begin to cry whenever a nurse is spotted.

Operant Conditioning

Operant conditioning is a form of learning that takes place through the association of a behavior with its consequence. The classic experiment in operant conditioning was performed by B. F. Skinner when he trained a laboratory rat to push a bar to receive a pellet of food or a drink of water. From this experience, Skinner theorized that behavior that is "reinforced" by a reward (positive reinforcement) or the absence of punishment (negative reinforcement) is likely to be repeated. Operant conditioning can be used to teach new skills through a training process that involves reinforcing behavior that increasingly approximates the desired final behavior. This process is called *shaping*.

Operant conditioning allows an individual to adjust to a changing environment through *adaptive behavior*. In other words, behavior that is no longer being reinforced is "extinguished," to be replaced by behavior that is receiving more reinforcement.

Operant conditioning begins very early in life. A simple example is a parent reinforcing an infant's smile by smiling in return. As an infant grows older, parents begin to find themselves withholding reinforcement in order to extinguish behavior. For example, parents of a very young baby respond immediately to a baby's cries, because crying is the only way the infant can communicate need. Later, when parents are sure that an older baby is crying solely to get attention, they may withhold reinforcement to extinguish the behavior.

Social or Observational Learning

Both Piaget and the behaviorists believe that children learn through watching others, then imitating their behavior. A child's ability to imitate increases with age. That's why parents have to be very careful about what kinds of behavior, or "models," to which their young children are exposed.

The Development of Memory

To understand how we learn, it's useful to draw a comparison to how we nourish our bodies. In order to eat, we have to accumulate various kinds of food, store the food in places where we can easily find it, then remove the food from storage when we're ready to eat so we can cook it. Similarly, learning requires not only that we obtain information and experience through the methods above, but also that we store it so that it can later be retrieved for processing, or "thinking."

All of us use two types of memory. The first is short-term memory, storage of information for a few seconds or minutes. Short-term memory allows us to dial the number we just looked up in the telephone book without filling up our minds uselessly with every number we've ever heard. The second type of memory is long-term memory, which is the storage of information over an indefinite period of time. Long-term memory allows us to remember our own telephone number, social security number, and so on.

Infants develop short-term memory first, and this type of memory matures relatively quickly. Long-term memory, however, is developed much more slowly. The reason is that infants lack the mental ability to "code" information so that it can be easily retrieved. According to Piaget, it's only in the last half of the first year of life that young children are able to form mental pictures complete enough for them to remember where a ball rolled to in the past.

Research has shown that even the long-term memory of 2-year-olds is inefficient, because language is needed for a mature and sophisticated system of encoding and recalling information. Few people remember anything from the first 3 or 4 years of life because long term memories encoded by language replace memories that consisted of mental pictures.

The result is that young children "think" (process information) much more slowly and less capably than older children and adults. Interestingly, studies have shown that adults with "photographic" memories, or memories that produce mental pictures of objects and experiences, often have a great deal of difficulty using that information in creative thought. The reason is that creative thought depends on advanced language skills and recall of information encoded by language.

WHAT YOU SHOULD KNOW ABOUT . . .

SIGNS OF PROBLEMS IN LANGUAGE AND SPEECH DEVELOPMENT

Nelson's Textbook of Pediatrics *provides the following guidelines that indicate to parents and caregivers when they should consult their pediatrician about a possible problem.*

Age	Sign
6 months	Does not turn eyes and head to sound coming from side or behind
10 months	Does not make some kind of response to his name
15 months	Does not understand and respond to "no-no," "bye-bye," and "bottle"
18 months	Is not saying up to 10 single words
21 months	Does not respond to directions (e.g., "sit down," "come here," "stand up")
24 months	Has excessive, nonappropriate jargoning or echoing
24 months	Has no 2-word phrases
30 months	Has speech that is not intelligible to family members
36 months	Uses no simple sentences
36 months	Has not begun to ask simple questions
36 months	Has speech that is not intelligible to strangers
42 months	Consistently fails to produce the final consonant of words (e.g., "ca" for cat, "bo" for bone)
48 months	Noticeably stutters
Any age	Voice is monotone, of inappropriate pitch, unduly loud, inaudible, or consistently hoarse

THE PROCESS OF LEARNING LANGUAGE

For all their differences, Piaget and the behaviorists have equally emphasized the importance of language in a child's intellectual growth. Similarly, all parents cherish a baby's first words as an important milestone, the symbols of the beginning of lifelong communication with their child.

The importance of language has led to extensive research into language acquisition. But of all the human mysteries that psychologists have tried to solve, language acquisition has proven one of the most difficult to fathom.

Among the information that has been conclusively proven is that all normal children acquire language in the same pattern at approximately the same time all over the world, regardless of the complexity or simplicity of the native language, cultural differences, or widely varying child-rearing techniques. Not only do all children begin to coo, then babble at about the same age, but the sounds they make are also similar all over the world.

One early explanation of this language acquisition was provided by the behaviorist B. F. Skinner, who put forth his *reinforcement theory*. Skinner believed that all babies babble the same "universal sounds," which are common to all languages. He suggested that mothers, or other primary care givers, reinforced the sounds common to their particular language, while other useless sounds were extinguished. Skinner further suggested that young children learned to form words, then sentences, through imitation and reinforcement.

Research has proven that children who are neglected and kept in isolation don't develop normal language. But the behavioral theory fails to account for the fact that young children put together words, such as "he goed out," that they've never heard before. The reinforcement theory also fails to account for the fact that parents often reinforce bad grammar ("her bring milk") because the sense is correct, while disputing grammatical sentences ("Walt Disney comes on Tuesday") because the sense is wrong.

A dramatically different theory of language acquisition was put forth by the famous linguist Noam Chomsky. Chomsky theorized that language ability was inborn, the result of a "language acquisition device" genetically programmed in the human brain. He argued that while imitation and reinforcement built vocabulary, grammatical rules and originality were innate.

What theory is closest to the truth? Most experts find some truth in all the major theories, while still acknowledging that an enormous number of questions still need to be answered.

The Sequence of Language Development

Charting a baby's growing language skills requires looking at two separate abilities. The first is the ability to understand what's being said to him and around him. What a child understands is called *receptive* language. The second ability is being able to use language by speaking (or in the case of deaf infants, by signing). This is called *productive* language.

A baby's receptive language skills advance more quickly than his productive language skills. One major reason is that speaking requires not only learning vocabulary and language rules, but also the physical maturity and muscle control necessary to form all the sounds we use in our language. Some babies master the physical part of speaking earlier than others, just as some babies walk much earlier than others.

Another reason productive language capability may be hard to judge is that some babies don't talk as much as others because they communicate effectively in other ways. Some young children develop physical gestures to indicate their desires, which are well understood by their caregivers, so they have less need to talk. Still other children don't talk as much as others because there's no one interested in listening.

The result is that although developing receptive and productive language skills are equally important, the level of receptive language ability is a more reliable measurement of overall language development in the first 2 years of life than is productive language skills.

Developing the Ability to Understand

Babies seem to be born with a predisposition toward the human voice. At birth, a baby can determine where sounds are coming from and can differentiate between sounds of various pitch, intensity, and rhythm. Studies have shown that by just two weeks of age, a baby can tell the difference between human voices and other sounds. By about 2 months of age, a baby can tell the difference between the voices of his parents and those of strangers, between Dad's voice and Mom's voice, and can pick up emotional clues (affection, anger, etc.) from human speech.

By age 4 to 5 months, a baby has a keen ear for human speech, so much so that he can discriminate between such similar sounds as "bah" and "gah." Based on studies that measured heart rate when certain words were spoken, babies of about the same age appeared to respond different-ly to familiar words such as *bottle* or *bye-bye*. By 6 months of age, a baby is very aware of the intonation and rhythm of his native language.

At some point between 8 and 11 months, a baby will demonstrate that he's beginning to understand words by responding to commands such as "no" or even "hot." By the end of the first year, he'll respond with the appropriate gestures when he hears "say bye-bye" or "let's play patty-cake."

In the second year, a baby's vocabulary soars from a handful of under-stood words to an average of nearly 300 words by 24 months of age. Some children seem to know the names of nearly every object in their environment. During this period, children also begin to respond to simple commands, such as "come here" and "give me that bottle." Toward the second birthday, some children will begin to understand the meaning of prepositions such as "in," "on," and "up."

Developing the Ability to Speak

Here is the pattern of speech development:

CRYING   An infant begins producing sounds from the moment of birth. Crying, the first form of communication, soon becomes expressive, with parents being able to tell the difference between a "hungry" cry and an "angry" cry.

As he cries, breathes, and swallows, a baby produces about eight distinguishable sounds, about one-fifth the sounds that an adult uses in speaking. These sounds, five vowels and the consonants *h*, *l*, and *g*, are made by babies in all cultures around the world.

COOING   At some point between 1 and 3 months of age, a baby begins to make non-crying sounds that are called *cooing*. Early cooing consists primarily of vowel sounds, which may be linked to a baby's mood. *I* and *e* sounds are more common when a baby's upset, *a*, *o*, and *u* sounds are more common when he's relaxed and happy. Later cooing may include some repetitive sounds such as "ga."

BABBLING   Between 4 and 7 months of age, babies begin to repeat vowel and consonant combinations, an activity called babbling. Early babbling usually starts when a baby is contentedly playing, in contrast to the earliest sounds, which were made when he was tired or hungry. Early combinations, which include "mama," "dada," "baba," "gaga," and "mimi," are babbled by babies all over the world.

Within another month or 2, however, babies begin to babble in their native languages. They drop sounds that aren't used in their language, and the intonation and rhythm of their babbling are the same as that of actual speech. Babies often utter what sound like sentences but are in fact nonsense syllables, a practice called *jargoning*. Jargon sounds different in every language. For example, Chinese babies learn to jargon in a much higher tone than American babies, because spoken Chinese has a much higher pitch. This selectivity that changes babble to jargoning is an excellent example of the environmental influence on speech.

Another environmental influence leads directly to the uttering of words. A mother, father, or other primary care giver who pays close attention to a baby's babbling usually responds enthusiastically to such repeated sounds as "mama" and "dada." This feedback encourages a baby to make more of the "right" noises during babbling or jargoning.

THE FIRST WORDS   All parents eagerly await the utterance of that "first word." However, because a baby uses meaningful sounds amid his normal babbling, it's hard to pinpoint the very first time he intentionally uses "mama" to refer to his mother, for example.

Studies indicate that 7% of babies utter that first word before the end of their eighth month, with most babies following suit at 10 or 11 months. On the other hand, 2% don't attempt to use words until after age 2. The average baby has a productive vocabulary of three words on his first birthday.

About half of the first few words spoken by babies are the names of things (ball, kitty); 15% are names for specific people (Mommy, Daddy, Nana), 15% are action words (bye-bye, give); and the rest are divided between modifiers (red, dirty); social words (yes, no, please); and function words (what, for, and). A child is most likely to learn words that are most meaningful in his own world. For example, he'll learn "doggie" if he's got a favorite pet, "car" if that's a favorite toy. The average toddler's vocabulary increases to about twenty words at 15 months and twenty-five to fifty words at 18 months.

Some "first words" may not be real English words, but rather just syllables. What puts them in the category of words is that both the child and his care givers attach the same meaning to the syllables as to the actual term. For example, a baby and his parents may understand that "ba" means "bottle."

Even though his first speech consists of single words, a baby tends to use these words not only as identifying names, or "labels," but also as sentences. Using single words as sentences is called *holophrastic speech*. For example, when a child points to a toy and a shelf and says "car," he really means "I want that car." When he's away from home and says "bye-bye," he means "I want to leave."

SENTENCES   Between 12 and 18 months of age, a child may put two words together to form a sentence. Some examples are "Mommy milk" and "Daddy phone." These sentences lack pronouns, articles, adjectives, and other embellishments, but they contain all the meaning of longer sentences condensed, or *telegraphed* into two words.

Telegraphic sentences can often have several different meanings, depending on the circumstances. "Mommy milk," for example, can mean "Mommy, I want milk," "Mommy, I've finished my milk," or "Mommy, I spilled my milk." By age 2, a child may be using three-word telegraphic sentences, such as "Mommy go bye-bye."

IMPROVING VOCABULARY   A child's vocabulary undergoes two changes as his command of language improves. First, he adds words to the list of those he understands and uses. Second, he gains an increasingly precise knowledge of the meaning of the words he uses.

In his second year, a child has little mastery of *semantics*, or the exact meaning of words. Because a *ball* is round, he may use the word ball for the moon, an apple, or anything else that's round. This tendency to generalize is called *overextension*. Sometimes a child exhibits the opposite tendency, *underextension*. For example, he may believe that "Ryan" is only his name and applies to no other person.

ARTICULATION   When a baby begins to babble, he can normally articulate all the sounds used in normal speech. But as babble turns into speech, the ability to form such consonant sounds as *l* and *r* disappear. For most children, articulation lags behind vocabulary. At 24 months of age, only 25% to 50% of what the average child says is intelligible to someone who doesn't "speak his language." The level of articulation can vary widely from one child to another. In the first 2 years of life, the ability to pronounce words distinctly has no relation to the level of language skills attained.

Helping a Young Child Acquire Language Skills

In the absence of comprehensive knowledge of exactly how children acquire language, there's no program that parents can follow to guarantee that their baby will develop superior language skills. For example, there's no hard scientific evidence that improving a baby's vocabulary by drilling him with flash cards will permanently increase his overall mastery of language.

There are, however, a number of things parents and other care givers can do that have proven to promote normal language development. These include:

1. Talking and reading to babies, including newborns. Although young infants can't understand what's being said or read to them, they do become familiar with the patterns and rhythms of human speech. The interaction with adults also implants the very valuable idea that talking and reading are pleasurable activities.
2. Increasing feedback in response to an infant's babbling. For example, when your baby babbles "Mama," you can say, "Yes, Mama's here." This communication can and should be simple. But beware of falling into non-English baby talk. You can say, "give Mama a kiss," but you should avoid "give Mama kissy-kissy."
3. Model the use of polite speech for the child, using "please," "thank you," "excuse me," and similar words and phrases.
4. Encourage children to use speech instead of gestures to ask for things. Some parents are so attentive to every need of their young child, rushing to get a toy or a bottle at the first sign, that they don't give him a chance to practice speaking.
5. Use a technique called *expansion* to build a child's language skills. This involves enlarging a child's telegraphic sentences into full sentences, as well as filling in real words for unintelligible words. Two examples:
   Child: "Doggie sit."
   Adult: "Yes, the doggie is sitting in the chair."
   Child: "I want baba."
   Adult: "You want your bottle?"

6. Offer lots of encouragement and praise, not criticism, at every stage. Young children's speech is full of mistakes and mispronunciations. These will clear up over time if children are encouraged to practice.

Problems in Language Acquisition

Two physical problems that can inhibit language acquisition in the first 2 years of life are mental retardation and deafness. Mental retardation normally causes severe developmental lags in several areas, and can be detected by a test that evaluates overall development. This and other tests will be discussed in the next section.

The earlier deafness is detected, the more normal language acquisition can be. Deaf children will cry, coo, and even begin to babble, just like hearing children. Perhaps because they don't receive any verbal feedback, babbling soon fades away. However, if deaf infants are introduced to signing, their language development will proceed normally. In other words, they will sign their first words around their first birthday, increase their signing vocabulary to thirty to fifty signs by 18 months, and they'll make the same kind of language errors as hearing children.

A problem, which is not physical, that can inhibit language acquisition is neglect. Children who aren't spoken to, and whose early language efforts are ignored, will seriously lag in language skills. This kind of neglect can occur both at home and in inadequate day care.

EARLY LEARNING AND THE "SUPERBABY" MOVEMENT

No one who walks into a toy store, examines titles in a bookstore, or listens in on adult conversations at a preschool playground can escape the conclusion that a great number of parents today are obsessed with the intellectual development of their young children. Toy stores are filled with expensive "educational" toys, bookstores sell dozens of different "how to make your baby smarter" instructionals. Not only has the number of nursery schools increased 1,000% since 1965, but most communities have dozens of "early learning" programs, some of which are aimed at infants as young as 4 weeks.

The rational for these programs, toys, books, etc., stems from revolutionary research revealing that intellectual development is a logical process that begins at birth. Some educators, psychologists, and parents took the fact that very young children could learn and did so in a logical way to mean that the process could be significantly accelerated and improved. Since adults learn skills more quickly and effectively through intensive, organized instruction, the argument went, so could young children. Advocates of early learning maintained that not only could children be taught to read, write, and play musical instruments at a younger age, but, by accelerating their instruction, they'd eventually acquire a more complete store of knowledge and attain a higher level of reasoning ability, both of which would be reflected in a higher IQ score.

Some widely publicized programs aimed at young children seemed to provide concrete proof of the benefits of earlier learning. Out of the social upheavals of the 1960s came great concern for improving the lot of disadvantaged children. Young idealistic educators organized programs designed to compensate for the bleak home environments of children born into poverty-stricken families. Soon, evidence emerged that the enrichment provided these children enabled them to perform much more competently when they entered grade school. This evidence so impressed Congress that preschool education for the disadvantaged became a federal program known as "Head Start."

The term *Head Start* was used because the instruction gave enrolled disadvantaged children an advantage over disadvantaged children who didn't have the benefit of preschool programs. However, the phrase was immediately seized upon by some middle- and upper-class parents who believed that similar preschool programs would give their kids a "head start" over their peers.

These beliefs have become so widespread that many school systems have established "academic" kindergartens that emphasize reading and writing, while at the same time extending kindergartens from a half day to a full day. Some school systems have begun to admit 4-year-olds into these programs. Nursery schools, to prepare children for earlier academic training, have begun organized instruction in the alphabet, counting, even reading short words.

Among the more vociferous advocates of the advantages of early learning is Glenn Doman, whose Better Baby Institute advertises parental education seminars and learning materials designed to teach babies under 1 year of age to read words, learn foreign languages, and accomplish other sophisticated intellectual tasks. Doman's program gave rise to the expression "superbaby." Taking Doman's beliefs one step further, one California psychologist has founded Prenatal University, where he teaches pregnant mothers to communicate with their 7-month-old fetuses in order to stimulate their intellectual development and language acquisition. Similar programs have since spread across the country.

Is It Possible to Produce a Superbaby?

An exhaustive review of current research and experts indicates the following:

1. No study has yet proven that accelerated or intensive preschool learning significantly improves the intellectual potential of middle-

class children. In other words, there's no proof that teaching a child to read at age 4 rather than at age 6 will make him a more intelligent adult. There's also no proof that any type of preschool education can transform a child with a normal IQ into a genius.

This does not mean that some techniques developed by Glenn Doman or other advocates of early learning may not eventually prove to be helpful, or even revolutionary. It does mean that the evidence to date is strictly anecdotal.

2. Recent research into the early childhood experiences of unusually talented adults has revealed that their early childhood environments were exceptionally supportive and enriched. For example, Dr. Benjamin Bloom, a renowned educational researcher, recently studied 120 adults with superior records of achievement in a wide variety of fields. Bloom's findings, and those of others, strongly suggest that parental support plays a critical role in a child's eventually achieving his or her full intellectual, artistic, or athletic potential. But nothing in the findings suggested that any kind of formal preschool education played a part in the fulfillment of potential.

3. There's growing evidence that some kinds of accelerated or intensive preschool learning can cause moderate to severe developmental problems at some point between infancy and the teenage years. One common problem found by researchers is greatly increased stress that causes behavioral and emotional problems. Other studies indicate that some children who are pushed into learning to read at age 4 or 5 develop more reading problems than children who learn to read at age 6 or 7. Further evidence exists that some intensive early instruction inhibits the later development of creativity and decision making skills.

A majority of child psychologists believe that some advocates of early learning make the erroneous assumption that young children learn in the same way that adults learn, disregarding the fact that adults are physically, socially, and emotionally mature. An infant's intellectual development, on the other hand, is intricately related to his physical, gross motor, fine motor, social, and emotional growth. Researchers have found that children develop best when this growth is "balanced." When it's unbalanced by undue emphasis on intellectual growth, problems can easily develop in other areas. The effects of stress on children may not be immediately apparent, for two reasons. First, young children lack the experience to understand and verbalize what is happening to them. Second, young children have a strong urge to please their parents and the other adults in their lives. Children can seem perfectly normal, until developmental problems suddenly appear in future years.

The Balanced Approach to Early Learning

Current research shows that parents and other care givers play a much more significant role in the intellectual development of their young children than previosuly had been thought. This role, however, is a "supportive" one. Parents can enrich a child's environment, provide stimulation when needed, and encourage developing interests. They can also look for preschool programs that provide an enriched atmosphere while encouraging lots of social interaction and play.

This research also shows that serious problems can develop when early learning is parent or teacher directed rather than child directed. There's no evidence that academic training for children under age 6 has any lasting benefits. The majority of experts recommend that if parents have any doubt about a child's genuine enthusiasm for any type of program or instruction, the prudent response is to discontinue it.

The Organization of a Baby's Day in the First Two Years

During the first 6 or 7 months of life, a baby, with the help of his parents and care givers, increasingly organizes his twenty-four-hour day into a pattern of behavior that better fits with the schedule of the rest of his family. This pattern normally consists of three meals of solid food during regular eating times, morning and afternoon naps, and sleeping through the night. He's primarily alert and active during nonsleeping and noneating hours, and he's extremely interested in interacting with his care givers and exploring his environment.

By far the most important part of this schedule to most parents is a baby's sleeping through the night.

A BABY'S SLEEPING PATTERNS IN THE FIRST TWO YEARS OF LIFE

While science has yet to completely answer the question of exactly why we need to sleep, research indicates that sleep plays an important role in synthesizing protein, memory storage, and many other complex biochemical functions.

A newborn's body is growing at a faster rate than at any other time in life, and his need for sleep appears to be tied to that growth. As the growth rate begins to slow, the total hours of sleep needed fall from seventeen to twenty for a newborn to twelve to fourteen hours for a 6-month-old.

A newborn's sleep is broken up into as many as seven different segments, largely because his stomach isn't large enough to hold enough breast milk or formula to stave off hunger long enough to sleep through the night. The need for a middle-of-the-night feeding disappears at some point after 6 weeks of age, most commonly at around 3 months for bottle-fed babies and somewhat later for breast-fed babies.

However, hunger isn't the only reason babies don't sleep through the night. Another reason is a baby's sleeping patterns. As we explained about the newborn baby, a very young infant spends 50% of his sleeping hours in light, dreaming sleep (active sleep), in comparison to an adult's pattern of 20% of sleeping time in dreaming sleep. Because a baby is neurologically immature, he has trouble making the transition from deeper nondreaming sleep to light, dreaming sleep, then back to deeper nondreaming sleep. Adults often become conscious briefly during the night. But since adults are in the habit of sleeping through the night, they roll over and go back to sleep.

A baby, on the other hand, hasn't acquired the ability to put himself back to sleep. Coupled with the fact that he makes more transitions during the night than an adult, it's no wonder he tends to wake more frequently.

How soundly and how much a baby sleeps is also related to temperament. "Difficult" babies who tend to be fussy and sensitive to changes in schedule sleep less and wake more frequently than "easy" babies. Because sleeping through the night is partly dependent on physical maturation and partly on temperament, there is no fool-proof method to automatically produce this much desired behavior. Because sleeping through the night is also partly learned behavior, parents can encourage the process by giving a baby who wakes during the night adequate opportunity to learn to put himself back to sleep before they intervene.

A baby's basic sleeping schedule remains about the same from 6 to about 18 months. The primary change that occurs after a child's first birthday is that he may begin to resist going to sleep. This behavior comes primarily from the newly developed urge to control all aspects of his behavior. A secondary factor is that a 1-year-old who's just learned to walk is extremely active and easily becomes overstimulated, making the transition into sleep more difficult. The antidote to this behavior is normally the establishment of an enjoyable bedtime routine (a bath, reading stories, kissing good night, etc.) designed to quiet the child, coupled with firm insistence that bedtime is sleep time.

At some point in the middle of a baby's second year, one nap, usually the morning nap, disappears. A baby may go through a transition phase, during which one nap isn't enough and two naps may make it difficult to put the child to sleep at night. By age 2, most children are sleeping ten to twelve hours per night with one afternoon nap.

Feeding a Baby in the First Two Years of Life

HOW THE HUMAN DIGESTIVE SYSTEM WORKS

Before you make important feeding decisions affecting your baby (whether or not to breast-feed, when to start solid food, when to add cow's milk), you should have an idea of how the digestive system works, and how a baby's digestive system develops during the first 2 years of life.

The digestive process begins in the *mouth*. Our teeth break down the food and mix it with saliva, which contains enzymes that start the digestion of carbohydrates. Then our tongue forces the food to the back of our mouths, to the *pharynx*.

Next, a reflex action pushes the food into the *esophagus*, a tube that connects the mouth with the stomach. Various reflex actions prevent the food from entering the nose, trachea (windpipe), ears, and mouth. The food is then moved along into the *stomach*.

In the stomach, the food is "churned" by the muscular contraction of the stomach walls as it's mixed with gastric enzymes that partially digest the food. Some water and alcohol are absorbed into the bloodstream from the stomach before the liquified food is "squirted" through the *duodenum* into the *small intestine*.

The digestive process is completed in the small intestine, aided by gastric enzymes manufactured there, pancreatic enzymes made by the *pancreas*, and bile produced by the *gallbladder* and *liver*. Then the end products of digestion—sugars, fats, amino acids, vitamins, and minerals—are absorbed into the bloodstream.

What's left over is pushed into the *large intestine*, where water and some additional fats are absorbed. Whatever's undigestible is pushed along into the *colon*, then out of the body through the *rectum*.

Waste products—especially excess sodium and proteins—and excess liquid from the blood are removed by the *kidneys*, then passed to the *bladder*, where they're stored for elimination.

A BABY'S DIGESTIVE SYSTEM AND HOW IT MATURES

Let's take a tour of a baby's digestive system. We'll begin with:

The Mouth

At this starting point, there are three major differences between the digestive system of an adult and that of an infant:

First, and most obvious, a newborn doesn't have teeth, which makes chewing difficult. A baby won't be able to chew effectively for some time.

WHAT YOU SHOULD KNOW ABOUT . . .

HICCUPS

By the far the most important thing new parents should know about hiccups is that they're totally harmless. That's hard to believe when your newborn's whole body seems to be shaking. But while your baby's hiccups are new to you, your baby's used to them—he's been having hiccups in the womb for at least 5 months.

What is a hiccup? For some unknown reason, signals are carried by the phrenic nerves from a ''hiccup center'' near the top of the spinal cord to the muscles of the diaphragm and chest. The muscles suddenly contract, causing air to be sucked into the trachea (windpipe). Then the air is prevented from passing into the lungs by an abrupt closing of the vocal cords. The result: the characteristic ''hic'' sound.

Unlike other reflex actions such as a sneeze or a cough, hiccups serve no useful purpose. They don't clear the respiratory tract or block the passage of food into the trachea (windpipe). Although physicians have been investigating hiccups from the time of the ancient Greeks, no one's been able to discover exactly what triggers them or develop a foolproof method for stopping them.

Hiccups have traditionally been associated with distention of the stomach. Since it's very easy for young infants to take in too much liquid or air, that may be one reason babies get hiccups far more frequently than older children or adults. These bouts can last minutes or hours, but are invariably harmless.

What may not be harmless is trying traditional cures for hiccups on infants. It can be very dangerous to give little babies a mouthful of granulated sugar, a spoonful of honey, make them breath into a paper bag, try to frighten them, or force them to hold their breath. The only thing that may help but will do no harm is to offer some water in a bottle. In most cases, however, the hiccups will just stop, as suddenly and mysteriously as they started.

Although he may have some teeth in the first half of the first year, those front teeth aren't nearly as useful as the first molars, which probably won't appear until sometime in the second year.

Once he has all his first teeth, a baby has to learn how to use them. Effective chewing is a skill, like crawling or walking, that takes practice and some concentration—even adults lose concentration sometimes and can easily choke.

Second, a newborn produces enough saliva to keep his mouth moist, but he doesn't produce enough to adequately moisten the carbohydrates in solid foods until the third or fourth month.

Third, an infant can't use his tongue to transfer solid food from the front of his mouth to the rear for swallowing until he is at least 4 months old. He also can't move his head to indicate that he's had enough food.

The Esophagus

The sphincter muscles at the top of the esophagus are immature at birth, so they do a poor job of insuring that food always moves downward. That's why babies regurgitate food frequently. These muscles don't work with adult efficiency until about 1 year of age.

An infant has the ability to breathe and suck at the same time, meaning that air often precedes liquid down the esophagus. This ability disappears at about 6 to 8 months of age, when a baby has to interrupt breathing to swallow, just like an adult.

The Stomach

The first thing to know about the baby's stomach is that it's small:

Average for a newborn	1-3 ounces
At 1 month	3-5 ounces
At 1 year	7-10 ounces
At 2 years	17 ounces

When air fills up part of the stomach before milk or formula arrives, it's easy for the stomach to overfill—you know the result. Their small stomachs also mean that babies need to consume foods that are nutritionally efficient. For example, a commonly recommended adult diet that provides a high percentage of fiber would be disastrous for a child under age 2.

The baby's stomach walls, like his entire gastrointestinal system, are more sensitive and immature than an adult's. Spicy foods cause more irritation, as do substances like caffeine. Certain proteins, such as those found in cow's milk, form hard curds that can produce internal bleeding. Until about 3 months of age, the stomach muscles can't produce a single, coordinated spasm to push food along. In this period, the baby's stomach empties more slowly than an adult's.

The Small Intestine

The pancreas, the liver, and the gallbladder are immature at birth, so the fluids they pump into the small intestine aren't as effective as in a child over the age of 1 year. Certain kinds of proteins and fats aren't absorbed well. Almost 100% of the fats in breast milk are absorbed compared to only 75% to 85% of the fats in formula.

Another feature of the baby's small intestine is its more permeable walls, which are, therefore, open to the passage of large molecules. This causes infants to be prone to food sensitivity—that is, more foods can cause digestive problems.

Finally, the small intestine serves as the conduit for gas and for air bubbles that have been swallowed. This gas and air, which take about four hours to pass through the entire digestive system, can be uncomfortable, even painful—as many exhausted parents with colicky babies can attest to.

The Large Intestine and Colon

The bowel movements of infants and toddlers are much less regular than those of an adult. A normal, healthy infant can have a bowel movement as infrequently as once a week or as often as three or four times a day.

The Kidneys

The kidneys at birth are very immature. Excess salt and protein in a baby's diet can very easily overload and damage these vital organs.

PLANNING A CHILD'S DIET

Mother Nature knew that parents had a lot of impressive demands on them in the first few months of their babies' lives, so she thoughtfully eliminated the need for meal planning for newborns by providing a "perfect" food—breast milk. As we've said previously in this book, breast milk will take care of all the nutritional needs of a baby in the first 6 months of life or longer, provided the mother is eating a well-balanced diet. Modern formula also is a nutritionally complete food that serves as a "one-food" diet for infants, if properly used and prepared.

Within a few months after birth, however, all babies should and need to be introduced to other sources of nutrition. That's when meal planning begins to be important. A baby's growth can't take place without the right foods as "raw materials," any more than a brick building can be built without mortar. Although there seems to be little scientific evidence to support claims that you can make your child a genius by feeding him the right foods, it is well established that the right diet is necessary for a child to achieve all of his potential. One reason is that the right amount and types of protein and fat are required for brain growth and the myelinization of the central nervous system that take place rapidly in the first 2 years of life. One study reported that the brains of low-income, big-city children weighed 15% less than the brains of children from middle-class homes, primarily because of poor nutrition. These children had significantly lower intelligence scores.

The right diet is also an important factor in reducing the risk of obesity. Yale University Psychologist R. H. Milstein found that overnourished in-

WHAT YOU SHOULD KNOW ABOUT . . .

FOOD INTAKE FOR GOOD NUTRITION BY FOOD GROUP AND AVERAGE SIZE OF SERVINGS

According to recommendations developed by the Institute of Home Economics of the U.S. Department of Agriculture and the Children's Bureau of the U.S. Department of Health and Human Services, a 1-year-old's balanced diet should include:

Food Group	Servings per Day	Average Size of Serving
Milk and cheese	4	1/2 cup
Meat group	3-4	
Eggs		1 egg
Meat, fish, poultry		1 ounce
Fruits and vegetables	4-5	
Citrus fruits, berries	1	1/3 cup
Green/yellow fruits and vegetables	1	2 tablespoons
Other vegetables (inc. potato)	2	2 tablespoons
Other fruits (apple, banana)	1	1/4 cup
Cereals	4-5	
Breads		1/2 slice
Ready-to-eat cereal	1/2 ounce	
Rice, pasta, cooked cereal		1/4 cup
Fats and carbohydrates		
Butter, margarine mayonnaise	1-3	1 tablespoon
Desserts, sweets	1	1/3 cup ice cream 2 3-inch cookies 1 ounce cake

fants grew to prefer sweet, high-calorie foods and ignored internal clues that they were full. Jule Hirsch found that nutrition in the first 2 years of life was critical to the development of fat cells. Hirsch discovered that overweight infants had an excess of fat cells that no amount of dieting in later life could reduce.

Because nutrition is so important, everybody has an opinion about what and how much a baby should eat. Even the most independent of new parents are susceptible to seemingly expert advice, because of the many problems in feeding young children. The problems include the fact that babies can't talk, they're very fussy, their appetites vary wildly from meal to meal and from day to day, and they often consider being made to sit in a high chair an act of high treason. As badly as parents want advice, however, many of the solicited and unsolicited opinions they receive are wrong, some even harmfully so.

You don't need a degree in nutrition to feed your baby. What's important is that you have a basic understanding of your baby's nutritional needs, how his digestive system operates, and a few of the psychological implications of eating. Then you can see that you're providing the right foods in the right quantities at the right times.

A Baby's Energy Needs

Our bodies run on the energy provided by food, just as a car runs on the energy provided by gasoline. The energy we need is usually measured in calories (compared with gallons for gasoline), and how much energy we use is measured in calories per pound of body weight (compared with miles per gallon for a car).

Every body, including that of a baby, uses energy in five different ways:

1. To keep warm. A body is a miniature furnace, burning fuel to maintain the right temperature. The measure of how much fuel we burn to keep warm is our *metabolism*. People with higher metabolisms burn more fuel (and stay thinner) than people with lower metabolisms. Keeping warm is the single largest use of energy for us, consuming about half the calories we take in. Because babies have so much body surface area compared to their weight, their metabolism is high—they burn about twice the fuel per pound of body weight as an adult.
2. To grow. Babies grow fastest right after birth, so their energy needs for growth are highest in the first year. The number of calories needed for growth declines from birth through the grade school years, increases after puberty, then drops to zero in adulthood.
3. Activity. Our muscles need fuel to move. Even young infants are active, kicking their arms and legs. The more active any of us are, the more energy we need.
4. Digestion. All food takes some energy to digest, with the amount determined by the type of food. Protein is harder to digest than carbohydrates, so about twice the calories are used.
5. Losses through excretion. The digestive system isn't totally efficient, so adults lose about 1 in every 8 calories taken in. Since babies' systems are immature, they lose more calories per pound than their parents.

The total calories per pound needed by babies depend on their age, with one exception. The calorie needs of babies with low birth weights, whether they're premature or just small for their age, are much higher than for full-term infants in the "normal" birth weight range. Below are the calorie needs per pound of body weight broken down by use:

Age of Child				
	Low Birth Weight	Birth to 6 Months	6 Months to 1 Year	1 Year to 2 Years
Metabolism	27	25	25	20
Growth	23	9	5	5
Activity	7	8	9	11
Digestion	3	3	3	3
Excreted	9	5	5	4
Totals	69	50	47	43

What does this mean in terms of how much food your baby needs? An 8-pound infant needs about 400 calories a day, a 10-pound infant needs about 500 calories, a 20-pound older infant needs about 940, and a 25-pound toddler will need almost 1,100 calories a day.

A Baby's Fluid Needs

Water is second only to oxygen as a necessity of life. That's particularly true for infants, for two reasons. First, water makes up about 70% of the body weight of a newborn, compared with about 60% of the body weight of an adult. Second, a baby loses (by evaporation through the lungs and by urinating) about 20% of his total body water each day, compared with just 2% to 4% for an adult. That's why babies dehydrate very quickly, and why such dehydration is dangerous.

Fortunately, Mother Nature again comes to the rescue of parents. A baby's calorie needs are met by almost exactly the amount of breast milk needed to meet his fluid needs. Except in the first few days of life, when babies aren't likely to be taking their full quota of breast milk, young infants don't need any supplemental water or other liquids. The same is also true of bottle-fed babies, since formula has slightly fewer calories per ounce than breast milk.

The situation changes only slightly when a baby starts solid food, since baby foods contain between 60% and 90% water. But fluid intake becomes more important when your baby starts to become more active, especially if he's outside on a hot day. Even children under age 2 should always have access to liquids.

Fluid needs can vary according to room temperature and the activity level of the baby. Under normal conditions (meaning the child isn't losing an abnormal amount of fluid from vomiting or diarrhea), the average daily fluid needs at sample weights are:

7 pounds	13-17 ounces a day
12 pounds	25-29 ounces a day
16 pounds	32-37 ounces a day

21 pounds   38-42 ounces a day
26 pounds   46-51 ounces a day

How Much Protein a Baby Needs

Protein provides the building blocks of the human body and is vital to adequate growth. Too much protein, however, taxes the digestive system and the kidneys. That's why breast milk is perfect for infants, because it has one-third the protein of cow's milk. In order to adapt cow's milk into an adequate infant formula, half the protein content is removed and the rest is treated to make it more digestible.

Infants under 6 months of age need 1 gram of protein per pound of body weight every day. Children aged 6 months to 2 years need slightly under a gram of protein per pound every day.

A Baby's Vitamin and Mineral Requirements

The National Academy of Sciences' recommended daily allowance (RDA) for vitamins and minerals is:

	0-6 Months	6-12 Months	1-2 Years
Vitamin A (IU)	420	400	400
Vitamin D (g)	10	10	10
Vitamin E (mg)	3	3	5
Vitamin C (mg)	35	35	45
Thiamin (mg)	0.3	0.5	0.7
Riboflavin (mg)	0.4	0.6	0.8
Niacin (mg)	6	8	9
Vitamin B_6 (mg)	0.3	0.6	0.9
Folacin (g)	30	45	100
Vitamin B_{12} (g)	0.3	0.6	2
Calcium (mg)	360	540	800
Phosphorus (mg)	240	360	800
Magnesium (mg)	50	70	150
Iron (mg)	10	15	15
Iodine (g)	40	50	90

MAKING THE BIG DECISIONS ABOUT FEEDING A BABY

By this time, you've probably made one big feeding decision, whether or not to breast-feed. Soon afterward, however, you'll begin to face more decisions about how, when, and what to feed your growing baby. Since nearly everyone claims to be an expert on the subject, knowing the facts will help you to resist pressure and make informed decisions.

Decision One: When to Start Solid Foods?

Until the last decade, babies were commonly started on solid foods as early as 6 to 8 weeks of life. Today, however, the American Academy of Pediatrics recommends waiting until 4 to 6 months to start feeding solids.

One reason for this change is that research has disproved the two major reasons for starting babies on solid food much earlier. The studies failed to reveal any nutritional advantage in feeding young babies solid food. They also showed that solid foods play absolutely no part in helping a baby sleep through the night.

A second reason for the recommendation was evidence that starting solid food very early may contribute to overfeeding, which in turn increases the chances of obesity later in life.

Finally, and most important, pediatricians have come to understand more clearly the dangers of forcing solid food into an immature digestive system. As we described above, until at least the fourth month of life, a baby doesn't have the ability to move food from the front to the back of his mouth with his tongue, he can't refuse food, he doesn't produce enough saliva to adequately moisten carbohydrates in his mouth, and his stomach isn't mature enough to efficiently begin the digestive process.

How to introduce solid food is nearly as important as when. Most experts recommend starting with cereal that's been diluted until it's watery. The baby should be comfortable, and the atmosphere quiet and relaxed, to build the association of eating with pleasant experiences.

At first, the baby should be given only a half teaspoon at a time. Because swallowing is a physical skill that takes some practice, it's likely that as much food will be spit up as consumed. A baby is likely to gradually increase the quantity consumed, but he may refuse to eat completely at any given meal. Food should never be forced.

Decision Two: Commercial or Homemade Baby Food?

Intense consumer pressure over the last ten years has resulted in a drastic lowering of the salt and sugar content of commercial baby foods. The major brands are now considered safe and adequate sources of nutrition for babies.

If you're wondering about preparing your own baby food to save money, you should know that a number of studies have shown little difference in cost between homemade and commercial baby foods. If a dollar value is placed on food preparation time, the advantage is definitely with commercial food.

Homemade baby food is an advantage if high-quality, very fresh food is used. However, researchers have found that a significant number of parents who make their own baby food don't prepare an adequate variety of foods. Menu planning and food preparation require reading one or more books on the subject, as well as the purchase of a good baby-food grinder.

In addition to variety and convenience, an advantage of commercial baby foods is that they contain nutritional supplements, particularly vitamin C. However, some still contain preservatives that may contribute to food allergies.

Decision Three: Does Your Baby Need Dietary Supplements?

Whether or not your baby needs vitamin and mineral supplements is ultimately a decision to be made in consultation with your pediatrician. Giving vitamins to babies without medical advice can lead to possibly dangerous overdoses, especially of vitamins A and D.

Fluoride presents the clearest need for supplementation if the drinking water in your home isn't fluoridated. You can find out the fluoride content of your drinking water by calling the utility that supplies it or, if your water comes from a well, by obtaining a chemical analysis from a laboratory. Then inform your physician of the fluoride content in case a prescription for a supplement is required.

Decision Four: When to Add Cow's Milk to the Diet?

The official recommendation of the American Academy of Pediatrics is that a small amount of cow's milk can be added to a baby's diet after the age of 6 months, upon approval of the child's pediatrician. However, because the hard curds formed by cow's milk have been shown to cause bleeding in the stomachs of even older infants, many experts recommend waiting until 1 year of age.

When cow's milk is given to babies, only whole milk should be used. Skim milk or low-fat milk should never be given to children under 2 years of age. Sufficient dietary fat is crucial to the growth of brain cells, myelinization of the nervous system, formation of bone marrow, and development of subcutaneous fat that aids in maintaining a proper body temperature.

Decision Five: When to Wean from the Breast?

Today, about one-quarter of all mothers, and 40% of college-educated mothers, are still breast-feeding their babies at 6 months of age. As we discussed earlier, the nutritional and immunological benefits of breast-feeding are very substantial in those first 6 months and continue to be important in the next 6 months.

Research has failed to show any "right time" to wean a baby. There is little concrete evidence to back up arguments put forth by some breast-feeding advocates to continue nursing to age 2 or 3. At the same time, no disadvantages to continued breast-feeding have been proven. The decision is and should be a strictly personal one.

Decision Six: When to Start Feeding Table Food?

Strained baby food doesn't require any chewing. It's also very bland and, after a while, a bit boring for a baby. Adding texture to a baby's diet makes eating more enjoyable.

The right time to add texture, by feeding "chunky" baby foods or table food, varies widely from baby to baby. One reason is that in order to chew, a baby needs teeth, and to chew anything "tough," such as meat, he needs molars. A baby whose teeth come in early will be handling table food much earlier than a baby who doesn't get his first teeth until nearly a year of age.

A second factor is how well a baby chews. Chewing is a motor skill, and some babies become proficient at it months earlier than other babies, even those with the same number of teeth.

The rule of thumb for parents, when it comes to adding texture to a baby's diet is, *be cautious*. Over 1,000 babies choke to death every year. There are three major causes for these largely preventable deaths. The first is giving inappropriate foods that can easily be swallowed whole, such as grapes or popcorn. The second cause is giving a baby pieces of food that are too large. The third, and most common cause, is failure to supervise a baby while he's eating. Parents should never leave a young baby who's eating table food. Even more important, babies should never be allowed to crawl or walk while eating.

FEEDING IN THE SECOND YEAR OF LIFE

A baby's growth rate drops dramatically in the second year of life. The average weight gain per month between 12 and 18 months is only about one-third of the average weight gain per month at 6 months of age. The much slower growth rate means a lower caloric need, and a much reduced appetite.

The result is that a baby who wolfed down meals with glee at 9 months may refuse to take a single bite at some meals at 14 months. At the same time, the 9-month-old who eats everything put in front of him may evolve into a 14-month-old with strong food likes and dislikes. Both trends can greatly frustrate parents who don't understand what's going on. Being naturally concerned that their child isn't getting an adequate, balanced diet, they tend to try to force food. Then meals turn into battles, resulting in long-lasting feeding problems.

Feeding problems can be largely avoided if parents understand the reasons for the fussy behavior. Studies have shown, as *Nelson's Textbook of Pediatrics* points out, that "children tend to select diets which, over a period of several days, assume a balanced nature." Experts recommend that children be allowed to determine how much they eat of a specific food or of a specific meal. The goal of mealtime is to eliminate stress, not force-feed the child.

One caution to letting a child determine what and how much he eats concerns snacks. Many parents whose young children skip a meal are tempted to compensate by offering high-calorie snacks, which are often junk food. Nutritionists have found that this practice builds bad eating habits.

DEVELOPING SELF-FEEDING SKILLS

To quote *Nelson's Textbook of Pediatrics*, "Acquisition of the ability to feed one's self is an important step in the infant's development of self-reliance and of a sense of responsibility." One reason is that if a child attains the ability to feed himself and is proud of that ability, mealtime is less likely to turn into a battle than if a parent regularly feeds him.

Feeding one's self requires mastering a series of complicated motor skills, which a child acquires over about a 2 1/2-year period, from age 6 months to 3 years. The process can be a messy one, and understanding the steps can help parents deal with the frustration of progress that is often slow.

Perhaps the first steps of self-feeding take the longest to develop—the complicated process of learning to pick something up in one's fingers and direct it into one's mouth. By about 6 months of age, most babies are beginning to master that part of the process. By age 7 or 8 months, they're beginning to learn to bite and chew, so they can start feeding themselves a cracker. At the same time, they can hold their own bottle and can drink a little from a cup held by an adult.

Here is a timetable of self-feeding milestones after that period:

9 to 12 months:

· Masters finger-feeding
· Can hold a spoon, but turns it over on the way to mouth
· Holds a bottle easily and drinks from it
· Holds a cup, with much spilling

13 to 15 months:

· May drink from a straw
· Holds a cup, with moderate spilling
· Can direct a spoon into mouth, with much spilling
· Can take food off the end of a fork

16 to 18 months

· Lifts cup to mouth and drinks well
· Hands empty cup to parent

- Can fill spoon
- Can put spoon in mouth, but turns it over in mouth
- Still needs considerable assistance in eating
- Still spills considerably

19 to 24 months

- Handles cup well, lifting, drinking, and replacing on tray
- Inserts spoon into mouth without turning
- Refuses disliked foods and plays with food
- Continues to need some help with meals
- Can drink from small glass held in one hand

25 to 36 months

- Can eat with a fork
- Uses spoon with little spilling
- Pours well from a pitcher
- Usually eats without assistance
- Becomes interested in setting table

FEEDING PROBLEMS

Underfeeding

Despite the fears of parents and grandparents, undereating is seldom a problem in healthy children. Although it may seem at times that a toddler "doesn't eat a thing," children generally do consume the nutrients they need, if an adequate diet is made available to them.

They key words here are *adequate diet.* One new problem increasingly encountered by pediatricians is nutritional deficiencies in young children whose parents put them on a "health food" diet. Low-fat, low-cholesterol, and high-fiber foods make a healthy diet for adults, but a dangerous diet for children under 2 years old. Such a diet can produce vitamin and mineral deficiencies and retarded growth.

Great care also has to be taken if either a child or nursing mother is on a vegetarian diet, especially one that excludes dairy products and eggs as well as meat. Vitamin B12 and mineral supplements are recommended for nursing mothers who are vegetarians.

Overfeeding

Breast-fed infants almost never overeat, and formula-fed infants rarely consume more than they need. But overfeeding is a major problem for a large percentage of young children who have begun to eat solid food. One important reason is that many parents greatly overestimate their children's caloric needs. A second reason is a diet that includes frequent high-calorie snacks such as cookies, cupcakes, potato chips, etc. A third reason is the old-fashioned belief that a fat baby is a healthy baby.

It is normal for some babies to look "chubby" but not be overweight. At every checkup, however, parents should ask their pediatrician about their child's height-to-weight ratio. The earlier a weight problem is corrected by a proper diet, the less chance the child will become obese later on.

Food Allergies

A recent study presented to the American Dietetic Association revealed that 43% of children aged 3 and under showed some signs of a food allergy. Most of the problems occurred in the first year of life. The most common offending foods were fruit, milk, peanuts, eggs, soy, and wheat.

Possible allergic reactions are the reason all pediatricians recommend that new foods be added to a baby's diet one at a time and about two weeks apart. During those two weeks, the baby should be watched for a skin rash or diarrhea that could indicate a reaction.

The good news, however, is that the same study showed that most allergic reactions are very mild and disappear quickly. Most foods can be tried again within two to four months without problems.

Severe reactions, however, can be dangerous, in which case you should consult a doctor.

The Importance of Play in the First Two Years of Life

Play is a young child's "job" and has a crucial role in normal development. Through play, a child learns to gain control over his own body; strengthens and exercises his body; discovers the nature of the world around him; practices language skills; learns and practices social skills; acts out roles he sees around him (Mommy, Daddy, doctor); gains independence; builds self-esteem and self-confidence; and acquires practical knowledge of such concepts as shape and size, colors, numbers, and the alphabet.

Play is so important that it can't be left solely to children. Parents and other care givers have two major responsibilities in this regard. The first is to provide the right kinds and amounts of stimulation for the child. This requires taking the time to learn about the normal course of child development, then evaluating the child's development to determine the level of his progress.

The second is allotting sufficient time to play with the child. Optimum physical, social, and intellectual growth takes place when play is interactive, even at very young ages. Since infants and toddlers don't have the skills to interact with each other, parents, older siblings, and other care givers have to take the time to be play partners.

PROVIDING THE RIGHT STIMULATION

Stimulation takes several different forms. The first involves environment. Even a young baby appreciates a home with interesting things to look at on the walls, the sounds of music, smells coming from the kitchen. Careful exposure to other environments, from a supermarket to a zoo, is also a rich learning experience.

Stimulation also means freedom to explore. Researchers have noted significant developmental differences between crawling infants who are given the opportunity to move around in a safe environment and those who are restricted to cribs or playpens for major portions of the day.

Finally, as every parent knows, stimulation means objects to play with, or toys.

THE BEST TOYS IN THE FIRST TWO YEARS OF LIFE

What Is a Toy, Anyway?

Contrary to what manufacturers would like parents to believe, a toy doesn't necessarily come in a fancy package and cost so much it has to be paid for with a credit card. Neither is a toy just a "trinket," to use the dictionary definition; that implies toys are merely frivolous, which they definitely are not.

Instead, it's most useful to think of toys as "baby tools." The best toys are any objects that stimulate a baby's five senses, allow him to test his growing control over his body, expand his mental capabilities, and allow him to explore the physical nature of the world. A toy can be a rattle, a mirror, the fabric on the couch, a dog or cat, the sound of church bells in the distance, a picture torn from a magazine, a plastic food container with a lid, the scent of a flower, and a parent's voice.

Selecting the Best Toys

Selecting the right toys for a baby takes some work. But that work is a very good investment. One recent eight-year study found the home environment of gifted children to be strikingly different from the home environment of less talented children. The parents of gifted children recognized their children's natural abilities very early and fostered them with appropriate stimulation. The babies in turn grew more demanding of stimulation, mastering toys more quickly and asking for new ones.

What this research doesn't mean, however, is that a baby's IQ is related to the size of his parents' toy budget. Quality and versatility in toys have

WHAT YOU SHOULD KNOW ABOUT . . .

AGE LABELS ON TOY PACKAGES

You've probably noticed that almost all toys for young children have packages that include an age level. These labels are placed on the toy by the manufacturer to help parents determine whether that product is appropriate for their child.

Age-labeling toys is voluntary. Most large toy makers, however, do follow a voluntary toy age-grading guideline established by the Toy Manufacturers of America, an industry association. According to this guideline, toys are graded according to four criteria:

1. The physical ability of a child to manipulate and play with the features of a toy.
2. The mental ability of a child to understand how to use a toy.
3. The play needs and interests applicable at various levels of child development.
4. The safety aspects of the toy itself.

In addition to age labels, toy packages may also include cautionary labels that alert consumers to special hazards posed by the toy. One common caution warns about small parts. Toys designed for children under age 3 must be constructed without small parts, as described by a rigid U.S. government safety standard. This caution is based on the fact that children under age 3 are more likely to place small objects in their mouth than children age 3 and over. However, the industry association cautions that the tendency to put an object in one's mouth doesn't automatically stop at age 3. The small-parts warning is thus an alert to parents of any preschool child.

The toy association also cautions that all grading is based on average levels of development and that the methods used by toy manufacturers to ensure that a toy meets these criteria for a certain age vary widely. Some may use only written child-development material, while other manufacturers conduct elaborate play-testing, in which child psychologists and other experts observe children actually using a new toy. For both reasons, the final responsibility for proper toy selection and toy usage rests on parents and other care givers.

very little relation to their price. If you're just interested in keeping a baby happy and stimulated rather than in impressing your friends with status toys, you can combine household objects, used toys purchased at resale shops or garage sales, and some select new toys.

The Best Toys in the First Three Months

In the first 3 months, you want to give a baby an idea that the world around him is a fascinating place that deserves his attention. You can accomplish much of this by simply moving a baby around with you, preferably in a good infant seat that puts him in an upright position and gives him a different perspective on his environment.

The right toys are also important. Among the types of toys recommended by child psychologists and other experts are:

MOBILES Mobiles are colorful objects suspended over the baby from a frame that attaches to the side of a crib, a changing table, or some other piece of furniture. Some mobiles have windup or battery-driven motors that rotate them like a carousel, and some have music.

The characteristics of the best mobiles are:

1. A design that's fun for the baby to look at. You'll see dozens of adorable mobiles on display in a baby store. If you take the trouble to look at most of them from the viewpoint of a baby in a crib, you'll discover they look a lot more interesting from the side than from the bottom. Only recently have companies begun to design mobiles with the objects tilted so the baby gets the best view.
2. Movement. A mobile that moves encourages an infant to develop his ability to track objects.
3. Music. The auditory stimulation of a simple tune is well worth the extra cost.
4. Adjustable height. A mobile should be adjustable, so the toys can hang at the ideal 7- to 8-inch height for newborns, and can then be raised as the baby grows.
5. Bright colors. Babies show a preference for bright primary colors and objects with faces.

BOOKS You may be surprised to see books on the list of toys for newborns. But if you think about it, what better way to provide colorful things to look at and the sound of a parent's voice than reading from a book? According to the latest research in child development, one characteristic that separates the upbringing of children later identified as "gifted" from the upbringing of normal children is that a large majority of gifted children were read to right from birth.

The best books have simple, large, brightly colored pictures on sturdy board pages with little or no text. You "read" the books by holding them at the right distance (7 to 8 inches) from a baby and pointing at parts of the picture you describe.

BABY MIRROR By age 4 months, a baby will love to watch his reflection in a mirror. But even before a baby learns to deliberately watch himself in a mirror, the play of light and reflections of colors in a mirror make great stimulation. The types of baby mirrors available include small hand-held products and larger mirrors designed to be attached to the side of a crib or playpen.

TOY BARS A toy bar looks like the miniature frame of a swing set—two legs on each side in an A shape, connected by a top bar. The bars come with colorful plastic loops that allow toys to be hung from the top bar as a swing hangs from a swing frame.

Toy bars are a nearly indispensable tool for keeping a baby stimulated and happy from birth until he can sit up on his own. Set up over his infant seat, over the baby lying on his back on the floor or playpen, or even over his car seat, a toy bar allows a baby to watch, bat, then play with a wide variety of toys without a parent or care giver having to sit next to him, handing him toys, and fetching dropped toys off the floor.

Babies under 6 to 8 weeks of age merely need something stimulating to watch. Colorful ribbons, strips of aluminum foil, pictures cut out from magazines, empty thread spools, or any other interesting small objects can be suspended from the toy bars' loops. When a baby begins to start batting at the hanging toys, you can start attaching rattles and other objects that it's safe for him to touch.

RATTLES, CLUTCH TOYS, SQUEEZE TOYS, TEETHERS Babies are born with a grasp reflex that makes them clench their fist when their palm touches an object. However, newborns primarily keep their hands tightly closed—if you find a newborn's hands open, you may get him to hold a small rattle, but he'll have no idea he's holding it. The grasp reflex fades in a few weeks, but at the same time he'll be keeping his hands open more of the time. His next developmental steps will be first holding an object when it's placed in his hand, then reaching for an object.

You can aid this development and have some fun with your baby with an assortment of toys that are designed to be grasped by young infants. A baby will make the most use of these toys when he's in the 3-to-6 months age range, but you can start accumulating them shortly after his birth. Experts recommend looking for:

1. Toys with a variety of textures. These toys are a baby's introduction to the physical world. Look for toys made of fabric, soft rubber, hard rubber, plastic, and wood.
2. Toys with a variety of shapes. Try not to buy toys that look alike. Instead of two dumbbell-shaped rattles, buy one dumbbell rattle and a soft clutch ball.
3. Toys that can be chewed. By age 4 months, a child will be putting absolutely everything in his mouth. Make very sure the toys are too large to choke a baby and are sturdy enough to survive chewing and dropping. If in doubt, crack a toy on the floor yourself. If it breaks, return it. When buying fabric toys, make sure they're washable—if they're not they'll soon be too disgusting to touch.
4. As many toys as possible that can be hung from toy bars. Some ex-

cellent toys (e.g., clutch balls) don't fit this description, but the general rule of thumb should be, the more versatile the toy, the better.

The Best Toys for Babies Aged Three to Six Months

TOY BARS Toy bars can be used when a baby's on the floor, in his infant seat, in his playpen. The more practice he gets in reaching for, batting, and manipulating objects, the more quickly he'll refine his hand-eye coordination.

RATTLES, CLUTCH TOYS, SQUEEZERS, TEETHERS The more, the better. As a baby starts to reach out for objects, however, another type of toy becomes appropriate: toys that affix by suction cups to a flat surface, such as the trays on infants' seats, walkers, etc. Two or three of these toys will provide a lot of amusement for a baby between age 5 and 7 months, the time when he's most likely to be bored.

BOOKS Every month, a baby responds to more complex visual stimulation, and books provide a great source. At about 4 months of age, he'll start responding to his own image in the mirror, and at the same time he'll really enjoy looking at photographs of other babies, either in board books or magazines. During this period, a baby will also want to touch and manipulate what he's looking at. He'll get pleasure out of turning the pages of board books. Babies also begin to enjoy some of the many books that contain different textures (soft fur, sponge, rough "sand," etc.).

Plastic books, which are often advertised as "bath books," are easy for a baby to hold, they've got bright pictures, and they're very easy to clean.

ACTIVITY CENTERS These toys are often called "busy boxes." They are normally plastic boxes designed to give a baby several different things to look at and do. For example, they usually have a telephone dial to stick a finger in and turn, spinning cylinders, bells to ring, "peek-a-boo" windows to slide back and forth, squeakers, rotating pictures, etc. Most of these toys are designed to attach to the side of a crib or playpen. But for a baby who doesn't sit up yet, a busy box can be placed on the floor or tied to toy bars so he can reach the box while reclining in his infant seat.

CRIB GYMS OR BABY EXERCISERS These devices include toys that are suspended over the crib, where the baby can reach them on his back. The exercise provided is great, with one large exception: any crib gym suspended by elastic or string is too dangerous—one major manufacturer of "educational" toys had to recall a product involved in two infant strangulation deaths.

PLAY QUILTS Play quilts are colorful blankets with toys (mirrors, rattles, squeeze toys, etc.) sewn on. They're designed to stimulate a baby while he's lying on the floor, as well as providing a clean, safe play surface while you're away from home.

CAR-SEAT TOYS If he's not napping, a baby's likely to get fussy in his car seat, especially before he's old enough to ride facing the front. If a car seat has a handle like an infant seat, you can suspend toys from it, using the links from your toy bars. Many manufacturers make car-seat toys for convertible car seats that don't have handles.

STROLLER TOYS Some babies are so absorbed with what they see and hear when they're out in their strollers that they don't need toys to keep them occupied. On the other hand, many younger babies do need diversion on longer shopping trips. That's where a stroller toy, a mini-activity center that attaches to the stroller, comes in handy.

The Best Toys for Babies Aged Six to Twelve Months

As a baby becomes more mobile and begins placing objects in his mouth, a number of infant toys should be stored out of reach. At the top of the list are crib gyms and mobiles, which ought to go well before a baby's able to pull himself to a standing position. Toy bars aren't necessary when a baby can sit up and reach toys on his own. Finally, the toys of older children must be kept well out of reach—many are dangerous to infants, especially those with small parts that can be swallowed.

Some favorite objects for babies in this age range aren't toys at all. For example, we've yet to discover a crawling baby who didn't love a cabinet full of pots, pans, and plastic containers that he could manipulate and bang with a spoon. Remember, at this age a house is a playground—if you don't want something touched, remove it or secure it.

The toys you should make available during this period are:

BOOKS A baby is beginning to build his vocabulary during this period. You can help by reading him books that have large, easily recognizable pictures of objects, books that show simple everyday activities, and books that demonstrate concepts such as opposites (up and down) in visually interesting ways.

A second benefit of books at this age is that turning pages promotes fine motor development. Especially useful in this regard are "chunky" board books (3 3/8 inch square), which a baby can easily hold in one hand.

A third benefit of books at this age is that they are a great source of distraction at mealtimes. Many companies tout high chair toys, but when a baby's in his high chair three times a day, seven days a week, any toy soon loses its appeal. Books, on the other hand, offer a great variety of stimulation. In fact, this may be the only time of day you can get a baby to pay attention to books.

ACTIVITY CENTERS A baby will be spending more time with "busy boxes" when he's able to sit up on his own. Again, variety is important, so look for used activity centers you can buy or borrow (or trade toys with friends).

Eventually, however, a baby is going to look for activity toys that are a little more challenging than busy boxes. He'll want toys that include objects he can hold in his hand and doors that open and close. He'll also love surprises, such as doors that pop open when a button is pushed or turned.

BALLS AND PUSH TOYS When a baby starts moving around, creeping, then crawling, he'll often be interested in objects that move along with him. Lightweight balls of different colors and sizes are inexpensive and provide great diversity. You'll also see balls that do more than just roll—some are transparent and have objects inside, some chime, some have textured exteriors for a varied tactile experience.

Another type in this category is the "roly-poly" toy. These include inflatable figures with weighted bottoms that pop back up when they're hit by a baby. Other inflatable objects are meant to be rolled or climbed on. Your baby might also be interested in push or pull toys on wheels. Be careful, however, of any toys with strings—they can be swallowed.

NESTING TOYS Nesting is a fancy name for putting one object inside another. The concept seems simple enough to adults, but the process is extremely important in infant development, for two important reasons. First, babies learn about relative sizes, shapes, colors, and numbers by putting different objects inside one another. Second, the process of putting objects inside one another and removing them refines hand-eye coordination.

Store-bought toys aren't necessary to give a baby opportunities for nesting. He'll get satisfaction from putting objects into pots and pans, into shoe boxes, and into plastic containers. As he nears his first birthday, he can also practice with paper cups.

STACKING TOYS This category includes many variations on a classic toy, which consists of five plastic rings that stack on a cone attached to a rocker base. Each ring is a different color, and the rings get progressively smaller from bottom to top. A 6-month-old will be primarily interested in chewing on the rings, but simply holding two rings of different sizes is a step in learning about spatial relationships. As a baby gets older, he'll learn to fit the rings over the cone, first in random order, then by size.

BLOCKS Blocks are also a stacking toy, but the right blocks can teach a baby a lot more than stacking. Cloth and vinyl blocks are especially appropriate for babies under 1 year of age. Several companies make soft blocks with different colorful pictures on each side. A baby will examine the pictures, probably between a little chewing (the blocks are washable). They're also the right size for first attempts at stacking, but they won't bring tears if a baby falls on them.

BATH TOYS   A baby will begin to enjoy playing in the bathtub when he can sit up on his own, and the experience is very good for him. Even the simplest water play, pouring water out of a cup, is a complex activity with important developmental benefits, such as teaching cause and effect.

PUZZLES   Simple puzzles are wonderful toys for babies 9 months of age and older. The appropriate puzzles have large, precut pieces that fit into separate holes. While a baby is not likely to be able to fit a piece back into its hole, removing the piece and manipulating it is great for improving dexterity.

The best puzzles have another benefit—there's a picture hidden beneath the picture on the puzzle piece, so removing the piece is another way to play "peek-a-boo."

WALKING TOYS   When a baby is able to pull himself to a standing position and strong enough to take steps holding on to your hand, he may enjoy a walking toy. These toys have a bar about baby-chest high attached to a stable base on wheels. The baby can use the bar for support as he pushes the toy across the room.

The Best Toys for the Second Year of Life

The second year of life is dominated by a toddler's seemingly inexhaustible urge to explore his environment. He has a growing appetite for gross motor play to exercise his newfound ability to walk, run, and climb. Not far behind is an interest in exploring the environment through such fine motor activity as poking, lifting, dropping, banging, and other methods of manipulation.

At times toddlers resist slowing down for more quiet play. But they should be given the opportunities for quiet play, including reading books and other activities designed to encourage language ability, the development of which accelerates in the second half of the second year.

The major types of toys appropriate for the second year include:

GROSS MOTOR TOYS   A child begins to enjoy trips to the playground in his second year, but the equipment is often too big for toddlers. At home, he'll enjoy:

- A slide: A small, safe, durable plastic or wooden slide is good for climbing as well as sliding
- Large riding toys: Stable toys that encourage pushing with legs while riding are fun—and good exercise
- A swing: Toddlers enjoy swinging—any standard home swing set should be specially equipped with a toddler safety seat

SAND TOYS Sand play promotes cognitive and fine motor development, in addition to endless hours of enjoyment. A sandbox for a toddler should have both a bottom and a cover to keep out insects, animals, and debris. Sand toys for toddlers should be made of durable plastic, with no small parts.

WATER TOYS Water play is excellent for encouraging a toddler's development. Bath toys can be used in the tub and, under strict supervision, in a small outdoor wading pool. Plastic food-storage containers make excellent water toys.

FINE MOTOR ACTIVITY TOYS A toddler is ready for more complex activity toys, similar to the types described among the recommended toys for babies age 6 to 12 months. Shape sorters build knowledge of shapes, colors, and textures. A toddler also likes well-built tops and other spinning toys.

BLOCKS Toddlers are too young for sophisticated block play, but they do enjoy manipulating small, lightweight blocks. Both cloth and hollow plastic blocks are appropriate for this age.

MUSIC AND MUSICAL TOYS Several companies make sets of musical instruments, such as cymbals and drums, built rugged enough for toddlers. Young children at this age begin to enjoy banging instruments as they listen to recorded music. Exposure to music is fun and encourages a sense of rhythm. Children this age will begin to dance, although not in time to music.

PULL TOYS Toddlers enjoy putting things into and dumping them out of containers. Well-built plastic, wooden, and metal wagons serve this purpose, and also provide practice in pulling.

HOUSEKEEPING TOYS Toddlers love to imitate their parents and other care givers. Among the safe items they'll enjoy are toy brooms, toy vacuum cleaners, toy lawn mowers, toy telephones, and toy pots and pans.

DOLLS AND STUFFED ANIMALS Toward the end of the second year, young children begin what's called *pretend play*. In other words, they begin using their imagination, and dolls and stuffed animals become play partners.

CARS AND TRUCKS When pretend play begins, toddlers also like large, well-constructed toy cars and trucks; they should have no small parts and no sharp edges.

CRAFT MATERIALS Children can begin to do crafts when they stop automatically putting everything in their mouth. A child's modeling compound, such as Play-Doh, is a good introduction. Some toddlers also love to finger-paint.

BOOKS As a child's vocabulary grows, the choice of reading material expands. In the second year, your choice of reading material can progress from "baby" books that consist primarily of labeled pictures to real stories. Look for material with easy words and simple messages. Toddlers are particularly attracted to rhyme, so nursery rhymes are an excellent choice.

TOY SAFETY

Toy safety should be a major concern during the entire period of childhood—an estimated 130,000 toy-related accidents occur every year. Infants and toddlers aren't more vulnerable to injury than older children, but *almost all the toy-related injuries they suffer are preventable.* Parents and other care givers are in more control of a child's environment during the first 2 years of life than they will be in any future years. If they provide safe toys, their children will be far more likely to play safely.

Parents and other care givers need to educate themselves about toy safety. One excellent source of information is the book *Toys That Kill* by Edward M. Swartz. Swartz is an attorney who's spent over two decades crusading for toy safety and representing the parents of children who've been killed or severly injured by unsafe toys. Although we don't necessarily agree with everything Swartz says, the hard facts and heart-rending stories in the book will keep toy safety in the forefront of your mind as you shop for your baby. We think it's essential.

Another essential step in ensuring the safety of your baby's toys is to send for the no-choke testing tube designed by the Consumer Products Safety Commission. This plastic tube is designed to emulate the throat of a child—if a toy fits in the tube, it's a choking danger to young children. For more information, write:

Toys to Grow On
Dept. Safe Toys
P.O. Box 17
Long Beach, CA 90801

The third step is to think toy safety every time you give a baby something to play with. Although the Consumer Products Safety Commission has regulations on toy safety and major toy companies proclaim that their toys are thoroughly tested for safety, use your own judgment—even major companies have made tragic mistakes.

It's especially important to exercise good judgment when a baby receives a toy as a gift. Grandma and Grandpa, among others, may not be as knowledgeable about toy safety as you are—they might buy a toy that's designed for much older children or that's flashy but not well made. The temptation will be to let a child play with a gift for a little while so the giver won't be offended. Don't give in.

WHAT YOU SHOULD KNOW ABOUT . . .

WHO ADOPTS BABIES?

Americans adopted 141,861 babies in 1982, according to the Adoption Factbook, prepared and published by the National Committee for Adoption.

Sixty-four percent of all adoptions were by relatives, up from an average of 50% of adoptions during the years from 1951 to 1971. The rise was probably due to the increase in stepparents adopting the children of their new spouses after remarriage.

Children of unwed mothers, the traditional source of babies for adoption, were less frequently given up in 1982 than in 1972. The percentage of babies of unwed mothers given up for adoption fell from 16% in 1972 to 7% in 1982. The percentage varied greatly by race, however. In 1982, 12% of the babies of white, unwed mothers were given up for adoption, compared with less than 1% of the babies of unwed, black mothers.

Keeping the babies, however, was a great sacrifice for the mothers. The National Committee for Adoption found that 40% of women who kept their babies had incomes below the poverty level, compared with 18% of the women who gave up their babies. Only 60% of unwed mothers who kept their children finished high school, compared with 77% of mothers who gave up their children. Half the women who kept their babies eventually married, compared with 75% of the women who gave up their babies for adoption.

Eight thousand foreign-born children were adopted by Americans in 1982, twice as many as in 1972. Sixty-two percent were from Korea, 7% from Columbia, 5.6% from India, and 4.9% from the Philippines. Sixty percent of the foreign children adopted were girls.

Mothers who adopted babies were older than the average mother of a first baby, better educated, and had a higher-than-average income. The vast majority were unable or unwilling to have their own children.

Adopted children tended to be very well off after their adoptions—only 2% lived in families below the poverty level, compared with 13% of all children. That may be one reason why only 2% of adopted children ever searched for their biological parents.

Social and Emotional Development from Birth to Age Two

The desire to have children and form a family is so basic that expectant parents tend to take it for granted that they'll love their baby and that their baby will love them in return. The truth is, however, that a strong, healthy attachment between a baby and his parents isn't automatic. Rather, building such an attachment is as important a task for parents as seeing that their baby is fed and clothed. And in the first 2 years of life, parents have to be as conscious of their baby's social and emotional needs and development as they are of his physical needs and development.

ATTACHMENT

Attachment is that enduring emotional bond that develops between a child and his parents, siblings, and other significant people in his life. Forming a strong attachment is critical to healthy social and emotional development. While forming this attachment is a relatively easy, natural process for most babies and parents, the importance of the process is such that it can never be taken for granted.

The process of forming an attachment with a baby has received enormous attention since 1976, when Marshall Klaus and John Kennel published a book entitled *Maternal-Infant Bonding.* Their research, based primarily on animal studies, suggested that a "sensitive period" existed during the first few hours after birth, during which close contact between mother and infant was essential to the infant's normal emotional and social development.

The bonding concept produced a dramatic change in hospital procedures and pediatric practice. Prior to 1976, newborns were routinely separated from their parents immediately after birth, and generally were kept in a hospital nursery until they and their mothers went home. In the last decade, however, most hospitals have begun to allow mothers to hold and breast-feed their infants immediately after birth, and many allow newborns to spend the majority of their hospital stay in their mothers' room.

The widespread publicity surrounding the bonding concept has had both negative and positive effects. The unfortunate aspect of the publicity was that mothers who couldn't have close contact after birth (because the baby was delivered by cesarean section or for other medical reasons), fathers, and adoptive parents all felt disadvantaged or guilty. These parents have had to understand that subsequent research has failed to provide any proof of the existence of this "sensitive period" for human babies. Even Klaus and Kennel later retracted their previous insistence on the crucial importance of immediate bonding. Experts now believe that while close contact between mother and baby after birth is desirable, bonding is a complex process that takes place over a long period. Research has proven that bonding does take place even without the initial contact.

The positive effects of the bonding concept were threefold. First, the importance of attachment was underscored for parents and health professionals. Second, they were reminded that forming an attachment was not an automatic process. Third, Klaus and Kennel's work pointed out that attachment problems could seriously affect a child's normal development.

Parents' Attachment to Their Newborn

Parents are often shocked, then overcome with guilt, that they don't feel an immediate, overwhelming love for their newborn baby. But this lack of immediate strong feelings is common and normal. For example, one study of fifty-four mothers reported in the *Journal of Pediatrics* found that only half the mothers reported positive feelings for their newborns after birth, and only 13% identified any positive feelings as "love." The study found that most mothers took about three weeks to love their babies, and that the strongest attachments weren't fully formed until the babies were 2 to 3 months old.

The most important factor in the feelings of parents for their baby immediately after birth is the parents' previous expectations of the birth process and their unborn child. Parents who expect an uneventful labor but experience a difficult birth often have conflicting feelings about their newborn. Even more commonly, the sex, appearance, temperament, or behavior of a newborn fails to match the parents' expectations. For example, parents who desperately wanted a girl may have initial problems warming up to a male newborn.

Fortunately, infants are born with behaviors that attract parents' attention and facilitate attachment. As we've noted before, a newborn baby can focus on objects about 8 inches from his eyes, almost the exact distance of a mother's face during breast- or bottle-feeding. A newborn spends a lot of time gazing at his mother's face, and this eye contact normally arouses strong feelings of affection. The more affection the parents feel, the more they cuddle their baby, and this physical contact in turn increases attachment.

At some point between birth and 6 weeks, a baby begins to smile in response to external stimuli. Research has shown that the amount of time parents spend with their infant increases dramatically when the baby starts to smile. By 3 months of age, a baby gains enough control to track his parents as they walk around the room, causing additional eye contact and positive feelings. At the same time, the infant begins to coo, giving the impression that he's communicating with Mom and Dad. By this point, attachment is normally cemented.

Problems in Parents' Attachment

Among the signs that one or both parents are having difficulty attaching to their newborn are:

1. Parent doesn't hold, touch, or examine the baby.
2. Parent talks about the baby as unattractive, or refers to the baby as "it."

3. Parent doesn't make eye contact with the baby.
4. Parent doesn't talk to or play with the baby.
5. Parent is concerned that the baby has a defect, even though that possibility has been ruled out.
6. Parent can't find anything to admire in the baby.
7. Parent handles the baby roughly or without warmth.
8. Parent believes the baby judges him or her.
9. Parent believes that the baby doesn't love him or her.
10. Parent is disgusted by normal infant behavior and habits, such as sucking, drooling, and soiling diapers.

The problems that can cause these symptoms include:

1. Lingering disappointment. Some parents have such strong expectations about a baby's sex or appearance that they have severe problems getting over their disappointment.
2. Personality conflict between parent and child. The newborn's personality often conflicts with a parent's personality or expectations. A parent who expects an easygoing baby who is content in any situation may have trouble attaching to a baby who's difficult or slow to warm up.
   A special problem often occurs with a baby who suffers from colic. Anyone who hasn't been the parent of a baby who cries incessantly doesn't appreciate the emotional havoc such behavior causes.
3. Stress. Marital or financial problems that produce stress in the parents' lives can influence the way they relate to their infant. Mothers commonly have emotional conflicts about their newborns when the father is jealous of the baby or distances himself from contact with his new child.
4. Babies with special needs. Parents often have difficulty loving premature babies or infants born with disabilities or other serious medical problems.
5. Severe postpartum depression. Hormonal changes after birth normally produce occasional moderate depression in new mothers. In some cases, however, this depression is so deep and prolonged that mothers may not only be incapable of caring for their baby, but may even be capable of causing him harm.

Special counseling is important if any of these problems arise.

Infant's Social Behavior and Attachments

An infant's attachment to his parents, siblings, and others progresses through three stages in the first year of life.

BIRTH TO THREE MONTHS During this time, a baby's social responses become more sophisticated, as he begins to smile from outside stimuli, maintain eye contact as someone walks around the room, and vocalize apart from crying. Although a young infant learns to recognize familiar faces and prefers to look at his mother or other primary care giver, he'll respond enthusiastically and pleasantly to almost everyone.

THREE TO SEVEN MONTHS As a baby advances from what Piaget called the "primary" level of concentration on his own body to the "secondary" level of looking to outside events and objects, two social changes take place. First, he becomes increasingly fussy and bored if left alone, and he increasingly enjoys social contact. At about 4 months of age, he can laugh as well as smile, and he'll show excitement in his entire body at even the sound of footsteps.

Second, over the course of time, he'll begin to make more and more of a distinction between familiar people, especially his mother or other primary care giver, and unfamiliar people. By 6 months, he'll strongly prefer his primary care giver's company, even to that of other family members.

SEVEN TO TWELVE MONTHS By this time, a baby is beginning to grasp the concept of object permanence, that is, the idea that objects exist even when he can't see them. He's also beginning to understand that he's a separate person from his mother, and that his mother is separate from other people. This new knowledge produces two rather dramatic changes in his social behavior:

· Stranger anxiety—a baby begins to react with shyness or outright fear when a stranger approaches
· Separation anxiety—a baby becomes obviously upset when his primary care giver is out of sight, often even when another familiar person such as the other parent, a grandparent, or a babysitter is in the room

Some parents tend to become concerned that their baby is not developing normally when these two behaviors begin. In fact, it is the absence of these behaviors that may be cause for concern. Stranger anxiety and separation anxiety are the direct result of normal cognitive development and a strong, healthy attachment to the primary care giver.

Problems in an Infant's Attachment in the First Year

Incomplete or insecure attachment between an infant and his primary care givers has been linked to emotional and social difficulties later in life, including overaggressiveness and poor self-esteem. The most common reasons for insecure attachment are the parental problems previously discussed. Children with physical or mental disabilities or conditions can also have problems with attachment.

Finally, separation from the primary care giver can produce attachment problems if a baby doesn't receive warm, responsive care from another care giver. No harm generally results from temporary separations such as hospitalization, but long-term or permanent separations caused by such events as death or divorce can have an effect in the absence of special attention by other care givers and, possibly, professional counseling.

Day Care and Attachment

At a time when over half of all mothers of babies under 1 year of age are employed outside the home, the effect of day care on an infant's attachment to the primary care givers is both extremely important and extremely controversial.

To date, research has produced no definitive answers to guide parents. One major problem is the wide variety of types of care lumped under the general term day care. One infant may be cared for in his home by a full-time, live-in professionally trained nanny, while another may spend most of the day lying in a crib with a dozen other infants under the lax supervision of a poorly paid, poorly trained child care aide. The effects of these two kinds of care on the infants in question are likely to be very different.

Until recently, much of the existing research into the effects of day care failed to find any significant developmental differences between infants raised by a primary care giver and those placed in day care. Critics have charged, however, that most of these studies involved children in high-quality day care, such as day care programs administered by the child development departments of major universities. Recently, a great deal of controversy has been raised by the results of a major study by a former day care advocate that found a high rate of insecure attachment in infants under 1 year of age who spent more than twenty hours per week in day care.

At this time, parents can only be guided by the following general points:

1. Research has failed to find any significant benefits in placing a child under 1 year of age in day care instead of a normal home environment.
2. Parents should choose the highest quality care possible and closely monitor their child for any signs of emotional problems.
3. Parents of infants in day care should make a special effort to attend to their baby during available hours.

SOCIAL DEVELOPMENT FROM TWELVE TO TWENTY-FOUR MONTHS

During the first year of life, a baby's social development is dominated by his growing attachment to his primary care givers. The relationship with his parents also dominates social development in the second year of life, but in a different way. The second year begins the long course of *socialization*; that is, teaching a child to adapt his behavior in order to fit in, to fulfill his role in society.

The socialization in the second year primarily involves teaching a young child his place in the family unit. Among other things, this process involves gaining some control over emotions and accepting discipline.

The Emotional Development of Young Children

The emotions that dominate the first 6 months of an infant's life are positive emotions, such as happiness and pleasure. An infant begins to express happiness by smiling in response to external stimulation in the first few weeks of life, and by the age of 3 or 4 months he can recognize pleasurable emotions expressed by others.

Some psychologists believe that infants are born with the capacity to express negative emotions such as anger and fear. However, the crying of a young infant is an expression of physical need, such as hunger, tiredness, or discomfort. Young infants don't seem to be angry or fearful, and they don't seem to recognize the emotions of anger or fearfulness in others.

However, as discussed above, fear and anxiety do begin to express themselves in the second half of the first year. Infants also begin to express frustration, and perhaps anger. These emotions are a normal part of development over which the child has no control.

The latter is a very important point for parents, especially those worried about spoiling a child. At 8 to 10 months of age, the time when a child becomes mobile, parents find themselves frequently using the word "no." At the same time, the child begins to comprehend what the word means. Understanding the command, however, does not mean that an infant has any control over the actions or emotions that led to the prohibition.

The reason for the lack of control is that during the first year of life, an infant has a very incomplete concept of himself as a separate entity. As we saw in Piaget's description, he also has a very limited knowledge of cause and effect. That's why the concept of discipline, especially discipline by punishment, is both ineffective and highly inappropriate for infants.

The emotional condition of the infant has been described by psychologist Erik Erikson, whose theories are in part based on the pioneering work of Sigmund Freud. Erikson has explained emotional (or, in his own words, "psychosocial") growth in terms of a series of different conflicts. He defines the conflict in an infant from birth to 12 to 18 months as "Trust versus Mis-Trust," by which he means that the role of parents is to create in an infant a trust in the world and his care givers by sensitive response to his physical and emotional needs.

Sometime after his first birthday, an infant gains an understanding of his own identity. He has moved on to confront Erikson's second crisis, that of "Autonomy versus Shame and Doubt." Autonomy means that the toddler has a tremendous need to be independent, to assert his newfound individuality. On the other hand, he still has a strong emotional need to be dependent on his parents and others close to him, and he's subject to feelings of shame and doubt when his desire for independence brings about the disapproval of his care giver.

Aggressively asserting his independence leads to what child development experts call negativism and what parents call "the terrible twos." When thwarted, toddlers in this age typically express a wide range of negative emotions, such as jealousy, envy, possessiveness, fear, aggressiveness, and the violent anger that we call a temper tantrum. On the other hand, they're also prone to equally strong outpourings of love and affection.

This conflict between autonomy and doubt covers much of the second year of life, and nearly all of the third.

Socialization in the Second Year

According to Erikson, a child should emerge from this second conflict with a sense of balance between self-assertiveness and self-control, with a rudimentary knowledge of when it's appropriate to hold on (be dependent) and to let go (be independent).

The very difficult task of parents and other care givers during this period is to chart a consistent middle course for their child. A child at this age needs the opportunity to positively assert his independence by making decisions in minor matters (e.g., what to wear, what to have for breakfast, etc.). On the other hand, too much leniency will not only make a child difficult to live with, but may be dangerous physically and emotionally.

Research is beginning to show that the matter in which discipline is applied during this period has a strong influence on the development of a child's personality. If a child's transgressions routinely produce anger and physical aggression by the parents, the child is likely to be over-aggressive and have trouble controlling anger. A number of studies of children who are bullies have shown that they invariably received severe physical punishment when young. The studies also show that the over-aggressive tendencies of childhood bullies lead to serious problems when they reach their adult years.

Social Relationships with Other Children in the Second Year

A child's relationship with other children his own age (his peers) is much less significant to his development in the second year than is his relationship with his parents and family. During much of this period, a child engages almost exclusively in "solitary play," playing alone and independently. Other children may be nearby, but he pays no attention to them and makes no attempt to share or communicate. If he does pay attention to other children his age, he tends to treat them as objects, just as he treats his toys, observing them or briefly touching them out of curiosity. Being egocentric, he's also likely to grab toys out of their hands or to shove them if they get in his way.

As a child nears his second birthday, he becomes more interested in other children. In the company of his peers, he may begin to engage in *parallel play*. That is, he plays beside, but not with, another child. Both children play with similar toys in similar ways (e.g., both dig in the sandbox), but communication or sharing aren't significant parts of play.

A child of this age may engage in *onlooker play* when in the company of older children. That is, he spends most of his time watching their activities. This observation has some value, for it can lead to more sophisticated play. However, a toddler shouldn't be left unsupervised with older children. In these situations, the toddler often becomes an object of play or a "victim" of the older children, with obviously damaging results.

Standardized Testing in the First Two Years of Life

IS MY BABY A GENIUS?

Few parents don't ask this question, at least of themselves, during infancy. Unfortunately, there are no reliable ways, including tests, to answer that question during the first 2 years of a child's life.

The problems begin with the obvious: Children under age 1 can't be asked questions at all, and children under age 2 have a far too limited command of language to express what they know or how they think. As a result, the testing of young children is largely limited to observing their behavior.

For young infants, that presents a second problem: They don't do very much. Older babies and toddlers can exhibit more kinds of behavior, if they're motivated to do so. As anyone who deals with young children knows, that's a big if. A child who's hungry, tired, bored, or frightened by strangers or strange places, or simply obstinate, can't be accurately tested.

The third major problem with trying to determine the intelligence of young children is the most difficult to overcome. That problem is accurately relating measurable behavior, such as motor skills, with future intelligence. After decades of experimentation, no testing program for children under age 2 has proven an accurate predictor of superior intelligence. In fact, no test has been shown to be as reliable an indication of high IQ as the long-established rule of thumb that children of highly educated parents tend to have superior intelligence.

The Value of Standardized Tests

Even though standardized tests can't predict if a baby will be a genius, they are extremely valuable in detecting slower-than-normal development that can be an early sign of physical problems, disease, emotional difficulties, malnutrition, and abuse. Developmental problems detected in the first 2 years are far more easily correctable than those same difficulties detected in the school years.

Throughout this book, we've provided details of normal development in every area for the infant and toddler. Parents and other care givers who are familiar with normal development can far more easily pick up signs of developmental lags. If any doubts arise, parents should consult their pediatrician, who will help make arrangements for professional testing.

General Developmental Testing

The "father" of developmental testing was Dr. Arnold Gesell of Yale University, who meticulously charted the development of the children of 109 middle-class families in New Haven, Connecticut, in the 1920s. Gesell compiled a list of developmental norms in four areas: motor behavior, adaptive behavior, language behavior, and personal-social behavior. In 1928, in his book *Infancy and Human Growth*, he presented the first tests for infants and preschoolers. The test was subsequently modified several times by Gesell and his colleagues at the Yale Clinic of Child Development, and it was published in its modern form in 1940.

The Gesell developmental schedules, as the test was called, produced a combined score called a *developmental quotient*, or DQ. The DQ was arrived at by matching a child's behavior in every area with the norm for his age. A DQ of 100 meant that the child was exactly average, while scores below 100 meant below-average development.

In the succeeding decades, several other tests have come into general use, all of which are generally modeled on the work of Gesell. The most commonly used general development tests are:

1. The Gesell Developmental Schedules cover children from 4-month-olds to 6-year-olds and measure four areas of development: motor behavior, adaptive behavior, language behavior, and personal-social behavior.
2. The Bayley Scales of Child Development were designed for babies from birth to 15 months and compare the child's development with established norms in 150 areas.

3. The Cattell Infant Intelligence Scale tests babies from 2 to 30 months. It is a downward extension of the Stanford-Binet intelligence scale that uses developmental norms from the Gesell test and others.
4. The Denver Developmental Screening Test is for children from birth to age 6 and measures development in four areas: gross motor skills, fine motor-adaptive behavior, personal-social behavior, and language.

Language Development Tests

Although the general tests do measure language acquisition, tests are available for children over age 7 months to provide a more detailed look at development. Because children under age 2 have limited ability to speak, the two major tests concentrate on evaluating receptive language ability, or what a child understands. These tests are the Harvard Preschool Project language abilities test and the Reynell developmental language scale.

Social Competence Tests

The social interactions of young children are so limited that sophisticated testing has proven difficult. Serious interpersonal or emotional problems may be detected by the Harvard Preschool Project social competence test.

SOME DEVELOPMENTAL NORMS

No short list of developmental norms can substitute for the kind of knowledge of the course of child development provided in the sections of this book. However, for quick reference, below are some norms compiled from the Denver developmental screening test:

6 Weeks
Holds head up at 45 degree angle when lying on stomach
Follows an object with eyes for a short distance
Communicates by sounds other than crying
Keeps head erect when held in a sitting position
Smiles

3 Months
Holds head and chest up when lying on stomach
Sits, head steady
Follows an object moving from one side to the other
Brings hands together
Laughs, squeals, coos
Listens to voices; recognizes care giver's voice
Smiles and responds socially to others
Reaches for but misses an object hanging overhead

4 Months
Turns head in all directions and supports self on straight arms
Rolls from front to side or back

Grasps an holds an object; reaches for and sometimes grabs an object that is offered
Babbles in wordlike syllables; coos, gurgles, squeals
Anticipates care giver's approach and becomes excited
Smiles at self in mirror
Recognizes care giver and siblings
Crying can be quieted by voice or music
Bears some weight on legs when held standing

5 Months
Sits up for half hour with back support
Lifts head and shoulders while lying on back; brings feet to mouth and sucks on toes
Reaches for objects and often grasps them
Shifts objects from hand to hand; may drop one deliberately to pick up another
"Talks" to self and others
Reacts to name
Anticipates a whole object by seeing part of it; recognizes familiar objects
Shows emotions, including anger and frustration; may protest loudly when something
   is taken away
Raises arms to be picked up
May hold bottle with one or two hands, pat bottle or breast

5-6 Months
First tooth erupts
Sits well with support
Gets a toy that is out of reach
Bears some weight on legs
Pulls on a toy when adult pulls
Turns toward a voice
Tries to recover an object that falls nearby
Recognizes a familiar face

8 Months
Grasps object with thumb and finger
Plays peek-a-boo
Says "Dada" and "Mama"
Sits without support; gets self into sitting position
Stands well while holding adult's hands
Creeps on stomach
Is shy with strangers
Holds a block in each hand and bangs them together

8-10 Months
Plays patty-cake
Calls "Mama" and "Dada" by name
Pulls to a standing position
Stands without support, briefly
Walks holding on to furniture
Waves bye-bye

12 Months
Stops a rolling ball, then rolls back
Indicates desires without crying
Drinks from a cup, not spilling much
Takes a few steps
Stands alone, bends down, comes back to standing position
Understands many words
Says two or three words besides "Mama" and Dada"
Says "no" decisively

12-15 Months
Uses a spoon; spills only a little
Imitates care giver doing housework
Builds a tower with two blocks
Scribbles with a pencil or crayon
Walks backward and forward

18 Months
Takes off clothes
Builds a four-block tower
Walks up steps, holding rail or using wall for support
Uses own name

18-24 Months
Uses words in combination to make simple statements or ask questions
Identifies parts of body
Follows directions most of the time if only a single step is required
Tries to put on some items of clothing, usually not successfully
Washes and dries hands, with supervision
Identifies pictures of animals by name
Builds a tower of eight blocks
Pedals a tricycle or propels a kiddie car
Kicks a ball forward or throws it overhand, not accurately

Practical Aspects of Parenting in the First Two Years of Life

THE COSTS OF CARING FOR A CHILD

The cost of raising a child places a strain on the budget of most new parents, and that strain continues past infancy to the end of the teenage years. Several separate studies have estimated that total expenditures on a child born in 1988 from birth to age 18 could range from $150,000 to $175,000 (taking inflation into account), a figure that is projected to be about 30% of the after-tax income of the average family.

Of that total, an estimated one-third will go to added housing expenses (e.g., a bigger house or apartment than needed by a couple); one-quarter will be spent on food; 5% on clothing; 11% on transporation; 8% on health care; and 15% on child care, education, and other expenses.

Because of added child care expenses, the Urban Institute has estimated that families in which the husband and wife both work will spend about 23% more to raise a child than a family with only one working parent. The only good news for those starting a family is that each subsequent child requires expenditures of only an additional 10% of family after-tax income, one-third the amount required for the first child.

Expenditures in the first year of life are higher than in any other precollege year, and the second year requires the second highest expenditures. Costs decline significantly after a child turns 2, stay relatively low through age 12, then rise again in the teenage years.

In the early 1980s, economist Lawrence Olsen, in his study "The Costs of Children," found that the average family spent $7,118 on child-related expenses in the first year of their first baby's life and $6,216 in the second year. Most recent estimates place the total cost to the average family for the first 2 years of a first baby's life at $15,000 to $17,500.

EQUIPMENT, SUPPLIES, TOYS, AND FURNITURE

Expenditures for baby furniture, equipment, supplies, and toys are the primary reason that the costs of raising a baby in the first and second years are much higher than in subsequent years. It's impossible, however, to find any accurate statistics on average expenditure on individual pieces of equipment or furniture. The major reasons for the difficulty are that most parents have some used and borrowed products and receive others as gifts. One family may buy a new crib, use a second-hand changing table, and receive a stroller as a gift. Another family at the same income level may purchase a used crib, receive a changing table as a gift, and buy a new stroller. Total expenditures are very similar between families in the same income level, but the dispersion of those budgets varies.

Here is a master list of the products that the average family acquires, one way or another, in the first 2 years of their first child's life:

Master Shopping List

Nursery Furniture and Accessories
Cradle/bassinet
  Cradle/bassinet sheets
Crib
Crib mattress
Nursery chair
Changing table
Clothes storage
  Dressers
  Other storage
Toy storage
  Toy chests
  Other storage
Soft goods
  Crib sheets
  Bumper pad
  Quilts/blankets
  Mattress pad
  Crib skirt
  Wall hangings
  Diaper stacker
  Other soft goods
Climate control
  Air conditioner
  Fan

Humidifier
Vaporizer
Thermometer
Diaper pail
Lighting
  Lamps
  Night light
  Dimmer switch
Window coverings
  Shades
  Blinds
  Curtains
Decorating supplies
  Paint
  Painting equipment/supplies

Baby Equipment
Car seat
Infant seat
Infant front carrier
Nursery monitor
Stroller/carriage
Baby swing
Baby bathtub
  Bath thermometer

Bath seat
High chair
Portable high chair
Playpen/portable crib
  Playpen
  Portable crib
  Through-the-door playpen
  Portable playpen
  Portable play space
Walker
Back carrier
Baby jumper

Toys and Books
Birth-3 months
  Mobiles
  Books
  Baby mirror
  Toy bars
  Rattles/clutch toys/teethers
3-6 months
  Rattles/clutch toys/teethers
  Books
  Activity centers
  Crib gym
  Car-seat toys
  Stroller toys
6-12 months
  Books
  Activity centers
  Balls and push toys
  Nesting toys
  Stacking toys
  Bath toys
  Puzzles
  Walking toys
12-24 months
  Gross motor activity toys
  Sand toys
  Water toys
  Fine motor activity toys
  Blocks
  Music and musical instruments
  Pull toys
  Housekeeping toys
  Dolls and stuffed animals
  Cars and trucks
  Craft materials
  Books

Baby Supplies and Accessories
Diapers
  Disposable diapers
  Diaper inserts
  Diaper services
  Cloth diapers
  Diaper pins/waterproof pants

Diapering supplies
  Baby wipes
  Petroleum jelly
  Diaper tape
  Zinc oxide ointment
Diaper bag
Breast-feeding equipment
  Breast pump
  Nursing bras
  Nursing pads
  Nursing cream
Bottle-feeding equipment
  Bottles
  Nipples
  Hoods/collars
  Pacifiers
  Nipple brush
  Bottle brush
  Nipple/collar caddy
  Bottle warmer
  Bottle sterilizer
  Bottle covers
Training cups
Baby dishes
Baby cutlery
Bibs
  Drooler bibs
  Feeding bibs
Formula
Baby food
Baby-food grinder
Medical supplies
  Rectal thermometer
  Medicine syringe
  Acetaminophen drops
  Nasal aspirator
  Syrup of ipecac
  Antiseptic for cuts
Rubbing alcohol
  Bath supplies
  Baby shampoo
  Comb
  Brush
  Wash clothes
  Cotton balls
  Hooded bath towels
Teething supplies
  Teethers
  Teething gels
Sun protection
  Sun block
Safety equipment and supplies
  Outlet plugs
  Outlet covers
  Electric cord shorteners
  Drawer latches
  Cabinet latches
  Cabinet locks

Sliding-bathroom-cabinet locks
Hinged-bathroom-cabinet locks
Doorknob covers
Corner and edge cushions
Refrigerator latch
Stove-knob covers
Range-top guard
Oven-door latch
Toilet-lid latch
Safety gates
Window guards
Smoke detectors
Shopping-cart harness
Memories of the first year
  Baby book
  Camera
  Film
  Film processing
  Professional photography

Baby Clothing
Newborn clothing
  Stretchies
  T-shirts
  Receiving blankets
  Hat
  Snowsuit
  Socks
  Sweaters
  Onesies
  Dress clothes
3-12 months
  Overalls
  Jogging suits
  Pants/shorts
  Shirts
  T-shirts
  Dresses
  Dress clothing
  Shoes
  Socks

CHILD CARE

In 1986, over half of all women with babies under 1 year of age were in the work force. That figure rose to 62% of all women with children under age 6. The greatest concern of families in which both parents work is finding reliable and affordable day care.

In 1986, the Census Bureau found that the 8,686,000 employed mothers with children under age 5 made the following day care arrangements:

Type of care	% of children
Care in child's home	31.0
By father	15.7
By other relative	9.4
By nonrelative	5.9
Care in another home	37.0
By relative	14.7
By nonrelative	22.3
Group care center	23.1
Mother cares for child while working	8.1

ENSURING THE SAFETY OF A BABY

Accidents are by far the leading cause of death and serious injury of children over 6 months of age. About one in five children under age 2 requires hospital emergency room treatment for an accidental injury during the course of a year.

That's why parents and care givers have to think about child safety at all times. By far the most important step they can take is child-proofing the home. We have included a complete list of the wide range of excellent commercial products that are extremely valuable in making a home safe for an active baby. Every person who cares for a child should become thoroughly familiar with these products and purchase those that are applicable. For detailed information on the use of these products, you can consult *Buying the Best for Your Baby* by Tom and Nancy Biracree.

Two areas of child safety are of special concern to parents and care givers of children under age 2. These are:

Nursery Equipment and Furniture

The Consumer Products Safety Commission estimated the following annual product-related injuries that resulted in trips to the emergency room:

Walkers	16,000
Strollers/carriages	11,300
High chairs	9,000
Playpens	4,000
Infant seats	3,700
Changing tables	1,330

Most of the injuries resulted from improper use of these products or inadequate supervision rather than from manufacturing defects or design problems. Parents and care givers must understand how these products are used and must think about safety first when using them.

Poisoning

An estimated 250,000 children under age 2 required hospital treatment for ingestion of household products, drugs, etc., in 1984. According to a study of poisoning incidents by the American Association of Poison Control Centers, the causes were:

Over-the-counter/prescription drugs	60%
Aspirin/acetaminophen	10%
Cleaning agents	9%
Toxic plants	9%
Cosmetics	5%
Alcohol	4%
Insecticides/pesticides	3%

The two leading causes of death from poisoning were drugs and alcohol. Eighty-three percent of all alcohol poisonings involved children under age 6.

3

The Preschool Years

Physical Growth in the Preschool Years

MEASURING GROWTH

Body Proportions

Most of a child's growth between his second and fifth birthdays is upward. The width to length ratio for both boys and girls drops, which means that children look slimmer. Since most of the increase in height occurs below the waist, preschool children have increasingly longer legs.

An additional change that makes a child look slimmer is that after age 2, his abdominal muscles become stronger, and the midsection bulge so evident on toddlers disappears. Baby fat in the archs of the feet and the cheeks also disappears.

Height

The rate of growth drops dramatically after a child's second birthday. A smaller decline takes place after his third birthday, then the growth rate levels off through age 5. The average height gain in each six month period from age 2 to 5 is:

Age (in months)	Height Increase (in inches)
24-30	1.9
30-36	1.7
36-42	1.5
42-48	1.4
48-54	1.4
54-60	1.3

By percentile, the height in inches of children from age 2 to 5 is:

Boys

Age (in years)	5th	10th	25th	Percentile 50th	75th	90th	95th
2.0	32.5	32.75	33.5	34.25	35.0	36.25	37.25
2.5	33.5	34.0	34.75	35.5	36.5	37.75	38.5
3.0	35.0	35.5	36.5	37.25	38.5	39.5	40.25
3.5	36.5	37.0	38.0	39.0	40.0	41.25	41.75
4.0	37.75	38.25	39.25	40.5	41.5	42.5	43.25
4.5	39.0	39.5	40.75	42.0	43.0	44.0	44.75
5.0	40.25	40.75	42.0	43.25	44.5	45.5	46.0

Girls

Age (in years)	5th	10th	25th	Percentile 50th	75th	90th	95th
2.0	32.25	32.25	33.0	34.25	35.25	36.25	36.75
2.5	33.25	33.5	34.5	35.5	36.5	37.5	38.0
3.0	34.75	35.25	36.0	37.0	38.0	39.0	39.5
3.5	36.0	36.5	37.5	38.5	39.5	40.5	41.25
4.0	37.5	38.0	39.0	40.0	41.0	42.0	42.75
4.5	38.5	39.25	40.25	41.25	42.5	43.5	44.0
5.0	39.75	40.5	41.5	42.75	43.75	44.75	45.5

Many researchers have explored the relationship between height in these early years and full height at maturity. No absolutely foolproof formula has been found—and until someone can read an individual's genetic imprinting and factor in nutrition and health, no such formula will be found. However, parents might find interesting the following formula relating eventual height to height at age 3, developed by J. M. Tanner. The formulas, using height in centimeters are:

Boys: $1.27 \times$ Height at $3 + 54.9$
Girls: $1.29 \times$ Height at $3 + 42.3$

One centimeter equals 0.39 inches. A sample computation for a boy who's 37.5 inches tall at age 3:

Step 1: Convert height to centimeters.
$37.5 \div 0.39 = 96.2$ centimeters.
Step 2: Use formula
$1.27 \times 96.2 + 54.9 = 177.0$ centimeters.
Step 3: Convert to inches.
$177.0 \times 0.39 = 69.0$ inches.

In other words, a boy who's about average height at age 3 will, according to the formula, be 5-foot 9-inches tall, exactly the average height for an adult American male.

Weight

The average rate of weight gain drops off less dramatically from the second to the third year of life. A child's average annual weight gain is very consistent from age 2 to 5. The average preschool boy or girl gains a little over 1 pound every 3 months. The average total yearly gain is 4.4 pounds between ages 2 and 4, and 4.6 pounds between ages 4 and 5. By percentile, the weight in pounds of a child from age 2 to age 5 is:

Boys

Age (in years)	Percentile						
	5th	10th	25th	50th	75th	90th	95th
2.0	23.25	24.55	25.5	27.25	29.5	31.75	34.25
2.5	24.75	26.0	27.75	29.75	32.25	34.75	36.5
3.0	26.5	27.75	29.75	32.25	34.75	37.25	39.25
3.5	28.25	29.5	32.0	34.5	37.25	40.0	41.75
4.0	30.0	31.5	34.0	36.75	39.75	42.5	44.75
4.5	31.75	33.75	36.0	39.0	42.0	45.25	47.75
5.0	33.75	35.25	38.0	41.25	44.5	47.75	51.0

Girls

Age (in years)	Percentile						
	5th	10th	25th	50th	75th	90th	95th
2.0	22.0	22.75	24.25	26.0	28.0	30.0	31.25
2.5	23.75	25.0	26.75	28.75	31.25	33.5	34.75
3.0	25.5	27.0	29.0	31.0	34.25	36.5	38.0
3.5	27.25	28.75	30.75	33.25	36.5	39.25	41.0
4.0	29.0	30.5	32.75	35.25	38.75	41.75	44.0
4.5	30.5	32.0	34.25	37.0	40.75	44.25	46.75
5.0	32.0	33.75	36.0	39.0	42.75	46.75	49.75

Except for children whose weight is under the third percentile, lower-than-average weight in this age range is much less of a concern than higher than average weight. Obesity in preschool children has been tied to obesity in adolescence and adulthood. Unfortunately, many parents believe "pudginess" to be a sign of good health. In fact, a trend toward lower appetite and leanness is the norm for healthy preschool children.

Head Circumference

The head circumference of the average child increases 5.4 inches between birth and age 2, but just 0.8 of an inch (from 19.2 inches to 20.0

inches) from age 2 to age 5. The head circumference of a 5 year old reaches 90% of his eventual adult measurement. The rate of increase in head circumference parallels the rate in brain growth, with the brain of a 5 year old having 90% of the mass of the adult brain.

The shape of the head changes more dramatically. The jaw grows in preparation for the emergence of permanent teeth in the early school years. As a result, the face becomes longer and more angular.

Chest Circumference

The chest measurement of a two-year-old is normally the same as his abdominal measurement. After age 2, the chest circumference increases at the rate of about an inch per year (increasing from an average of 19.5 inches at age 2 to 22.0 inches at age 5). At the same time, the abdominal muscles tighten, reducing the circumference around the abdomen.

Bone Growth

Bone growth proceeds at a steady rate from age 2 right up to the onset of puberty in early adolescence. The fastest-growing bones are those of the arms and legs, with the major leg bones (femur, tibia, and fibula) growing about 2 inches a year. Proper bone growth requires good nutrition, particularly an adequate supply of calcium.

The processes of ossification, or the changing of soft cartilage into hard bone, continues through the preschool years. While the major bones of the body have ossified earlier, the hardening of joints (knee, ankle, elbow, etc.) isn't completed until shortly before the teenage years. This means that preschoolers are more flexible than teenagers and adults. At the same time, their joints are much more prone to injury from carrying too much weight or from overuse.

How a Child's Body Works in the Preschool Years

THE BRAIN

The ferocious rate of brain growth in the first 2 years now slows down. Still, the growth from 75% of adult size at age 2 to 90% of adult size at age 5 is more substantial than at any succeeding time of life. At age 5, the average child's brain weighs about 42 ounces, compared with 47.25 ounces for the average adult.

The brain and the rest of the central nervous system are still larger in comparison to the rest of the body than are the brain and central nervous system of an adult. The entire nervous system of a 5-year-old represents one-twentieth of his entire weight, compared with one-fiftieth of the entire weight of an adult.

WHAT YOU SHOULD KNOW ABOUT . . .

A CHILD'S HEALTH IN THE PRESCHOOL YEARS

Preschool children today are much less prone to serious illness than they were twenty-five years ago. The death rate for children aged 1 to 4 was cut in half between 1960 and 1985. One major reason for the decline in fatal illness was widespread immunization against serious childhood illnesses. From 1960 to 1985, the number of cases of rheumatic fever fell from 9,022 to 117; the cases of measles from 441,000 to 2,700; the cases of whooping cough from 14,800 to 3,300; the cases of polio from 3,190 to 5; and the cases of diphtheria from 918 to 2. In 1985, 73.7% of children under the age of 14 were immunized against whooping cough, tetanus, and diphtheria; 69.7% against polio; 71.5% against measles; and 71.6% against mumps.

Preschool children are, of course, still prone to the common cold, influenza, chicken pox, and other routine illnesses. The incidence of these conditions peaks when a child begins to attend preschool programs or spends time in a day care center. Studies have found that children between the ages of 3 and 5 have some symptoms of illness on one of every five or six days of the year. The average child under age 5 sees a doctor four times a year. About 8% of all visits are in a hospital emergency room.

About 7% of preschool children are hospitalized during the course of an average year. Respiratory disease accounts for almost half the hospital admissions of children aged 1 to 4, with injuries from accidents or abuse being the second leading cause (12% of admissions). The death rate for children aged 1 to 4 was 1 in 1,754.

The process of myelinization, or the connecting of the nervous system, still lags behind brain growth. One major sign of increasing brain organization in the preschool years is the clear emergence of hand preference by age 4. In other words, by age 4, about 90% of children are clearly right-handers and about 10% are left-handers. Heredity is the primary determinant of hand preference, but the child's environment or a brain injury can alter the genetic predisposition.

The environmental influences are primarily parents, some of whom still cling to the discredited beliefs that left-handedness is socially unacceptable or leads to "odd" behavior and attempt to force their children to become right-handers. This coercion does work, but research has shown that children suffer less emotional upset and perform better at fine motor activities if they are allowed to use the hand they are genetically predisposed to use. The same research has indicated that left-handers may have an advantage in some sports and artistic activities.

The emergence of hand preference is, in turn, a sign of an extremely important and more comprehensive organization of the brain that's called *lateralization*. The brain is divided into two halves, the right half, or hemisphere, and the left hemisphere. As children move through the preschool years, each hemisphere begins to develop different functions. In almost all right-handed children and half of all left-handed children, the left hemisphere assumes control of reasoning, understanding, and speech. The right hemisphere assumes control of creativity, musical, and artistic skills, spatial relationships, facial recognition, emotional expressions, and other nonverbal activities. In half of left-handers, the organization is different, in that the speech center may be in the right hemisphere, or speech centers may be in both hemispheres.

While this lateralization begins in the preschool period, it's far from mature then. That's why young children have trouble coordinating thoughts and actions. Their brains are considered more flexible or "plastic."

Brain flexibility means that the brains of young children can overcome serious injury far more successfully than the brains of older children and adults. A 4-year-old whose left hemisphere speech center is damaged has little trouble transferring speech control to the right hemisphere. An adult with the same severity of injury may never speak again. The half of left-handers whose brains are less strictly lateralized are an exception to this general rule.

THE SENSES

Because the central area of the retina, the fovea, isn't fully developed until about age 6, preschoolers tend to be farsighted, focusing better on distant objects than they do on close objects. That's why reading books for young children should be printed in larger type.

The other four senses, hearing, touch, taste, and smell, are fully developed by the preschool period. In fact, a preschooler's sense of taste may be sharper than an adult's because of extra taste buds in the cheeks and throat that disappear in later years.

The major changes involving the senses in the preschool years aren't in their sensitivity, but rather in the way they're used by the preschool child. When confronted with a new object, a child under age 2 normally explores it with his sense of touch. After age 2, he's increasingly likely to use vision for that first inspection.

Because he's new at it, a 2-year-old isn't very efficient in his use of visual scanning. For example, he has a difficult time picking out his parents in a crowd. Visual scanning ability improves rapidly, and along with it comes improved coordination of vision, hearing, and touch to refine inspection of a new object or place. By age 5 or 6, a child is nearly as skilled as an adult in coordinating these senses.

THE CIRCULATORY SYSTEM

The child's circulatory system matures gradually over the preschool period. His resting heart rate is still more rapid and fluctuates more than an adult's. The average rate declines from about 110 beats per minute for a 2-year-old to 95 to 100 beats per minute for a 5-year-old. Blood pressure increases very slightly, reflecting a strengthening of the heart muscle. The weight of the heart increases in proportion to overall weight gain, reaching an average of 3 ounces by age 5.

THE RESPIRATORY SYSTEM

Babies are almost exclusively "stomach breathers," using their diaphragm to inhale and exhale. By age 3, a child's breathing movements combine chest and abdominal movements in an adultlike pattern. Thus a preschooler can take in a relatively greater quantity of air with each breath. As a result, the number of breaths per minute drops from an average of 25 to 30 for a 2-year-old to an average of 20 to 25 for a 5-year-old.

The air passages of a preschooler are relatively smaller than an adult's. That's why breathing difficulties are more obvious, with swelling of the nasal tissues during a cold or allergy attack. Since parts of the lymphatic system such as the tonsils and adenoids are relatively larger in the preschool period, their inflammation causes more severe problems.

THE DIGESTIVE SYSTEM

The stomach of the average 2-year-old is big enough to hold approximately 2 pints of liquid, about 40% of the capacity of an adult's. The stomach of a preschooler is positioned more vertically than an adult's, sitting in a shape most commonly described as a "cow's horn." This position means that the stomach empties upward relatively more easily, leading to more frequent vomiting during illness or other gastric distress.

By age 3 or 4, digestive enzymes in the system reach adult levels, so a child is capable of digesting the same types of foods as adults. However, for reasons that are not completely understood, the digestive system of a preschooler is more sensitive to certain foods and spices. As a result, a preschooler may have more loose stools and more frequent stools (diarrhea) that are not caused by disease.

THE URINARY SYSTEM

A preschool child typically urinates between one-half and three-quarters of a quart of liquid per day, as much as half the amount of liquid passed by an adult. That's why the amount of fluid per pound of body weight he needs is at least three times that of the average adult. Those needs are 100 to 120 milliliters of fluid per kilogram of body weight, or roughly a pint of liquid for every 10 pounds of body weight.

One consequence of this fluid need is that preschoolers are more prone to dehydration, especially after frequent vomiting, diarrhea, or exertion in hot weather.

A second consequence is more frequent urination than an adult. The average 2-year-old urinates ten times a day, half as frequently as an infant, but about twice as often as an adult. The average slowly declines to about nine times a day for a 3-year-old and eight times a day for 4- and 5-year-olds.

Children begin to gain bladder control after age 2, with girls gaining control relatively sooner than boys. Most children gain daytime control by age 3, although accidents are frequent.

Feeding the Preschool Child

EATING PATTERNS

There's an old medical saw that goes "pediatricians eat because children don't," that is, pediatricians get a lot of business from parents worried that their kids aren't eating enough. The age range for which that's most true is the preschool years, ages 2 through 5.

The goal of most parents is to have their child eat three well-balanced meals a day, with a light, nutritious snack in mid-morning and mid-afternoon. Very few preschoolers manage that schedule for an entire day, much less over the course of a year. The normal eating pattern of preschool children is the absence of any regular pattern at all. Days of voracious eating may be followed by days on which hardly anything is consumed.

Some characteristics of preschool eating patterns are:

1. Significant fluctuation in calorie needs. Adults don't need any energy for growth; rather, we eat to have energy for our daily activities. Since these activities change little from day to day, we tend to have regular eating habits.

   Children, on the other hand, need calories for growth as well as for energy. Preschool children grow much less rapidly than younger children, but that growth often comes in spurts. The amount of energy expended also varies much more widely than does an adult's. The result is that the number of calories children burn changes significantly from day to day.

2. Significant fluctuation in appetite. A preschool child's appetite can be affected by many factors other than his calorie needs at mealtime. He may not feel like eating because he's tired, he's overstimulated, or he's just too restless to sit. He's also likely to be very sensitive to the entire ambience surrounding eating. For example, his appetite may disappear if he doesn't like a strange smell in the kitchen, if he objects to the color of a new food, or if he can't use his regular fork or spoon.

3. Very limited likes and many violent dislikes of foods. A recent survey of the eating habits of preschoolers found that the average young child ate only six of twenty-nine vegetables (three cooked, three raw), four of seventeen fruits, and six of twenty meats. The typical 3-year-old, for example, is very resistant to any new foods or any favorite food prepared in even a slightly new way. These limited dietary preferences frustrate parents, who want their child to eat a varied, balanced diet.

4. The periodic emergence of negativism. Everyone's heard of the in-famous "terrible twos," when "no" seems to be the only word in a child's vocabulary. All the preschool years, however, are punctuated by periods of rebellion against authority. Mealtime is a favorite focus for a little revolutionary. The more insistent Mom and Dad are about eating, the bigger the battle becomes.

NOW, THE GOOD NEWS

Research has shown that although one-third of mothers were convinced that their children were not getting enough to eat, the overwhelming majority of the preschoolers were actually consuming more than enough calories and protein. Other studies have produced reassuring evidence that young children presented with a well-balanced diet do, over the long run, eat enough to meet all their nutritional needs. In other words, preschoolers may not eat three balanced meals every day, but they do consume a balanced diet.

There are three major exceptions to the above rule. The most common involves junk food. Some parents who are so concerned that their child eat something, anything, gradually give in to the demand for candy and other junk food. For example, we once ate dinner at the house of a high school teacher and his wife who served their 3-year-old a chocolate milk shake not only for dinner, but for all three meals a day, every day, because "that's all he'll eat." In other households, children eat primarily junk food because of lack of attention from their parents or other care givers. Given enough junk food to allay hunger, children will ignore a balanced diet.

The second major exception is in households where confrontations about eating have become so heated that mealtime has become a traumatic event for the child. The result can be a strong aversion to food, and the situation may require professional counseling.

The third major exception is loss of appetite caused by a physical problem or disease. While it's normal for a child's appetite to fluctuate dramatically, consistent refusal to eat over a long period of time is a sufficient reason for a visit to the pediatrician.

THE NUTRITIONAL NEEDS OF THE PRESCHOOL CHILD

Calories

As we explained in our discussion of the nutritional needs of infants, children need energy for five specific bodily functions:

1. Basal metabolism, or the energy needed to generate body heat, circulate blood, think, and operate other internal organs.
2. Specific dynamic action, or the energy needed to digest food.
3. Activity, the energy needed to run, jump, play, etc.
4. Growth.
5. Excreta, or the calories lost in undigested food.

A child's calorie needs can be roughly calculated from his body weight. A child aged 2 to 5 needs about twice as many calories per pound of body weight as an adult does. The fact that a child is growing is only one reason for the disparity. Even more significantly, preschool children burn over twice as many calories per pound of body weight through activity and 60% more calories in basal metabolism.

The calorie needs per pound for the average preschool child are:

Basal metabolism	18
Specific dynamic action	3
Activity	11
Growth	5
Excreta	3

Total calories per pound 40

Once again, calorie needs can vary considerably from day to day, depending on growth rate and activity. But on the average, a 30 pound child needs to take in 1,200 calories a day, and a 40-pound child needs 1,600 calories.

Composition of the Diet

A preschooler thrives on a diet that's balanced differently from the ideal adult diet, for two reasons. First, a preschooler needs over twice as

WHAT YOU SHOULD KNOW ABOUT . . .
FOOD INTAKE FOR GOOD NUTRITION BY FOOD GROUP
According to recommendations developed by the Institute of Home Economics of the U.S. Department of Agriculture and the Children's Bureau of the U.S. Department of Health and Human Services, a 2- or 3-year-old toddler's balanced diet should include:

Food Group	Servings per Day	Average Size of Serving
Milk and cheese	4	3/4 cup
Meat group	3-4	
Egg		1 egg
Meat, fish, poultry		1 ounce
Peanut butter		1/2 ounce
Fruits and vegetables	4-5	
Citrus fruits, berries	1	1/2 cup
Green/yellow fruits	1	3 tablespoons
and vegetables		
Other vegetables (inc. potato)	2	3 tablespoons
Other fruits	1	1/3 cup
(apple, banana)		
Cereals	4-5	
Breads		1 slice
Ready-to-eat cereal		3/4 ounce
Rice, pasta, cooked		1/3 cup
cereal		
Fats and carbohydrates		
Butter, margarine	1-3	1
mayonnaise		
Desserts, sweets	1 1/2	1/3 cup ice cream
		2 3-inch cookies
		1 ounce cake

The recommended diet of preschool children aged 4 or 5 should be:

Food Group	Servings per Day	Average Size of Serving
Milk and cheese	4	3/4 cup
Meat group	3-4	
Egg		1 egg
Meat, fish, poultry		2 ounces
Peanut butter		1 ounce
Fruits and vegetables	4-5	
Citrus fruits, berries	1	1/2 cup
Green/yellow fruits	1	4 tablespoons
and vegetables		
Other vegetables	2	4 tablespoons
(inc. potato)		
Other fruits	1	1/2 cup
(apple, banana)		
Cereals	4-5	
Breads		1-1/2 slice
Ready-to-eat cereal		1 ounce
Rice, pasta, cooked		1/2 cup
cereal		
Fats and carbohydrates		
Butter, margarine	1-3	1 tablespoon
mayonnaise		
Desserts, sweets	1 1/2	1/3 cup ice cream
		2 3-inch cookies
		1 ounce cake

much protein, the building blocks of growth, as does an adult. Insufficient protein can stunt growth and produce a loss of appetite. The average preschooler needs slightly less than a gram of protein per pound of body weight per day. The National Academy of Sciences recommends that a 30-pound child consume 24 grams of protein per day and a 44-pound child consume 30 grams per day. These needs can be met if protein represents about 20% of the child's diet.

The second major difference between the ideal preschool and adult diets are that young children need relatively more fat and less carbohydrates. Fat is a nasty word to most diet conscious parents, but even the slimmest of us need fats for repair of body tissues, absorption of fat-soluble vitamins such as A and D, and synthesis of hormones. One reason that preschoolers need relatively more fat is that their bodies are building more tissue and have more need for the steroid hormones essential for growth. A second reason is that because of their relatively greater body surface area, young children have to burn significantly more calories to keep warm. Research has shown that these additional calories must come from fat, which appears to be essential to the proper functioning of the mechanisms by which a child's body regulates its temperature. For these reasons, fats should make up 35% of a preschooler's diet and carbohydrates should make up 40%. In comparison, a good adult diet may have 60% carbohydrates.

The remaining 5% of a preschooler's diet should be fiber from breads, vegetables, and other sources. This fiber is important for proper elimination of food wastes.

Vitamins and Minerals

The recommended daily allowances for vitamins and minerals for 2- to 3-year-olds and 4- to 5-year-olds are:

	2- to 3-year olds	4- to 5-year olds
Vitamin A (R.E.)	400	500
Vitamin D (IU)	10	10
Vitamin E (mg)	5	6
Vitamin C (mg)	45	45
Thiamin (mg)	0.7	0.9
Riboflavin (mg)	0.8	1.0
Niacin (mg N.E.)	9	11
Vitamin B_6(mg)	0.9	1.3
Folacin(mcg)	100	200
Vitamin B_{12}(mg)	2.0	2.5
Calcium (mg)	800	800
Phosphorus (mg)	800	800
Magnesium (mg)	150	200
Iron (mg)	15	10
Zinc (mg)	10	10
Iodine (mg)	70	90
Vitamin K (mg)	30	40

	2- to 3-year olds	4- to 5-year olds
Sodium (mg)	975	1,350
Potassium (mg)	1,650	2,325
Chloride (mg)	1,500	2,100

In addition to the above, children also need small amounts of copper, manganese, chromium, selenium, molybdenum, and fluoride.

A well-balanced diet will generally provide all the above requirements, with one exception. If your water supply is not fluoridated, a pediatrician may prescribe fluoride supplements. A physician should also be consulted before any other vitamin or mineral supplements are given to a child.

Sleep in the Preschool Years

AMOUNT OF SLEEP

There's an old saying that goes "Never was there a mother so fond she didn't welcome the sight of a sleeping child." A significant number of parents are concerned that their preschoolers don't get enough sleep. Like eating, sleep is a major nonillness-related reason for parents' contact with pediatricians.

However, the overwhelming majority of children get enough sleep to meet their needs, if not their parents'. Although the average amount of sleep for children aged 2 to 5 is about twelve hours a day, the normal range can vary from nine to fourteen hours. A child who is basically cheerful, active, and not obviously tired during waking hours is probably getting enough sleep.

SLEEP SCHEDULES

Most children have reduced their naps from two to one per day by their second birthday or shortly thereafter. The remaining nap is usually taken in the afternoon and averages slightly longer than one hour. About 7% of two-year-olds, 10% of 3 year olds, and 30% of 4-year-olds don't take a regular nap.

A significantly longer-than-normal nap seldom affects the nighttime sleep of a child under age 3. An older preschooler who takes an especially long nap may have more trouble going to sleep at night. A child who naps for three hours or more during the day, then sleeps less than eight hours at night has a sleep schedule disturbance that can cause problems in the school years if not corrected.

To the dismay of their parents, many preschoolers seem to be part rooster, awaking at the first ray of dawn. Unfortunately, sleep specialists have failed to find a way to train a child who's getting enough sleep to sleep an hour longer.

SLEEP DISTURBANCES

By age 2, children's sleep has assumed the adult pattern of four progressively deeper stages of nondreaming sleep, alternating with a lighter, dreaming sleep. Because a young child's nervous system is still immature, the transition between stages is often not as smooth as the transitions in adult sleep. In particular, a child may have trouble with arousal from deep nondreaming sleep to lighter, dreaming sleep, which can cause three common sleep disturbances.

Night Terrors

Night terrors commonly afflict children between the ages of 2 and 5. Night terrors typically occur in the first three hours of sleep. The child suddenly arouses from deep sleep, sits up in bed, and screams. Parents rush in to find him obviously terrified, covered with sweat, his heart beating rapidly. The child, however, doesn't recognize his parents and is totally unresponsive. The attack can last from a few seconds to as long as thirty minutes. Eventually, the child suddenly relaxes, may wake briefly, then goes back to sleep. Because the attack took place during non-dreaming sleep, the child has no memory of it in the morning. Attacks of night terrors seldom affect a child's daytime behavior.

The tendency to have night terrors appears to be inherited. They usually disappear as the child's nervous system matures. If they occur sporadically, they're generally not treated. A physician may prescribe medication to alleviate very frequent attacks.

Bed-wetting

Most preschool children don't achieve nighttime bladder control until about age 4, and even older children have occasional accidents. However, bed-wetting in children approaching school age is often a sleep disturbance, not a bladder control or psychological problem. These children wet the bed because they have trouble arousing from the first cycle of deep, nondreaming sleep. Since the cause is an immature nervous system, the same children often have night terrors. The tendency to wet the bed is inherited and most commonly disappears with age.

There are, however, other reasons for bed-wetting than a disturbance in the sleep cycle, so a physician should be consulted.

Nightmares

The most common sleep disturbance of preschool children is bad dreams, or nightmares. Nightmares result from tension or anxiety that's carried over into sleep. As children emerge from infancy, their days inevitably include more conflicts with parents, siblings, and friends. As they get out into the world, they have more frightening experiences (a barking dog, a fall from playground equipment) and more exposure to frightening entertainment (television, books). They have attacks of separation anxiety that make them feel lonely or frightened to be alone at night. Finally, vigorous horseplay or exercise right before bed can produce physical tension.

Because of all the above experiences are common, many children have occasional nightmares, which occur during dreaming sleep. The difference between nightmares and night terrors is that a child having a bad dream is easily awakened and remembers the dream.

Unfortunately, nightmares can cause sleep problems. Preschoolers lack the cognitive ability to distinguish between dream and reality. Believing his nightmares are real, a preschooler may become afraid of going to bed. This fear may produce even more nightmares in a vicious circle that results in more fearfulness.

The age-old solution to this fear is the establishment of a bedtime ritual that revolves around quiet, soothing activities. Reading warm, happy stories, saying good night to family members and toys, arranging favorite stuffed animals in bed, all have the effect of relieving tension and anxiety. If nightmares occur frequently despite parents' best efforts, counseling may be necessary to uncover and treat deep-seated anxiety.

Gross Motor Development in the Preschool Years

THE IMPORTANCE OF GROSS MOTOR DEVELOPMENT

Gross motor activity consists of walking, running, jumping, climbing, kicking, throwing, and other activities involving the large muscles of the body. In the first 2 years of a baby's life, his parents are normally more interested in his gross motor development (sitting up, crawling, walking) than they are in any other area of his development, with the possible exception of language acquisition. An example of this interest is in a recent survey that found a baby's first steps were listed as the most important milestone by the largest percentage of parents.

Unfortunately, parents' interest in their child's gross motor development and activity all too commonly fades in the preschool years. Today's parents tend to be primarily concerned with their child's intellectual development at this time, with social development coming second. Increasingly, preschool programs have shaped their activities around "early learning" to meet this concern.

The impact of this concentration on early learning for children's later intellectual development is not yet clear. What is clear, however, is that lack of attention to gross motor activity is producing the least physically fit generation of elementary school children in America's history. Only 2% of 18 million young people passed the Presidential Physical Fitness test the last time it was administered. A study of 18,000 young people by the Amateur Athletic Union found that only 36% met the fitness standards for "average healthy youngsters." Forty percent of those surveyed had at least one risk factor for cardiovascular disease. Poor physical fitness is largely a result of lack of exercise, which in turn comes from a long-term failure to encourage gross motor activity.

Yet young children love movement, and toddlers seem obsessed with walking, running, and climbing. This vigorous physical activity is extremely important in developing a healthy cardiovascular system, respiratory system, and strong muscles. Exercise also alleviates tension and anxieties that can otherwise cause emotional and behavioral problems. And the process of gaining command over one's body is vital to building confidence and self-esteem.

There are several reasons why parents and other care givers fail to encourage gross motor activity as toddlers become preschoolers. The first is a simple failure to understand its importance at a time when parents concentrate on preparing their child for school. A second reason is that, as a child grows, gross motor activity needs space, equipment, and constant supervision—a preschooler confined to a playroom with toys and a television set needs much less supervision. A third reason is that some parents are overly fearful of injury, a fear that's soon instilled in their children. Finally, a lack of understanding of the process of gross motor development leads to either a failure to provide the proper materials and encouragement at the right time, or, on the other hand, unrealistic expectations of progress that can lead to a child feeling like a failure.

Our goal in this section is to explain in detail the process by which a child gains control over, coordinates, and exercises his large muscles. Understanding and encouraging the process may not turn a child into an accomplished athlete. But it will keep alive the child's innate love of movement that provides the impetus for exercise and fitness in the school years.

HOW MOTOR SKILLS ARE LEARNED

Certain ways of moving are characteristic of mankind, just as certain ways of moving are characteristic of dogs or horses. The current theory of human movement is called *patterning*. This theory states that man's major motor movements are genetically coded and laid down as specific nerve-muscle relationships that result in the coordinated responses of two or more body parts. These patterns are common to all children without a neurological or other handicap. For a motor activity to take place, however, the nervous system and muscles must be mature enough to carry out the pattern of activity. For example, walking can't take place until the legs are strong enough to carry a child's weight.

Just because the patterns for movements are genetically programmed, it doesn't mean that the skills can't be acquired without learning. The theory of patterning also states that motor movements are complex and developmental, meaning that they have to be acquired over a period of time. Acquisition of skills also requires sensory stimulation to begin the movement, then constant monitoring of sensory feedback to refine the skill and acquire the ability to use it in various ways in the future.

Learning motor skills requires three conditions. First, the child must be in good health. Second, the child must have the space to move, equipment to practice with and on, and adequate time to use the space and equipment. Finally, the third essential requirement is consistent encouragement and motivation from parents and other care givers.

Research hasn't discovered any way to make every child into an accomplished athlete. However, if the above requirements are met, children will develop smoothly operating movement patterns. Clumsiness in older children with no physical problem has been found to be primarily a product of a restrictive environment in the preschool years.

Basic Motor Tasks

Just as knowledge of the alphabet and of vocabulary is the basis for reading and writing, the movements of work and play that allow us to live our lives efficiently and enjoyably are founded upon basic, common movement patterns. The importance of these basic motor skills has been emphasized by recent research into the reasons why an increasing percentage of children have been dropping out of youth sports programs. Researchers have discovered that many children become quickly frustrated in their attempts to learn a sport because their motor skills are well below developmental norms.

We'll discuss the basic motor tasks by type:

BASIC LOCOMOTION SKILLS The basic locomotion skills are a child's ability to move around his environment. They are:

Creeping, a child's first efficient method of moving around, is also a significant milestone in his ability to control his body. Creeping is the first activity in which a baby coordinates all four limbs. It requires timing, as a child learns to stop one leg as the other leg starts to move. Finally, efficient creeping requires mastery of the sophisticated type of movement called opposition, in which the opposite arm and leg (e.g., left arm and right leg) move forward at the same time. Well-coordinated opposition is very important in more advanced motor skills. Almost all children can creep (or crawl) well before age 2. By age 2 1/2, most children master opposition and exhibit a smooth, rhythmic style.

Walking upright is man's basic method of getting around. The elements of walking include alternating leg movement in a smooth, symmetrical pattern, using the arms for balance, using arms and legs in opposition when walking quickly, pointing toes forward, walking in a straight line without looking at the ground, placing the foot on the ground in a heel-to-toe pattern, and maintaining proper posture.

By age 2, a child walks confidently without falling, but he occasionally watches his feet to deal with obstacles in his path. By age 2 1/2 he can walk backward. By age 3, he walks in a straight line without looking at his feet, uses a heel-to-toe foot placement, and moves his limbs in opposition.

Running, a faster and more demanding method of locomotion, requires opposition and smooth coordination of arm and leg movements. To run with speed, a child must learn to land on the ball of the foot, leaning forward from the waist to sustain his momentum. Elbows should be bent, and knees lifted. Running for a distance requires building endurance as well as maintaining good coordination and rhythm when tiring.

Most children don't run smoothly by age 2, and they can't turn sharp corners or stop abruptly. All these abilities gradually appear during the third year. By age 3 1/2, the average child develops some speed and endurance, and is able to run 50 feet in under six seconds. By age 5, a child runs with speed and agility, starting, stopping, and changing direction quickly and smoothly.

CLIMBING Climbing and descending ladders and steps are also important early motor skills. The separate tasks involved are:

Climbing is an all-fours activity, like creeping, and therefore it's a natural next step for babies. Like creeping, climbing requires synchronizing alternate leg and arm movements as well as opposition. It is also excellent and important exercise for the trunk and limb muscles. Climbing also builds physical confidence.

Young children will first attempt to climb up steps. Later, they'll move on to ladders or ladderlike playground equipment. At an average age of 2 1/2, a child can normally climb to the top of a short ladder by bringing both feet to rest on a rung before climbing to the next. By age 4, the average child can climb a ladder by alternating feet on the rungs, if the rungs are close enough together.

By age 3, about half of all children are relatively proficient at climbing jungle gyms and other appropriately sized playground equipment. Most children gain that proficiency by age 4.

Ascending stairs on two feet requires more balance than climbing. By about age 2, the average child can get up the stairs on two feet by holding on to the bannister or an adult's hand and bringing both feet to rest on each step. By age 3 or shortly after, he can climb stairs (with short risers) by alternating feet on each step as he holds on to the bannister. Without support, most children have to bring both feet to rest on each step. By age 4, the average child can alternate feet while climbing without support.

Descending stairs on two feet requires more balance, more coordination, and more leg strength than ascending stairs. At age 2, most children descend stairs by crawling down backward or bouncing down in a sitting position. Six months later, the average child can get down the stairs on two feet by holding on to the bannister and bringing both feet to rest on each step. He needs another 18 months, to age 4, to master descending the stairs by alternating feet, with support. The average child doesn't descend a long stairway by alternating feet without support until about age 5.

JUMPING   Jumping is another skill that requires a complex combination of coordination, leg strength, and balance. Jumping activities in the preschool years include:

Jumping off a step is normally a child's first attempt to leave the ground. Normally, a child will step off a low object with one foot at about age 18 months. By age 2, he'll be using a two foot takeoff to jump off the step, but he may lead with one foot as he descends to the ground. By age 3, with some practice holding on to the hand of an adult or older child, the average preschooler can jump down from a height of 8 inches and land on two feet without falling. During the next year, he learns to jump down from 12 inches, then 18 inches, and by age 4 he can land and remain on his feet from a height of 28 inches.

A *vertical jump* involves a two-foot takeoff straight up in the air. Since the direction of the jump is straight upward, vertical jumping requires more leg strength and coordination than jumping down off an obstacle. Most children can clear the ground with a two-footed jump at some point between ages 2 and 3. By age 4, the average child can jump up 2 inches, but he has trouble coordinating the act of jumping with the act of reaching up with one hand to touch an object. By age 5, he can jump up 2.5 inches to touch a balloon or other object.

The *standing broad jump* is a two-footed forward jump on a flat surface. Jumping for distance not only requires more leg strength, but also coordinating the push of the legs with a forward swing of the arms. Landing on two feet without falling requires good balance.

Most children can jump forward on two feet shortly after age 2. The average standing broad jump distance is about 12 inches at age 3, 24 inches at age 4, and 36 inches at age 5.

The *running jump* requires converting forward momentum to upward momentum in a one foot takeoff, a very complex movement. The object of a running jump can either be to clear a barrier (a rope, a box, a hurdle) or for distance.

The average child doesn't gain the coordination necessary to jump while running fast until about age 3 1/2. At that age, he can clear a barrier about 8 inches high by diving over it to land on a soft surface. At age 4, he can broad jump for a distance of 23 to 33 inches and land on his feet, but he has great difficulty jumping over a barrier and remaining on his feet. By age 5, he can hurdle a barrier about 12 inches high and can execute a running broad jump of 28 to 38 inches.

BALANCE Balance is a factor in the mastery of most motor tasks, but it is the primary factor in the following skills:

Balancing on one foot requires balance and leg strength. Children under age 2 have trouble balancing on two feet, for two reasons. The obvious one is that they're inexperienced walkers and are still developing the coordination to move confidently on two feet. The second reason is that young children have a very high center of gravity, which means they tip over much more easily than an older child or adult.

Most growth in height after age 2 takes place below the legs, lowering that center of gravity. That's one reason that at some point between ages 2 and 3, the average child can balance momentarily on one foot, and by age 3 he can hold that position for an average of two to four seconds. By age 4, his balance time is up to ten seconds or more. However, he still needs to stretch out his arms to maintain the position.

Balancing skills improve significantly by age 5. At that age, the average child can balance on either foot. He can also balance with his arms folded or placed on his waist. Finally, he may be able to maintain his balance with his eyes closed. This latter skill is difficult, because our sense of balance is closely connected with our vision. Balancing on one foot with the eyes shut requires a mature enough awareness of one's own body to substitute neuromuscular feedback for visual feedback.

Walking a straight line requires good balance and coordination, the reason it's a standard test for intoxication. A child acquires the ability to walk 10 feet on a 1-inch-wide straight line remarkably early, with 50% accomplishing the task by age 3. The ability to walk a 10-foot-long circular line is mastered about a year later.

Walking a balance beam requires a combination of balance, physical confidence, and sufficient visual-motor ability to focus on the beam while ignoring the drop to the floor. Most tests of this ability involve walking a 4-inch-wide beam set slightly above the floor. A 2-year-old may try to stand on the beam or walk with one foot on the beam and one foot on the floor. By age 3, the average child can walk 8 feet on the beam with not more than one step up. Most 4-year-olds are very confident on the 4-inch beam but have trouble with a 2-inch-wide beam. Success in walking a 2-inch-wide beam without errors comes, generally, at age 5 1/2.

Bouncing on a trampoline is a valuable exercise in developing balance, whole-body coordination, and awareness of body parts (because moving a hand or leg can cause a fall). It's also a favorite activity for most preschool children, who invariably begin their bouncing on their parents' bed.

Children can begin bouncing on special children's trampolines (holding on to special hand bars) or regular trampolines (holding on to their parents' hands) in their second year. By age 2 1/2, the average child can bounce four or more times without holding on. After this initial balancing ability is mastered, children work on increasing the height of their jumps by coordinating the flexing of their knees and ankles, pushing off with their legs, uncoiling the upper body, and thrusting upward with the arms. Mastery of this coordination normally comes by age 4 1/2.

SPECIAL LOCOMOTION SKILLS These skills are variations of movement that combine the skills of walking, running, and jumping. These skills are used primarily in play, but they are extremely beneficial in building coordination, balance, rhythm, endurance, and muscle strength.

Hopping is traveling forward on one foot, or on alternating feet. Obviously, a child can't hop until he can balance well on one foot. That's why the average child is 3 1/2 before he can hop from one to three steps on the same foot. By age 4, he can normally hop four to six steps on the same foot. After age 4, girls hop better than boys. For example, 80% of 5-year-old girls could successfully hop 50 feet, compared with 62% of all 5-year-old boys. Seventy-three percent of 5-year-old girls could hop in a straight line using each of two feet in separate trials, while only 37% of boys the same age completed that test.

Neither sex, however, achieved much success in rhythmic hopping by age 5. Less then 10% of boys and girls could maintain the rhythm of two hops on the left foot, two hops on the right foot, two hops on the left foot, etc.

Galloping has been used by generations of children playing "cowboys" and other games. The motion involves a two-part rhythm: the first forward motion is a hop forward on a front leg, then the rear leg is pulled up alongside of it. The motion is then repeated, with the same leg always leading.

Early success in approximating the galloping motion usually depends upon encouragement from parents or older siblings. Handclapping or playing lively music also helps children gain a sense of rhythm in the motion. Some children can do an identifiable gallop step between the ages of 2 and 3. By age 4, 43% can gallop over a distance with rhythm. Not until age 5 can a majority of children gallop well using either foot as the lead.

Skipping seems to develop almost as spontaneously as does running.

However, it is a much more complicated motor skill, and it develops much later in the preschool years. The average child can't skip a few steps until age 4 1/2 and can't sustain a skip over a distance of 20 feet or more until age 6.

AGILITY   Agility is the ability to move part or all of the body with quickness and ease. Because preschoolers are still mastering very basic motor tasks, they're not as agile as older children and adults. Certain activities, however, can contribute to the development of agility. One of the most valuable of these isn't a motor skill, but an age-old form of parent-child play called "roughhousing." If obvious precautions against injuring a child are heeded, gentle wrestling and similar activities are very valuable in building muscle strength, coordination, and body awareness in a wide variety of positions.

Two specific movement tasks can also be placed in this category:

The *forward roll*, or somersault, is a child's first introduction to tumbling, and it's very helpful in developing agility. Experts caution that children need some instruction and supervision when learning this skill. The key instruction is that the neck should be bent so the head is tucked into the chest when the roll is started. A straight neck can produce pain and possibly injury. The first few times a child attempts to somersault, the parent should hold his head in the proper position. Experts caution that the forward roll should be done on a soft surface, such as a mat or plush carpet.

With some instruction, most children can do a rudimentary forward roll at age 2 1/2 and are accomplished at the skill by age 5.

The *figure-8 run* involves weaving around objects in a designed course that requires rapid and alternating changes of direction. Running a figure-8 course with speed requires not only physical agility, but the ability to mentally rehearse the motions before starting the run. By age 4, some children can complete the course with an occasional stop, but the average child does not run a figure-8 course with moderate speed until age 5 1/2 or older.

BALL-PLAYING SKILLS   These are not only enjoyable in themselves but are fundamental to participation in many sports. Among the ball-playing skills are:

Kicking a large ball with force requires balancing on one foot while swinging the other. By age 2, a child understands the concept of kicking and is able to nudge the ball forward with one foot. The ability to kick with power and control, especially while running, develops slowly. By age 4, a child may occasionally kick with proper form, but basic mastery of kicking isn't normally attained until age 5 or older.

Throwing with force and accuracy is a complicated skill that involves coordination of several parts of the body. The feet are placed at right angles to the line of flight, body weight is shifted to the rear foot, the body is rotated toward the throwing arm, and the arm is rotated back with the wrist cocked. Forward motion is initiated by a forward step, weight is shifted to the front foot, the body rotates back, the arm comes forward, the ball is released with a snap of the wrist, then the back foot comes forward as the arm and body follow through.

Few preschoolers master the entire task. Throwing begins with toddlers who discover that it's fun when an object accidently slips out of their hand when they're moving their arm. The first real throwing motion is usually an underhanded motion with a stiff arm. Between ages 2 and 3, a child normally experiments with throwing overhand. The motion generally involves a backward and forward movement of the body and arms, with the body and feet facing forward, no weight shift, and no cocking of the wrist. By age 3, the average child can throw a small ball 4 to 6 feet. In the next year, the child begins to throw with some body rotation and, possibly, a step forward. The average distance a ball is thrown increases to 8 to 10 feet by age 4, 12 to 13 feet by age 4 1/2, and 19 feet by age 5. Between ages 5 and 6 comes dramatic improvement in accuracy and velocity as the child learns to shift his weight, rotate his body more fully, and cock his wrist.

Catching a ball requires both hand-eye and body coordination. Researchers have identified three stages in a preschool child's development of the ability to catch a thrown or bounced ball. In the first stage, typical of a child between ages 2 1/2 and 3 1/2, he stands with his arms extended rigidly out in front of him. Success depends on a large, soft ball or balloon being thrown from a short distance so accurately that the catch is primarily passive as the ball comes to rest between his arms and his chest. At this stage, a child makes no attempt to move in order to compensate for an inaccurately thrown ball.

In the second stage, typical of a 4-year-old, a child begins to await the ball with his hands open and his elbows slightly flexed. He begins to make definite attempts to judge the trajectory of the ball and compensate by moving his arms. A child will more actively move to corral a ball, but he largely uses his arms, not his hands. His elbows are in front of his body, allowing no "give" to cushion the impact of the ball.

In the third stage, accomplished at age 5, a child stands with his elbows flexed and close to the sides of his body, so they can "give." He now uses his hands more than his arms and can catch a small ball as well as a large one. He judges trajectory better than at age 4, but not always successfully. He may also begin to attempt to catch a small ball in one hand.

Bouncing a ball with two hands requires timing as well as body and hand-eye coordination. A child acquires the ability to bounce a ball and catch it at about age 3 1/2. By age 4, he may be able to bounce a ball four times in succession, and by age 5 he can walk while bouncing the ball at least six successive times.

Hitting a ball with a bat is fundamental to the sport of baseball and an important developmental step for more advanced activities such as tennis. It's also a skill few children master before the school years. Most experts recommend starting out by placing a large ball on a batting tee set at an appropriate height, then instructing the child to attempt to strike it with a plastic bat held in two hands. Most 2-years-olds can make contact with the ball three out of five times, but they can't hit with power. Gradually, they become more accomplished, and they begin to rotate their bodies and shift their weight as they swing, generating more power. They also benefit from practicing hitting a softly tossed plastic ball. But few children under age 5 can hit either a stationary or a thrown ball with consistent accuracy and power.

Fine Motor Development and Adaptive Behavior in the Preschool Years

THE IMPORTANCE OF FINE MOTOR DEVELOPMENT AND ADAPTIVE BEHAVIOR

As we've seen previously, fine motor development consists of a child's growing ability to use his hands, and adaptive behavior is the way in which he makes use of his fine motor skills (e.g., by building a tower of blocks). Since fine motor development and adaptive behavior are two parts of the same process, we'll discuss that entire process under the term *fine motor development.*

Just as developing gross motor skills is necessary to accomplish such everyday tasks as moving from room to room and climbing stairs, so too is the development of fine motor skills necessary to accomplish such everyday tasks as turning doorknobs, dialing a telephone, and unbuttoning a shirt. And just as gross motor activity also serves larger purposes (keeping the body strong and healthy through exercise, building physical confidence, providing enjoyment through sports), fine motor activity serves the larger and vitally important functions of providing information to and providing creative expression for the mind. The fingers and hands, through the sense of touch, provide information to the brain about the properties of the world. And through the fingers and hands, the mind expresses its thoughts and creativity through writing, drawing, sculpting, playing musical instruments, and a variety of other forms.

Many parents and other caregivers fail to realize the importance of fine motor activity in a child's "intellectual" development. Emphasis on purely intellectual activities such as memorization of the alphabet and recognition of numbers should not come at the expense of fine motor activity. Research has shown that the most effective "early learning" is encouragement of fine motor development and adaptive behavior that refines the mental concepts and motor skills necessary for academic learning in the school years.

THE DIFFICULTIES IN ACQUIRING FINE MOTOR SKILLS

In the first 2 years of life, children develop the hand-eye coordination necessary to confidently reach out and grab objects, and the hand and finger control necessary to manipulate those objects in basic ways, such as stacking and nesting. The more delicate fine motor skills are more difficult for preschool children than most gross motor skills, for four reasons.

The first is that fine motor skills require precise control of small muscles. To understand why small muscles are more difficult to control than large muscles, compare threading a needle to kicking a soccer ball. Threading a needle can be difficult for an adult, even though it's a relatively simple motion. A more complex fine motor skill such as writing a sentence requires coordinating many small muscles through numerous complex movements. This control can only be developed over time.

The second reason, one that's often overlooked, is that small muscles tire more easily than large muscles. Many young children have difficulty learning to write not because they lack the cognitive ability to grasp the concept, but because the small muscles of their hands tire so easily that they can't carry out the mind's commands. Strengthening the hand muscles in preparation for writing is the concept behind many of the fine motor activities planned by nursery school teachers.

The third reason that fine motor skills take longer to develop is that they're expressions of sophisticated cognitive concepts that develop slowly in the preschool years. For example, building with blocks requires developing the ability to think three-dimensionally. To add features to an incomplete line drawing of a man or woman, a child must understand that two-dimensional drawings can symbolize the features of real people and must be able to mentally compare the incomplete drawing with complete drawings stored in memory, mentally catalog missing features, then command the muscles of the hand and fingers to supply the missing parts. This coordination between mind and hand is much more complicated than the understanding and coordination necessary for most gross motor skills, such as climbing a ladder.

Finally, fine motor skills require patience, not the most outstanding quality of preschool children. Most preschoolers will spend hours running, climbing, and jumping in a playground. That same energy, however, makes it very difficult for them to practice drawing a circle over and over again.

PROMOTING FINE MOTOR DEVELOPMENT

Because the skills are more complicated and difficult to master, promoting fine motor development requires a wider variety of materials and activities than are needed for promoting gross motor activities. The major difficulty in encouraging gross motor development is finding the time to supervise a young child in a well-equipped backyard or a good playground. Encouraging fine motor activity requires choosing a much wider range of material and planning a much greater variety of activities. Selecting and acquiring appropriate materials can be time consuming and expensive. Planning activities using these materials requires some knowledge of cognitive development in the preschool years and an evaluation of the developmental progress of the child.

Children whose fine motor development is neglected are seldom adequately prepared for school, and they quickly fall behind. Inadequate preparation is a major problem for children in low income households because their care givers commonly lack the time or knowledge necessary to provide materials and plan activities. However, preschool programs such as Head Start can compensate for less-than-ideal home environments, which is why studies have shown them to be so valuable in preparing children for school.

A good nursery school can also encourage the development of any child's fine motor development by offering a wider range of activities and learning materials than parents could provide at home. Some children also exhibit more patience and willingness to try new activities in a setting outside the home and in the company of their peers.

Parents who understand fine motor development make better toy purchases, plan more varied and interesting activities, and are better prepared to evaluate nursery schools and other preschool programs. Because of the direct link between fine motor activity and cognitive development, that understanding has to be based on an overall appreciation of a preschool child's intellectual progress. Before we consider the materials and activities that help build fine motor skills, let's look at cognitive development in the preschool years.

Intellectual Development in the Preschool Years

PIAGET'S PREOPERATIONAL PERIOD

The milestone that marks a child's emergence from Piaget's first stage of cognitive development, the "sensorimotor" period, is his ability to form mental images that are not dependent on what he is experiencing through his senses at the moment—for example, a child describing a giraffe he saw at the zoo the day before.

This ability to store and recall mental images is called *symbolic thought.* Attaining symbolic thought is a milestone because it marks the beginning of a child's ability to perform the mental operations that we call *reasoning.* An example of a simple mental operation is looking at a poodle for the first time, then mentally comparing it to recalled images, and labeling it a "dog."

Most children begin performing mental operations by age 2. However, the ability to reason, to consistently perform basic mental operations well enough to reach accurate conclusions, takes years to develop. It takes several years for a young child to learn the basics of reasoning, just as it takes him several years to master the physical coordination necessary to ride a bicycle or play baseball.

After observing young children over the course of decades, Piaget discovered that the period from a child's first mental operations to his mastery of fundamental mental operations lasted from about age 2 until ages 6 or 7, when he started grade school. Piaget labeled this earlier stage the preoperational period, the time leading up to the operational period marked by mastery of basic mental operations. Piaget further identified several specific patterns of illogical reasoning, or errors in thinking, that were characteristic of the preschool period.

An understanding of Piaget's theory is extremely important for parents and preschool educators, particularly in light of the recent emphasis on early learning. Some advocates of early learning view a preschooler's mind as basically an "empty vessel" that needs to be "filled up" with knowledge, and the earlier, the better. They believe they can make children "smarter" by introducing flash cards and other activities designed to increase a preschooler's memory of words, numbers, and other facts.

The majority of experts, however, agree with Piaget that knowledge is useless unless children have gained the ability to process that knowledge. While there is much disagreement about the details of Piaget's theory, there is a strong consensus that the best way to encourage cognitive development in the preschool years is for parents and educators to understand the fundamental types of illogical reasoning that are characteristic of young children. Then parents and educators can provide toys, activities, and other assistance to help children gradually correct these logical errors and gain mastery over concepts that serve as a basis for learning in the school years.

The Characteristics of Preoperational Thought

Piaget identified several characteristics of the thinking patterns of preschool children. These are:

1. *Egocentrism.* A preschool child tends to see everything from his point of view. This self-centered viewpoint dominates what he sees and how he thinks.

   Because he's egocentric, a young child believes that because he sees a 14-year-old boy as "big," his parents see the 14-year-old as big. He also believes that animals and inanimate objects share his feelings and motivations—his stuffed animal gets hungry, the sun disappears at night because it's tired and has to go to sleep, a stream is alive because it flows. Egocentrism also leads a young child to assume that other people have the same reactions to things and events—they dislike spinach because he does, they want to have an ice-cream cone when he does, etc.

2. *Centration.* This is the tendency of young children to focus on one aspect of an object or situation while ignoring all others. For example, they believe that a tall, slender glass of water holds more than a short, wide glass. They also believe that they have more money if they see five pennies spread out in front of them, as compared with five pennies touching each other or stacked on top of each other.

3. *Irreversibility.* A young child can't play back events in his mind to reconstruct the original situation. A classic example involves showing a child two identical glasses that contain exactly the same amount of water. With the child watching, the water in one glass is poured into a taller, thinner glass. A preschool child, unable to mentally return the water to the first glass, will say the taller glass now has more water than the shorter one did.

   Irreversibility also affects relationships. A 3-year-old may say that Jeff is his brother. But when he's asked if Jeff has a brother, he responds "no."

4. *Inability to transform.* Transformation is the process of change from one state to another. An example is a ball of clay that's rolled into a thin sausage. Even though he watches the transformation, a preschool child sees the ball and the sausage shape as two separate images. An adult, on the other hand, sees the transformation correctly as a single, continuous behavior.

5. *Concreteness.* Young children tend to concentrate on what they sense directly, rather than on more abstract concepts. For example, a preschooler may understand that an ice cube is cold, but doesn't understand that a person can be cold, in the sense of "emotionally unexpressive." For the same reason, a preschool child can recall two events but not the period in between. A 3-year-old who's just enjoyed his monthly visit from his grandparents may wake up the next morning to ask if they're coming again that day, because he doesn't have a concept of how long a month is.

These characteristics of preoperational thought make it very difficult for young children to reason the way adults do. Some specific tasks that young children do poorly are:

1. Determining cause and effect. Young children often assume that one event causes another if they occur at the same time. For example, they may believe that rain falls from the clouds just so they can't play outside. They may attribute cause and effect based on random observations, such as the sun doesn't fall from the sky because it's yellow. Preschool children can also juxtapose cause and effect. For example, a child may say that he's eaten because he's not hungry.

2. Classifying objects and events. If a preschool child is given an assortment of blocks of various shapes and colors and told to put together the ones that are alike, he may put two squares together, then replace one square with a blue triangle because the other square is blue. Then he'll notice the size discrepancy between the triangle and the square and replace the blue square with another triangle. He'll fail to develop any system, because he tends to focus on one characteristic at a time.

3. Ordering objects in a sequence. A child may be able to count from one to ten, and even count ten objects. But he may not be able to figure out whether six is more or less than four. Another example is a preschool child who may be able to pick out the longest and shortest sticks from a group but has trouble arranging them from shortest to longest.

4. Understanding part/whole relationships. A young child has difficulty understanding that a single object can belong to more than one class of objects at the same time. One example involves placing three red plastic cups and four yellow plastic cups in front of a child. When he's asked if there are more yellow cups or plastic cups, he will reply that there are more yellow cups. He has trouble understanding that a cup can have the qualities of color and plastic at the same time.

5. Understanding age, time, and distance. Young children live in the present, and they have difficulty comprehending both the gradual changes produced by aging and the meaning of such measurements of time as a month or a year.

   They also have trouble separating time and distance. If it takes ten minutes to walk to the park and ten minutes to drive to the mall, the young child believes the park and the mall are the same distance from his house.

Encouraging Cognitive Development in the Preoperational Period

At about age 2 1/2, when a child begins to acquire enough language to effectively communicate and when he has some practice at mental operations, it's possible for the first time to administer intelligence tests. These tests, which measure verbal skills, motor skills, reasoning, and problem solving ability, produce a score that compares a specific child to a predetermined set of standard scores.

During the preschool years, intelligence tests are used primarily to diagnose specific learning problems rather than establish a level of intelligence that can be used to predict adult intelligence. Traditionally, child psychologists have been very cautious about interpreting IQ tests as predictors of superior intelligence, preferring to wait until a child is at least 8 before labeling him "gifted." In recent years, however, educators and psychologists have acknowledged that certain children score remarkably better than average on early intelligence tests, and that their performance tends to continue to be superior through the preschool period and into the school years. Research has shown that these children correct illogical thinking processes and master classification, serialization, and other skills earlier than Piaget considered possible.

The key question, of course, is why? Piaget believed that progress from preoperational to operational thinking was dependent on the process of maturation, or a genetically programmed schedule. He therefore believed that exceptional intelligence was genetically predetermined. Many of Piaget's critics have attempted to refute his maturation theories by conducting experiments showing that concepts such as transformation could be taught. However, to date, no specific program of instruction has been developed that has any significant lasting effect on improving a child's cognitive abilities.

Over the past twenty years, the most reliable overall prediction of a child's performance in the preschool and school years has been the educational and income level of his parents. Children of highly educated parents with upper-middle class incomes have significantly higher IQ scores and school grades than do children of parents with limited education and low incomes. Until recently, it was believed that the major factor in this correlation was that children of highly educated parents inherit their superior abilities. That assumption, however, has been called into question. One important reason has been the extraordinary academic success of children with Asian ethnic origins, many of whom have parents with limited education and incomes.

New research focused on the home environment of superior students of all races has revealed that children who score well on intelligence tests and mature into adults with superior intelligence tend to have a home life with similar characteristics. Parents of high-scoring children almost always place a high value on learning and education and have strong confidence that their children share those values. These parents actively encourage exploration, creativity, self-expression, and independence in their children by devoting significant time to reading to them, playing with them, and teaching them. These parents provide more books, more play materials, and more learning opportunities such as trips to zoos, museums, etc. They also tend to be loving and sensitive, and they strongly favor reasoning over spanking as the method of discipline.

Finally, one additional factor has been shown to have a significant positive effect on IQ scores—the extent to which the father is available to the child. The time a father spends with a child has a direct correlation to higher test scores, and the absence of a father produces significantly lower scores. A study of young children whose father was home with them all day discovered that their average IQ score was on average higher than the seventy-fifth percentile by the preschool years. This dramatic but puzzling finding has led to further research on the reasons a child's environment can have such a significant effect on his intelligence.

SKILLS AND CONCEPTS DEVELOPED IN THE PRESCHOOL YEARS

If parents and other care givers can encourage cognitive development, the logical question to ask next is, what specific skills and concepts should they encourage? One way to answer the question is to consider the preschool years to be a period of preparation for school. The better prepared children are for school, the better their performance will be. Vivid proof of this has been provided by studies of children who participated in Head Start, a preschool program specifically designed to teach children from disadvantaged backgrounds the concepts and skills important to success in school. One study of 1,200 children, half of them whom attended Head Start between 1964 and 1984 and half of them whom did not, showed that Head Start children were 58% more likely to graduate from high school, 79% more likely to attend college, and 90% more likely to hold a full-time job.

What are the important skills and concepts to be encouraged in the preschool years? Recently, World Book funded a study that consulted with 3,000 kindergarten teachers to develop a list of 105 important skills and concepts. By type, they were:

Colors and Shapes:

·   Recognizes and names primary colors
·   Recognizes circles
·   Recognizes rectangles
·   Matches shapes or objects based on shape
·   Copies shapes

Recognizing and naming colors and shapes are important classification skills. The concept of colors is the easiest for young children to grasp, because color is one dimensional. The developmental norms are that a child should name one or more colors by age 3, two or more by age 4, and at least four colors by age 5. With instruction, however, children can learn basic colors much more quickly.

The concept of shape is much more difficult because objects are three-dimensional and can be so different in mass, color, etc. Children learn to match objects by shape (e.g., fitting a square block in the square hole of a shape sorter) earlier than they can name or copy shapes. The developmental norms are that a child should be able to copy and identify a circle by age 3, a square by age 4, and a rectangle by age 5.

Numbers

· Counts orally through ten
· Matches objects one to one
· Understands empty and full
· Understands more and less

Thanks in large part to "Sesame Street," children learn to recognize and recite the numbers from one to ten as early as age 2 1/2. Understanding that those numbers are a means of classifying objects by quantity, however, comes much more slowly. The developmental norms are that a 3-year-old should be able to count three objects correctly, a 4-year-old should be able to count four objects correctly, and a 5-year-old should be able to count ten objects correctly. A 5-year-old should also be able to match in pairs two sets of objects, such as ten cups and ten saucers.

Understanding the relationship between numbers is more difficult than counting. To understand that four is less than seven requires understanding reversibility and sequence, which are characteristics of operational rather than preoperational thought, and the developmental norm is reaching this understanding by age 5. Some methods that help develop understanding the relationship between numbers are counting backward and simple addition-subtraction games ("If I have four blocks and give one to you, how many do I have left?").

Size

· Understands big and little
· Understands long and short
· Matches shapes or objects based on size

Size is another classification skill. Most 2-year-olds can identify some things as "big" and some as "little." Mature size-identification skills require some judgment independent of a preschooler's initial egocentric perspective. In other words, by age 5, a child should know that a 7-year-old may be big to him, but isn't big by adult standards.

Another important skill that isn't on this list, but one that can be mastered by older preschoolers, is understanding the concepts of "bigger," "longer," "shorter," etc.

Opposites

- Understands up and down
- Understands in and out
- Understands front and back
- Understands over and under
- Understands top, bottom, and middle
- Understands beside or next to
- Understands hot and cold
- Understands fast and slow
- Understands day and night

Opposites are important classification skills, observational skills, and concepts important in following simple instructions. Developmental norms are that a child can follow one or two simple directions based on opposites at age 2 1/2 (e.g., "put the block *on* the table), three directions by age 3, five by age 4, and all of the above concepts by age 5 to 5 1/2.

Gross Motor Skills

- Is able to run
- Is able to walk a straight line
- Is able to jump
- Is able to alternate feet walking down stairs
- Is able to stand on one foot for five to ten seconds
- Is able to walk backwards for five feet
- Is able to throw a ball

Gross motor skills are important for participation in the games and sports that are part of the school experience. As we've explained previously, children acquire most of the above skills well before the school years.

Fine Motor Skills

- Pastes objects
- Claps hands
- Matches simple objects

· Touches fingers
· Is able to open and close buttons
· Builds with blocks
· Completes simple puzzles (five pieces or less)
· Draws and colors rather than scribbles
· Is able to open and close zipppers
· Controls pencil and crayon well
· Cuts simple shapes
· Handles scissors well
· Is able to copy simple shapes

As we've previously mentioned, fine motor skills and activities are extremely important in preparation for school. Among the benefits are:
· Developing small-muscle strength and coordination necessary for writing, drawing, and other creative activities, as well as self-help skills such as tying shoelaces
· Developing hand-eye coordination necessary for sports and recreation
· Developing concepts of spatial relations that overcome the tendency toward egocentrism
· Creating art projects, drawing figures, building with blocks, and putting together puzzles teaches reversibility, counteracts centrism, encourages the concept of transformation, and builds knowledge of cause and effect

The developmental norms for building with blocks are:

Age 2:   Builds tower of six to seven blocks
Age 2 1/2:   Builds tower of eight blocks
               Aligns two blocks to form "train"
Age 3:   Builds tower of ten blocks
            Adds "chimney" to train
            Can imitate a three-block "bridge"
Age 3 1/2:   Makes a bridge from a model, without previously seeing process
Age 4:   Can copy a taller gate with five or more blocks
Age 4 1/2:   Can make gate from model
Age 5:   Can imitate six-cube steps

The developmental norms for drawing are:

Age 2:   Imitates a V-shaped stroke
Age 2 1/2:   Imitates V-and H-shaped strokes
               Scribbles circle

Age 3:   Copies circle
           Imitates cross
           Adds three parts (e.g., arm, leg) to an incomplete drawing of a
              human figure
Age 3 1/2:   Copies cross
                Adds four parts to incomplete man
                Eyes of incomplete man better than a scribble
Age 4:   Imitates square
           Adds five parts to incomplete man
           Arms of incomplete man are drawn straight out from body
Age 4 1/2:   Copies square
                Copies rectangle divided like a ladder
                Adds seven parts to incomplete man
Age 5:   Copies triangle
           Copies all forms on one page
           Adds eight parts to incomplete man

The developmental norms for doing puzzles are:

Age 2:   With practice, can place cutout forms into proper spot on a form
          board or puzzle
Age 2 1/2:   Places pieces into precut spots with little practice
Age 3:   Can do four-piece jigsaw puzzle with help
Age 4:   Can do five- to six-piece jigsaw puzzle
Age 5:   Can do seven- to eight-piece jigsaw puzzle

Self-knowledge

- Knows age and birthday
- Knows full name
- Knows own sex
- Knows parents' names
- Knows home address
- Knows home telephone number

Increased self-knowledge is a sign of cognitive development. A child who knows his name, address, age, birthday, and other information has gained some ability to accurately place himself in relation to his family and community.

Self-knowledge is also important to a child's safety, should he become lost. Security personnel in large shopping malls are often frustrated when questioning a 4 year old who says her name is "Cupcake" and her parents are "Mommy" and "Daddy."

Researchers have found that girls generally have more self-knowledge than boys. Girls know their sex and their age by age 3, while boys don't learn the same information until about age 3 1/2. Both boys and girls can tell their full names, their parents' first names, and part of their address between ages 3 and 4. Between ages 4 and 5, they know their birth month, their street name and number, and at least part of their phone number.

Verbal, Listening, and Memory Skills

- Follows simple directions
- Listens to a short story
- Listens carefully
- Recognizes common sounds
- Repeats a sequence of sounds
- Repeats a sequence of orally given numbers
- Retells simple stories in sequence
- Remembers objects from a given picture
- Recognizes some nursery rhymes
- Identifies parts of the body
- Identifies objects that have a functional use
- Knows common farm and zoo animals
- Pronounces own first name
- Pronounces own last name
- Expresses self verbally
- Identifies other children by name
- Tells meanings of simple words
- Repeats sentence of six to eight words
- Completes sentence with proper word
- Answers questions about a short story
- Tells the meaning of words heard in a story

The ability to understand what's being said, remember important facts, and answer questions about what's seen, heard, and remembered is a crucial part of intelligence and vital to success in school. The acquisition of language skills is so important that we're going to discuss the developmental stages for children aged 2 to 5 in a following section.

Exposure to Reading and Reading Readiness

- Has been read to frequently
- Has been read to daily
- Looks at books or magazines
- Has own books
- Understands that print carries a message

- Pretends to read
- Uses left-to-right progression
- Knows what a letter of the alphabet is
- Identifies own first name when printed
- Prints own first name

Preschool children who are read to daily do significantly better in school and have higher-than-average verbal skills. Reading to a child builds vocabulary, knowledge of cause and effect, and diminishes egocentrism. Reading also increases a child's attention span and ability to concentrate, both very important qualities. The habit of daily reading tends to imbue a child with a strong love of books and reading materials that continues through the school years.

Reading to a child is also an excellent way to begin teaching the alphabet. You'll notice that knowledge of the alphabet isn't one of the skills that kindergarten teachers considered important for a child to attain by the time he starts school. Children with good language skills can and do learn to read at a normal pace and level even if they can't recite the alphabet when they start school.

However, again due in large part to "Sesame Street," many children can recite the letters of the alphabet and identify many individual letters in the preschool years. A child who isn't given the opportunity to gain this knowledge may feel left out or "dumb," which does retard learning. Most parents use books and other materials to teach letter recognition.

Along with letter recognition, however, parents and other care givers should make sure to teach the concept that individual letters represent different sounds used in speech. It's equally important for children to learn that d makes the "duh" sound as it is for them to recognize the letter itself.

Social and Emotional Qualities and Skills

- Can be away from parents for two to three hours without being upset
- Takes care of toilet needs independently
- Feels good about self
- Is not afraid to go to school
- Cares for own belongings
- Dresses self
- Knows how to use a handkerchief or tissue
- Enters into dinner-table conversation
- Carries a plate of food
- Maintains self-control
- Gets along with other children
- Plays with other children

- Recognizes authority
- Shares with others
- Talks easily
- Likes teachers
- Meets visitors without shyness
- Puts away toys
- Is able to stay on a task
- Is able to work independently
- Helps family with chores

Social and emotional problems can severely affect a child's performance in school, no matter how intellectually developed a child has become. Very gifted children, in fact, tend to have more social and emotional problems than children who fall into the range of normal intelligence. Social, emotional, and moral development is so important that we will also discuss them in more detail in a following section.

Language Development in the Preschool Years

VOCABULARY

The period from age 2 to age 5 is marked by enormous growth in a child's vocabulary. The average child understands about 300 words and uses about 50 at age 2. That vocabulary soars to 1,000 words at age 3, and 8,000 to 12,000 words by age 5. A 5-year-old's vocabulary includes most of the words he'll use for the rest of his life.

Because he's preoccupied with concrete objects, much of the growth in vocabulary from age 2 to 3 consists of nouns. Verbs, the action words, are added next. As a child's ability to classify objects grows, he adds more adjectives and adverbs.

Many parents of preschoolers are shocked when they discover that their children have added profanity to their vocabulary. Young children pick up almost everything they hear. While they don't understand the meaning of "dirty" words, they very much appreciate the shock value. The best way to discourage use of profanity is not to react to its use.

SENTENCE LENGTH

Researchers have found that the average length of a sentence is one reliable indicator of the level of language acquisition of a young child. By age 2, one-word utterances have given way to two-word "telegraphic" sentences. Shortly after age 2, two-word sentences such as "Mommy

WHAT YOU SHOULD KNOW ABOUT . . .

THE FUNCTIONS OF LANGUAGE

The preschool years are the most crucial period in the development of language abilities. These abilities are, in turn, critically important to a child's future success in school and in life.

Parents can better understand both the importance of language and the process by which their child gains command of it by understanding how language is used. Experts have defined its seven basic functions:

1. *Instrumental function: This is the "I want" function, which allows a child to say what he wants and needs.*
2. *Regulatory function: This is the "do that" function, by which the child attempts to control the actions of others.*
3. *Interpersonal function: This is the "me and you," in which language is used to develop social relationships.*
4. *Personal function: This is the "I" function, which allows a child to express his own beliefs, emotions, and attitudes.*
5. *Heuristic function: This is the "tell me why" function, which allows a child to explore and understand his environment.*
6. *Imaginative function: This is the "let's pretend" function, which is the basis for creativity.*
7. *Informative function: This is the "I've got something to tell you" function, which is the means by which information is related.*

book" are replaced by three-word sentences such as "Mommy read book."

Linguists don't rely on the number of words to determine sentence length. Rather, they look at what is called a *morpheme*, the shortest unit of meaningful sound. An example is the word *walked*. Linguists would divide this word into two morphemes, *walk* and *ed*. The reason for this division is that a young child who replaces "I walk home" with "I walked home" demonstrates a jump in language ability that couldn't be measured by counting words. The average sentence length increases from 2.5 morphemes shortly after age 2 to more than 8 by age 5.

GRAMMAR

The elements of English grammar include use of singular and plural, sentence structure, word order, and rules for verb tenses. Children as young as 18 months demonstrate some knowledge of the rules of grammar, and by age 5 children have achieved a basic mastery of the use of the language. Some experts consider mastering grammar the most significant intellectual achievement of childhood.

By age 2, or shortly afterward, young children create plurals by adding s to words and begin using verb tenses. Understandably, they have some trouble with irregular nouns and verbs. When children first speak, they often use the correct grammar because they memorize such phrases as "two feet" or "baby went." Shortly afterward, however, when they become aware of the general rules of forming plurals by adding "s" and creating the past tense by added ed, these phrases become "two feets" and "baby goed." This tendency is called overregulation, because it results from applying the basic rules of grammar too rigidly.

Overregulation gradually disappears as a child's experience with language increases. By age 4, a child can use most irregular plural and verb forms properly. Trouble with certain plurals ("goose-geese" and "ox-oxen") can continue into the school years.

LEARNING WHAT WORDS MEAN

Preschool children often recognize a word but fail to understand part or all of its meaning. They tend to quickly understand the meaning of concrete nouns (ball, rock, chair) and action verbs (go, come, walk). Certain other types of words take much longer to understand. Among these types are:

Opposites
Children understand the meaning of the less abstract opposites such as "tall-short" before the more abstract opposites "before-after." A research study conducted by Eve Clark revealed a definite order in which preschoolers acquire the meaning of opposites. That order is:

big-small	up-down
long-short	in-out
tall-short	on-off
high-low	first-last
old-young	over-under
thick-thin	early-late
wide-narrow	above-below
deep-shallow	ahead-behind
in front-in back	before-after

Negatives
Anyone who deals with young children immediately realizes that they don't have any trouble using and understanding the word "no." A 2-year-old may have trouble picking up a negative contraction in the sentence "Don't drop that glass," hearing "drop that glass" instead. Use

and understanding of "don't," "can't," and other negative contractions comes by age 3.

Preschoolers take longer to understand "not," in a sentence such as "pick up the blocks that are not blue." The child at first hears "blue" but doesn't hear "not." The understanding of "not," in turn, comes before use of the prefix "un." A child will understand that a person is "not happy" before he understands that the person is "unhappy."

Connectives

Young children understand "and." Other connectives such as "but," "or," "if," and "because" are much more difficult to conceptualize. Difficulty with these words continues into the school years.

Descriptive Words

Children understand adjectives that relate to what they can feel, smell, or taste, such as "warm," "cold," "hard," "sweet," and "dry" before they understand visual words such as "bright" or "deep." They also have trouble understanding the nonsensory use of these words, such as the sentence "she is a sweet person." Use of these words in a figurative sense comes only in the school years.

Questions

By age 3, most children can—and do—ask questions. They can use the interrogatory words "what," "where," and "who" first. One reason is that questions using these words have a regular word order, such as, "Where is the ball?" A second reason is that these words refer to concrete objects.

The use of "how," "why," and "when" comes later. The word order of questions using these words is more complex, such as, "How did he do that?" They also refer to more abstract ideas, such as time and motivation.

The type of interrogatory word also determines when a child can answer questions. A 3 1/2-year-old will respond to the question, "Where is your sock?" but draw a blank on a question such as, "Why did you drop the cookie?" By age 4, preschool children will understand and answer more abstract questions.

Passive Voice

Preschool children generally don't understand or use the passive voice. For example, when they hear the sentence, "The ball was thrown by the boy," they're likely to believe that the ball did the throwing.

DEFINING WORDS

Defining words is a more complicated skill than using them. The way a child defines words proceeds developmentally. First, a child defines words according to function: "A ball is to bounce." Next, a child defines words according to a concrete quality: "A ball is round." Finally, a child gains the capacity to define a word in relation to some abstract class of objects: "A ball is a toy."

Two- and 3-year-olds have difficulty with any kind of definitions. Few children pass beyond the first stage of definition by the beginning of the school years.

INNER SPEECH

Language is an extremely important tool in memorizing, thinking, and problem solving. Shortly after he acquires some language ability, a child begins to use language not only to communicate with others but also to help him organize his thoughts and actions. This use of language is called *inner speech*.

Adults use inner speech constantly. They use it in rote learning, repeating mentally, "Bring home a quart of milk, a quart of milk . . ." They use it to rehearse before speaking or writing. They also use language to help solve a problem: "The car won't start. I'll check the battery first, then . . ." Young children learn to use language in the same way. However, they tend to speak to themselves out loud. Parents who misunderstand the purposes of this "talking to himself" sometimes try to break the habit, which can retard language development, memory, and problem solving ability. By the school years, a child will internalize inner speech as thought.

SOCIAL COMMUNICATION

Having a conversation is a more complex skill than learning to talk. Conversation requires understanding the concept of taking turns and the ability to listen carefully and form a response.

Children as young as 18 months begin to understand the rhythm of conversation, speaking less or not at all when adults are talking. By age 2, children begin to have conversations with adults.

Communication with playmates takes longer to develop. Young children age 2 and even 3 who are playing together commonly engage in "dual monologues." That is, they speak in turn, but what each one says has little or no relation to what the other is saying. By age 3 1/2, at least half of what two children say is actually conversation.

By age 4, children have become sophisticated enough to realize that younger children have more limited language abilities. A 4-year-old will speak more slowly and simply when talking to a 2-year-old than he does when speaking to an adult.

ENCOURAGING LANGUAGE DEVELOPMENT

Language development has a very strong correlation to academic and social success. Research has shown that parents and care givers can significantly accelerate their child's acquisition of language and improve his ability.

Helping a child learn language requires a commitment of time and patience. Care givers who are bombarded by "what," "why," and "how" questions from their preschoolers often wonder if it's worthwhile trying to answer when the response is often just another question. Answering, however, does appear to have a significant positive effect on a child's language development.

Answering questions, however, is just one of many ways in which adults can help a preschooler learn language. The following list was compiled from professional research-derived knowledge by Bernadine Chuck Fong and Miriam Roher Resnick:

1. Talk often to a child.
2. Narrate what is happening.
3. Explain the daily schedule, in order of occurrence.
4. Review past events ("Remember when we went to the zoo...").
5. Question the child frequently on people, places, and things that are part of his past experience.
6. Give many simple directions to teach concepts and logical processes.
7. Teach time by events ("We'll go to the store first. Second, we'll go to the library . . .").
8. Teach relationships ("Grandpa Jerry is Mommy's Daddy.").
9. Use photos to remind a child of people, places, and things.
10. Define words functionally ("A pot is to cook in." "To be patient means to wait quietly.").
11. Describe behavior to build vocabulary ("You look sad. Why are you sad?").
12. Read books to a child as part of the daily routine.
13. Translate overheard conversations into simpler language.

Intelligence Testing in the Preschool Years

A preschooler's rapid acquisition of language makes it increasingly feasible to test his intelligence. One critical question, however, is what abilities constitute intelligence. The second critical question is how scores on intelligence tests relate to success in later life.

WHAT IS INTELLIGENCE?

Hundreds of volumes have been written on the subject of intelligence without anyone succeeding in defining the word to everyone's satisfaction. One psychologist, L. Humphreys, wrote that "intelligence is defined by a consensus among psychologists. It is the repertoire of intellectual skills and knowledge available to a person at any one time."

Writing in *Psychology Today* magazine, Robert J. Steinberg assembled the following list of characteristics most commonly mentioned by psychologists when referring to intelligence:

Verbal Intelligence
Displays a good vocabulary
Reads with high comprehension
Displays curiosity
Sees all aspects of a problem
Learns rapidly
Appreciates knowledge for its own sake
Is verbally fluent
Listens to all sides of an argument before deciding
Displays alertness
Thinks deeply
Shows creativity
Converses easily on a variety of subjects
Reads widely
Likes to read
Identifies connections among ideas

Problem-Solving Abilities
Is able to apply knowledge to problems
Makes good decisions
Poses problems in an optimum way
Displays common sense
Displays objectivity
Solves problems well
Plans ahead
Has good intuition
Gets to the heart of problems
Appreciates truth
Considers the results of actions
Approaches problems thoughtfully

Practical Intelligence
Sizes up situations well
Determines how to achieve goals
Displays awareness of the world
Displays interest in the world-at-large
Displays curiosity

TESTING INTELLIGENCE

In the 1890s, French psychologist Alfred Binet was instructed by the government to help them find a way to determine who would benefit most from formal education. In 1905, Binet and his partner, Théophile Simon, completed a test that attempted to measure such abilities as memory, recall, symbolic thinking, and visual-motor performance. In the 1930s, Professor Lewis Terman at Stanford University adapted the French test for American children. The test was first called the Terman-Binet test, then later the Stanford-Binet test.

The basis of the Stanford-Binet test, and almost all other intelligence tests, is that intelligence will increase with age from birth through adolescence. Test makers try out questions on children of every age to develop a set of averages for each age. A child who takes a standardized test has his results compared with the standard responses for his age.

The Meaning of "IQ"

The intelligence quotient (IQ) compares a child's mental age with his chronological age. The theory is that a child aged 10 whose test scores equal the standard for a child aged 11 is more intelligent than a 10-year-old child whose test scores equal the standard for a child of age 9.

The quotient for intelligence is derived from the following mathematical formula:

$$\frac{\text{Mental age in years}}{\text{Chronological age in years}} \times 100 = \text{Intelligence Quotient}$$

For example, using a 10-year-old child with a mental age of 11:

$$11/10 \times 100 = 110 \text{ IQ}$$

The median IQ score is 100, with half the population above that mark and half below. Sixty-eight percent of the U.S. population has an IQ between 85 and 115. About 5% of the population has a score of 120 or more, meaning superior or very superior intelligence, while another 5% has a score below 80, which indicate borderline mental retardation or more serious problems.

How Important Is the IQ Score?

Intelligence quotient tests alone are not determinants of success in life. However, longitudinal studies that follow children over the course of decades have discovered that children with high IQs did better in school, were healthier, and were better adjusted socially than children with low IQs. Children with high IQs also tended to achieve impressive success in adult life.

The danger of IQ scores, however, is that they lead to premature labeling of children. Intelligence quotient scores in early childhood, especially those of disadvantaged children, handicapped children, children with learning disabilities, and others who may be developmentally delayed, can change substantially through the school years. Research has found that early labeling of a child as "retarded" can significantly reduce that child's likelihood of obtaining the educational counseling and assistance that might significantly raise an early IQ score.

Intelligence Testing of Preschool Children

The most widely used intelligence test, administered to children aged 4 through 6 1/2, is the Wechsler preschool and primary scale of intelligence. This test stemmed from the work of clinical psychologist David Wechsler, who believed that a more useful picture of overall intelligence could be obtained by breaking up intelligence into several different components. The current Wechsler test has twelve subtests, which yield two scores: a verbal score that tests language ability and a problem solving and a performance score that tests ability to perform fine motor tasks. These subtests are:

VERBAL SCALE
· General information, such as how many weeks there are in a year
· General comprehension, such as what course of action a person should take in a situation
  Arithmetic
· Similarities, in which a child is asked why two different things or concepts are alike
· Vocabulary
· Digit span, in which a child is asked to repeat a series of digits

PERFORMANCE SCALE
· Picture completion, in which a child is asked which component is missing from a picture
· Picture arrangement, a series of pictures that have to be placed in the correct order to tell a story
· Block design, in which a child has to copy a design with blocks
· Object assembly, of a jigsaw-type puzzle
· Coding, in which symbols are matched with numbers according to a simple code
· Mazes, in which a child must draw the correct route form beginning to end

The Wechsler test also yields a single IQ score. The results of the Wechsler test have a very high degree of correlation to the results of the standard Stanford-Binet test.

Play and Play Materials in the Preschool Years

THE IMPORTANCE OF PLAY

As we emphasized earlier in this book, play is a child's work, an activity vital to normal development. In part 2 of this book, we described the importance of play to the motor and cognitive development of children under age 2. Play continues to contribute to gross motor, fine motor, and cognitive development throughout the preschool years. Through play, children increase their strength and endurance, develop coordination, gain fine muscle control over their hands and fingers, increase their knowledge of cause and effect, understand spatial relationships, and achieve many other advantages.

In addition to the above, play in the preschool years has additional benefits beyond those achieved in the period before age 2. Three important benefits both derive from the child's growing capacity to perform what's called "pretend," "imaginative," or "dramatic" play. This play develops when a child becomes capable of calling up mental images. He combines his ability to think with use of toys and other materials in an increasingly complex variety of imaginative activities. The child pretends he's a doctor, imagines his fire truck is going to put out a real fire, or engages in a two-part conversation with a puppet in a short "play."

The first major benefit of pretend play is in developing social competence. Through make-believe, children can experiment with all kinds of roles without risk. They can be dominant or submissive, an adult or a baby, raucous or quiet. Through play, they can safely learn what constitutes acceptable behavior in preparation for their assumption of social roles in later years, when failing to abide by the "rules" can cause social problems. Fitting in to society is also easier after children experiment with being other people and pretending to look at life from other perspectives.

The second major benefit of pretend play is its importance to emotional development. Through pretending, children can deal with fears and stresses and develop solutions to problems. For example, a child who has trouble accepting anger in others may act out a situation in which a stuffed animal is angry at him. Since the child is able to control the animal, he gradually learns to deal with others' anger in real life. Through play, a child also learns self-control. For example, he learns that his own anger gets in the way of completing a task.

A third major benefit of play in the preschool years is its role in developing social relationships with other children. By learning to play with other children, a child discovers how to make friends, cooperate,

WHAT YOU SHOULD KNOW ABOUT . . .

PRESCHOOL CHILDREN AND TELEVISION VIEWING

Some children become interested in television as early as age 1. Viewing time increases after age 2, and by age 3 the average preschool child spends more time in front of the television set than he does on any other activity except sleeping. Surveys have found a range of viewing habits from a low of 5 hours per week to a high of 100 hours per week.

Heavy television viewing by preschool children has been almost universally criticized by child development experts. One reason for the criticism is studies that show the following effects of television on preschool children's behavior:

1. *Aggression. Several studies, including two by the surgeon general of the United States, have shown that children who watched a great deal of televised violence were more likely to act aggressively than children who didn't watch television violence. While this finding was true for children of all ages, preschoolers were found to be particularly susceptible because they had much more difficulty than older children in distinguishing fantasy from reality.*

2. *Antisocial behavior. Preschool children are unable to distinguish the difference between violence and other antisocial acts performed for good purposes and those done for evil purposes. Therefore, they often believe that if a hero uses violence, they can too.*

   Violent television also can lead preschoolers to believe that the world is a dangerous place in which defensiveness, selfishness, and hostility are better responses than friendliness, honesty, and generosity.

3. *Advertisements. Nine out of ten preschool children ask for products they've seen advertised on television. Studies have shown that the dietary preferences of preschool children who watch a great deal of television are far more strongly weighted toward candy and other junk food than children who watch little television.*

4. *Sex. There is growing evidence that young children who watch a great deal of commercial television, especially prime-time programming, absorb negative sexual stereotypes and exhibit more suspicion and aggressiveness toward peers of the opposite sex.*

As disturbing as some of these effects of television viewing on preschool children are, many child psychologists believe that the most damaging effect of television is not the behavior it produces, but the behavior it prevents. Children who watch a great deal of television spend far less time on gross and fine motor play, socialize much less with their peers, and spend significantly less quality time with their parents and other adults. By the time children reach the school years, those who watch television an average of six or more hours a day lag significantly behind their peers in all areas of development.

> These children have much lower grades in school, have lower reading scores, and show a much greater propensity toward obesity.
>
> The only exception to the preponderance of negative effects of television watching have been studies that show some positive effects on children who watch public television's "Sesame Street" and "Mr. Rogers' Neighborhood." Preschool children who regularly watch "Sesame Street" tend to have greater command of the skills stressed on the program than children who watch infrequently. Children who've watched Big Bird and his friends also tend to have a more positive attitude toward school. Other studies have shown that nursery school children who watch "Mr. Rogers' Neighborhood" are more likely to show friendliness and cooperation, tolerate delays, and observe rules than children who don't watch the program.

compromise, and a host of other social skills that are important in the school years and later life.

IMPORTANT TYPES OF PLAY AND PLAY MATERIALS

After age 2, a child increasingly enjoys playing independently. This independence means more time for nonchild-related tasks for parents and other care givers. But it doesn't mean that parents and care givers don't have to spend as much time planning for, supervising, and providing materials for a child's play. Just because a child is mature enough to choose a toy from a toy box and amuse himself for an hour doesn't mean he's old enough to schedule appropriate types of play, judge the quality of play materials, or evaluate the dangers of certain activities.

Parents and care givers have the responsibility to provide play opportunities and materials that are appropriate to a child's developmental level and encourage the acquisition of necessary skills and concepts. In our previous discussions of motor development, cognitive development, and language acquisition, we've covered in detail the skills and concepts a child should develop in the preschool years. In the follow pages, we review the basic types of activities and materials that portant to that development.

One important mistake parents and care givers sho avoid is the tendency to select specific play materials the sex of the child. Research has shown that ch with their gender very early in life, and that fluence their play. Even in an environm neutral as possible, boys and girls There is strong evidence that it' fluence girls to devote as much time playing with cars and trucks than they do with dolls, or boys to devote as much time to dolls as they do to cars and trucks.

However, parents should make decisions on play materials based on their quality and purpose, not solely on their child's preferences. For example, playing with blocks develops a young child's understanding of spatial relationships and quantity, an understanding that is important in learning mathematics in the school years. Decades of testing reveal that girls have more difficulty learning mathematics in the school years. Thus, parents and care givers may want to make blocks available to girls and encourage block play. On the other hand, preschool boys have spent less time on arts-and-crafts activities. Arts and crafts build hand strength and fine motor coordination, which are important in learning to write. Boys generally have more trouble with handwriting in the school years, a problem that may be partially alleviated by more attention to fine motor coordination in the preschool years.

Types of Play Materials

GROSS MOTOR PLAY   The equipment and space needed for running, jumping, climbing, and other gross motor activities can normally be found in public parks and playgrounds if it isn't available at home. Two- and 3-year-olds love swings, slides, sandboxes, children's wading pools, wagons, playhouses, tricycles, riding toys, sleds, and small climbing equipment. Four-year-olds can try rope ladders, larger jungle gyms, seesaws, and trapezes. They are also interested in and capable of learning how to swim. Five-year-olds can learn to use roller skates and ice skates and can ride bicycles with training wheels.

Finally, preschool children benefit from access to sports equipment. In addition to a large variety of balls, toy stores carry many well-designed and appropriately sized equipment such as basketball nets, soccer goals, croquet sets, baseball bats, baseball batting tees, football goalposts, racquets, and golf clubs.

ARTS AND CRAFTS   Arts-and-crafts activities are both a wonderful outlet for creative expression and a vital way to develop fine motor skills. The variety of appropriate activities and materials are vast, and most libraries, book stores, and educational materials stores carry a number of books, each listing hundreds of arts-and-crafts ideas.

Among the activities 2- and 3-year-olds enjoy are:

· Drawing with chalk, crayons, and markers
· Pasting and gluing
· Finger painting
· with brushes
· -Doh and other claylike materials

Appropriate equipment includes an easel, construction paper, safety scissors, nontoxic and washable paints, child-sized smocks, and a child-sized table and chairs to work on.

Older children can learn to use safety scissors to do their own cutting, and they begin to enjoy coloring books. They also can do more advanced craft activities, such as simple sewing.

TOYS FOR PRETEND PLAY Among the very favorite toys for preschool children are miniature farms with farm animals, miniature houses with small figures, minature schools and playgrounds, miniature zoos, and dollhouses. Most of these toys are appropriate throughout the preschool years, with the child's use of the toys becoming more sophisticated with age.

DOLLS, STUFFED ANIMALS, PUPPETS, AND "DRESS-UP" CLOTHES Another kind of imaginative play is dramatic play. At ages 2 and 3, dolls and stuffed animals are the favorite toys. After age 3, children increasingly enjoy puppets and costumes.

HOUSEKEEPING TOYS Preschool children continue to have fun pretending to be their parents and care givers. As their capacity to pretend increases, they like toy stoves, toy refrigerators, toy sinks, play food, toy workbenches, toy typewriters, and similar materials.

"REAL PEOPLE" TOYS We use this phrase to describe play equipment that allows children to pretend to be adults with whom they come in contact outside the home. This includes doctor kits, nurse kits, shopping carts, cash registers, and service station pumps.

BLOCKS There's no need to describe again the considerable benefits of block play. Fortunately, toy manufacturers have developed many different kinds of building materials beyond the traditional wooden blocks. One excellent item for young preschool children is plastic interlocking blocks that are larger versions of the long-popular Lego blocks, which are too small for children under age 4.

Other types of preschool building materials are magnetic blocks, tinker toys, bristle blocks, blocks that snap together, and construction straws. The best way to determine the kinds of blocks that will interest a child at a specific age is to take him to one of the growing number of stores that allow children to play with toys before they're purchased.

PUZZLES At some point between ages 2 and 3, a child is able to progress from puzzles in which individual pieces fit in a precut slot to real jigsaw puzzles. Jigsaw puzzles for young children have three or four large pieces that fit into a frame. Once a child masters these, puzzles with an increasing number of pieces can be substituted. Once a child is capable of doing puzzles with eight to ten pieces, he's ready to try floor puzzles without a frame.

LOTTO GAMES AND DOMINOES Lotto games require matching pictures on a small card with pictures on large game cards. As a game,

Lotto is played like a smaller version of bingo. Young preschool children don't understand the game concept, but preschool educators have found that using Lotto games to practice matching is an extraordinarily effective tool in teaching vocabulary, number recognition, alphabet recognition, animal recognition, colors, shapes, and other cognitive skills.

For an older child, domino games that substitute pictures for the dots on real dominoes are also valuable as matching exercises.

BOARD GAMES Children under age 3 are too young to play board games. By 3 1/2, preschoolers may be ready for very simple board games that don't require reading. These games teach number recognition, colors, shapes, and counting. They also promote such social skills as waiting for one's turn, following rules, and cooperation.

SAND AND WATER TOYS Sand and water play continue to be important playthings throughout the preschool years.

MUSIC AND MUSICAL TOYS Young children should be encouraged to listen to music, dance, march, and play along with instruments designed for their age group.

BOOKS We've already discussed the vital role of books in a preschooler's development. One type of book we haven't discussed yet is those that teach social, emotional, and moral concepts. Children over age 2 are ready for books that promote such things as sharing, having friends, and understanding one's own feelings as well as the feelings of others. As children approach school age, they're ready for books that cover dealing with strangers, child abuse and sexual abuse, grief, divorce, pet loss, and other difficult situations.

Social Development in the Preschool Years

Social development is the process by which a child gains the ability to interact effectively and responsibly with the rest of the world. Social skills are not inherited but are learned, through training by others, observing and imitating role models, and developing the ability to understand other people's feelings and attitudes. This last process, gaining the ability to emphathize with other people, is the foundation of moral development, the process by which we become "good people."

Social development goes hand in hand with cognitive development. A child has to gain the ability to recall and process mental images before he can imitate behavior he's seen in the past. Social development requires the ability to classify behavior and make judgments about what's appropriate and not appropriate. A child must have a sense of self and an appreciation of his own worth in order to define his place in a social order. Finally, he must have the ability to put himself in other people's places to understand how they think and predict how they will react in social situations.

As we explained previously, the primary social development that takes place in the first 18 months of life is the establishment of a sense of personal security or trust in the world. This sense of security is provided almost exclusively by parents and other regular care givers, who see that the child's needs are met and that he feels loved.

By a child's second birthday, he's attained the ability to form ideas, or mental images. His next social task, which Erik Erikson defined as the conflict between autonomy and shame and doubt, involves establishing a firm sense of self by learning to balance the need to assert independence with the need for emotional support of others. One part of this sense of self, which begins to form during the period from 18 to 36 months, is learning one's sex role.

DEVELOPMENT OF SEX ROLES

One of the earliest socializing results of cognitive development is learning one's sex role. All children learn to think of themselves as male or female by about age 3. At the same time, they learn the social expectations for their sex, which exert a strong influence on their lives.

The differences in development are partially biological and partially environmental. Biologically, males have a higher concentration of male hormones, called *androgens,* than do females. Androgen levels in the bloodstream are associated with aggression. Studies among boys have shown that those with higher levels of androgen are more active and more likely to compete in sports.

A second biological difference is that male brains tend to become more specialized or lateralized. A highly specialized right hemisphere leads to improved ability at solving visual/spatial problems, an important characteristic for success in science and mathematics.

Any biological tendencies, however, vary from individual to individual, and they can be strongly modified by the environment. Research has shown, however, that boys and girls are almost always treated differently from birth. Babies of different sexes are dressed differently, their environments are decorated differently, and they're given different toys. Mothers tend to talk more to girl babies and to treat them more gently. Fathers tend to talk more to male babies and to spend more time with them.

As babies gain the ability to explore their environment, risk taking is tolerated more in males than in females. Fathers roughhouse with boy babies more frequently. Girl babies are comforted more soothingly when they cry.

WHAT YOU SHOULD KNOW ABOUT . . .

DIFFERENCES BETWEEN THE SEXES

Psychologists E. Mavis Hethrington and Ross D. Park have compiled the following listing of proven differences between the sexes, possible differences between the sexes, and alleged differences that have not been validated by research:

Actual Differences

1. Physical, motor, sensory: Girls are more advanced physically and neurologically at birth, walk earlier, and reach puberty sooner. Boys have more mature muscular development, larger lungs and heart, and lower sensitivity to pain.
2. Susceptibility to disease. Males are miscarried more often, have a higher rate of infant mortality, and are more vulnerable to hereditary diseases.
3. Cognitive: From infancy, girls have superior verbal abilities, and the gap between the sexes widens through the high school years. From about age 10, boys have superior visual-to-spacial abilities, which make them better at manipulating objects and aiming at targets. From age 12, boys develop increasingly superior mathematical abilities.
4. Social and emotional development: Boys are more often aggressors and victims of aggression. Girls are more compliant to the demands of parents and other adults.
5. Atypical development: Boys are more likely to have school problems, reading disabilities, speech defects, and emotional problems.

Possible Differences

1. Activity level. Boys are found to be more active when differences in activity level are discovered. Some studies have found no differences in activity level.
2. Dependency. No difference has been found in younger children, but older girls consider themselves more dependent.
3. Fear, timidity, and anxiety. No consistent difference has been found in young children. Older boys are more likely to take physical risks.
4. Vulnerability to stress. Recent studies have indicated that boys are more vulnerable to family disharmony, such as divorce, and to interpersonal stress.
5. Orientation to social stimuli: Infant girls may recognize faces more quickly than boys, and may attach to their mother at an earlier age.

Mythical Differences

Contrary to popular opinion:

1. *Boys are not less social than girls.*
2. *Girls are not more suggestible and are not more likely to conform to peer pressure.*
3. *Girls are not better at rote learning and boys are not better at more complicated problem-solving situations.*
4. *Boys do not have more achievement motivation than girls.*
5. *Girls do not have lower self-esteem.*
6. *Boys are not more responsive to visual stimuli and girls are not more responsive to auditory stimuli.*

Sometime after age 2, young children understand their basic gender identity, or the knowledge that they are boys or girls. In the preschool period, however, they don't comprehend gender consistency, or the idea that they'll always remain male or female and that superficial characteristics, such as wearing a dress, don't alter basic gender. A young boy may say he wants to grow up to be a mommy, or a young girl may want to grow a beard. In this period, children are very tolerant of the sex role behavior of others. For example, a 4-year-old boy won't react negatively to another boy playing with a doll.

Parents and other care givers, however, tend to narrowly define the limits of acceptable behavior for boys, although they're much more tolerant of girls. Parents are unlikely to react to a girl playing with a truck, but may stop a boy from playing with a doll or other "girl" toys. This treatment leads even preschool boys to have a stronger concept of their own gender consistency than girls, and they demonstrate a more defined tendency to use their father as a role model.

SOCIAL RELATIONSHIP WITH THE MOTHER IN THE PRESCHOOL YEARS

Much of the social development of infancy involves the bonding, or the formation of a strong attachment, between baby and mother. The strength of this attachment is the most important factor in a baby's development of a feeling of security or trust.

In the preschool years, however, the physical distance between child and mother increases. Cognitive development gives the child the ability to represent mentally their relationship with their mothers. This means that the emotional bond between mother and child can be maintained even when the mother isn't present.

WHAT YOU SHOULD KNOW ABOUT . . .

THE FAMILY AS A SOCIAL SYSTEM

Traditionally, socialization was looked upon as a system in which parents shaped the behavior of their children. Today, however, developmental psychologists view the family as a social system in which the members interact and have tasks and responsibilities.

In his book, Socialization and the Family, *J. A. Clausen has provided a new perspective on early childhood socialization by defining the roles of both parents and the child:*

Parental Aim or Activity	Child's Task or Achievement
1. Provision of nurturance and physical care.	Acceptance of nurturance (development of trust).
2. Training and channeling of physical needs in toilet training, weaning, provision of solid foods, etc.	Controlling expression of biological impulses; learning acceptable channels and times of gratification.
3. Teaching and skill training in language, perceptual skills, physical skills, and self-care skills in order to ensure safety, etc.	Learning to recognize objects and cues; language learning; learning to walk, negotiate obstacles, dress, feed self, etc.
4. Orienting the child to his immediate world of kin, neighborhood, community, and society, and to his own feelings.	Developing a cognitive map of one's social world; learning to fit behavior to situational demands.
5. Transmitting cultural and subcultural goals and values and motivating the child to accept them for his own.	Developing a sense of right and wrong; developing goals and criteria for choices; investment of effort for the common good.
6. Promoting interpersonal skills, motives, and modes of feeling and behaving in relation to others.	Learning to take perspective of another person; responding selectively to the expectations of others.
7. Guiding, correcting, helping the child to formulate his own goals, plan his own activities.	Achieving a measure of self-regulation and criteria for evaluating own performance.

Between ages 2 and 4, children put more distance between themselves and their mother. Studies have shown that as children age, the average distance they stay away from their mother during outdoor play steadily increases. In the same age range, children become less and less upset at separations from their mother, so much so that separation anxiety under normal circumstances is rare for a 4-year-old. This anxiety can return, however, in periods of stress, such as illness or the presence of strangers.

During the preschool years, mothers actively work to change the relationship with their children, just as the children physically separate. From a relationship based on total dependence, mothers relax their supervision and reduce physical contact. The goal is a relationship of "partnership" or "friendship."

There is considerable controversy about the effects of day care on mother-child relationships. The preponderance of evidence is that if adequate bonding takes place in infancy and if the infant's needs are met by high-quality care, the relationship between mother and child in the preschool years is little different from between full-time mothers and their children. If bonding is inadequate or day care is not adequate to meet all the child's physical and emotional needs during daily separation, the child tends to become autonomous earlier and to be much more emotionally distant from the mother. This distance is tied to higher levels of anger and aggression.

THE RELATIONSHIP BETWEEN FATHER AND CHILD IN THE PRESCHOOL YEARS

As the intensity of the mother-child relationship diminishes, the father-child relationship becomes more prominent. Sometimes mothers may become jealous over the tendency of many preschoolers to prefer to play with their father and to work with them on problem-solving tasks. Several major studies have shown that fathers who are highly involved in their children's lives have children who progress at a superior level in both their cognitive and social-emotional development.

The involvement of the father has been shown to be particularly important to the normal development of preschool boys. In the case of the absence of the father, due to divorce, military service, death, overinvolvement with work, or simply disinterest in child raising, boys experience significantly more cognitive, social, and emotional problems. In such cases, boys have trouble concentrating, do less well in learning tasks, and exhibit more aggressiveness. The effects of father absence on preschool girls, on the other hand, has been shown to be minimal.

The negative effects of father absence can be counteracted by the presence of a father substitute. Studies have shown that boys living with

WHAT YOU SHOULD KNOW ABOUT . . .

BIRTH ORDER AND PERSONALITY

Extensive research has revealed that firstborn children in a family have markedly different characteristics from later-born children. Eldest children are born into an adult world that eagerly awaits their appearance. Eldest children are the most pampered, have the undivided attention of their parents, and don't have to share possessions with anyone in the first years of life. As a result, firstborn children tend to be adult oriented, mature, self-controlled, conforming, and responsible.

On the negative side, firstborns suffer from inexperienced parents who are often inconsistent in providing discipline. They tend to receive more parental pressure to perform and set a good example for younger siblings. As a result, firstborn children tend to have less self-confidence, less social poise, more anxiety, greater fear of failure, and more guilt.

The result is that firstborn children excel in academic and professional achievements, and they are overrepresented among people listed in Who's Who, among Rhodes scholars, and among famous writers and scientists. On the other hand, they're also overrepresented in the incidence of sleep problems, oversensitivity, and shyness.

Later-born children receive less attention from their parents, but they also tend to be less pressured. They are often more extroverted than firstborn children, more humorous, and more pleasure oriented. They are also more self-reliant, less anxious, and they perform particularly well in dangerous situations, such as flying an airplane in combat. However, middle children also tend to have poor achievement and short attention spans. Perhaps because they try too hard for attention, they are much more likely than firstborns to be hyperactive or aggressive.

The last-born child in a large family is often indulged by parents and older siblings. The last-borns tend to have most of the positive characteristics of firstborn children and few of the negative characteristics. Last-borns tend to be optimistic, self-confident, and secure.

Only children have traditionally been regarded as ''spoiled brats'' who lack self-control and have poor social skills. Research has failed to substantiate these opinions. Only children tend to be mature, adult oriented, self-confident, and achievement oriented. Perhaps because they never have to compete with siblings, they are more assertive, less anxious, more socially adaptable, and have higher self-esteem than firstborn children. However, only children have slightly lower IQ scores than firstborn children, perhaps because they don't have the opportunity to sharpen their intellectual skills by tutoring younger siblings.

stepfathers tend to progress as normally as boys living with their biological fathers.

SOCIALIZATION WITH PEERS IN THE PRESCHOOL YEARS

As we've seen, infants and toddlers show signs of enjoying each other's company. It is only after age 2, however, that the process of true socialization develops. Longitudinal studies that follow children from age 2 to adolescence have shown that the amount of time spent socializing with peers steadily increases from age 2 to age 11, while the time spent with parents and other adults steadily decreases.

Most of the interaction between two preschoolers involves play. The increasingly sophisticated course of this interaction was elegantly described by sociologist Mildred Parton as a series of stages. Around their second birthday, as we noted previously, children begin to engage in what Parton called *parallel play*. One child plays beside another, with each engaging in similar activities or playing with similar toys. For example, both may set in a sandbox filling and emptying containers. While the children apparently enjoy being together, there's no meaningful interaction or conversation between them.

By about age 3 or shortly afterward, children begin to engage in what Parton described as *associative play*. At this stage, children obviously are playing together, and they interact. For example, if two children are in a sandbox, they engage in the same type of activity, talk to each other about what they are doing, and may even exchange toys. However, each child is involved in a separate activity with a separate goal. The children don't cooperate with each other by agreeing on a shared goal and dividing labor to reach that goal.

Children don't normally begin to interact in what Parton called *cooperative play* until about their fifth birthday. In cooperative play, children may play a game under mutually accepted rules, work together to build a castle or playhouse, or engage in dramatic play with each child assuming a separate role. Cooperative play is the first stage in which a child assumes the role of a leader or supervisor, while other children assume the role of followers.

Selection and Relationship with Playmates

At about age 3, a child begins to establish a one-to-one relationship with one or more playmates. Because he's still highly egocentric, a three-year-old considers his playmates relatively interchangeable. He tends to identify his playmates because of their attributes or possessions; for example, "Johnny is my friend because he's got lots of toys." As a child's play becomes more associative, he starts to increasingly discriminate between playmates. He may not enjoy playing with a child who won't share toys or a child who's too quiet.

The onset of cooperative play brings about a more advanced relationship, in which a child identifies certain peers as special friends. Because preschool children are still egocentric, these friendships have been described as *one-way attachments*, in which the most important criterion of friendship is what the friend can do for the child. Relationships often change abruptly as a child complains, "George isn't my friend anymore because he wouldn't let me be the police chief."

Throughout the preschool period, children tend to choose as playmates children who are most like themselves. As early as age 3, boys show a decided preference for playing with boys and girls with girls. Children also tend to choose playmates of approximately the same age and of the same race. Until they're capable of cooperative play, preschoolers generally are able to play only with one other person at a time.

Researchers have found that boys tend to be more physical and more argumentative in their play, while girls are often more quiet, orderly, and less argumentative. When boys play with girls, the boys tend to be less physical and the girls more active. Children of both sexes often show more cooperation when an adult is present.

The Importance of Peers

Relationships with peers become increasingly important as a child progresses through the preschool years. Socialization is the process of learning the rules of interacting with other people. In early childhood, parents act as models and provide reinforcement for positive behavior, and they continue to play that role throughout childhood. As a child begins to be aware of his peers, they become an equally important source of information about the rules. Peers provide the perspective of equals, other people with common problems, goals, social status, and abilities. As the child grows older and his relationships with peers become more complex, they act as increasingly important models and sources of reinforcement.

Observers of 3- and 4-year-olds have noted the following three categories of positive social reinforcement they provide to each other:

1. Giving positive attention and approval, such as offering praise, offering help, smiling, and general conversation.
2. Giving affection and personal acceptance, both physically and verbally.
3. Submissive behavior, such as imitation, sharing, accepting another child's idea, allowing another child to play, following another child's orders.

Throughout the preschool years, children provide reinforcement to each other at a higher rate. Researchers have observed that children who offer positive reinforcement, which is considered friendly, were much more successful in establishing social relationships than children who offered negative reinforcement by whining or demanding.

Several investigators have traced a child's pattern of social reinforcement to the kind of reinforcement the child receives at home. One classic study found that children of middle-class parents, who tended to praise their children much more frequently than punish them, made much greater use of positive reinforcement than children from lower-income homes, who were more often punished than praised. This study also found that intervention by adults in a supervised situation could alter preschoolers' patterns of social reinforcement. That is another reason why low-income children who attend well-run preschool programs such as Head Start tend to be more cooperative, and thus more successful, in elementary school.

TRENDS IN PRESCHOOL SOCIALIZATION

Over the last three decades, researchers have noticed a dramatic decrease in the amount of time preschoolers spend socializing with their peers. The most significant factor in this decrease has been an equally dramatic increase in the amount of time preschoolers spend watching television. A second factor is the availability of much more elaborate toys, such as "talking" stuffed animals that encourage solitary play. A third contributing factor is a reduction in family size that has decreased the number of available playmates in many areas of the country.

Many experts are disturbed by this reduction in peer socialization in the preschool years. They are finding signs that less social experience in the preschool years makes children more prone to negative reinforcement and more aggressive in the school years.

Emotional Development in the Preschool Years

The preschool years are dominated by the third of psychologist Erik Erikson's crises in psychosocial development. Erikson described this basic conflict from about age 2 to about age 6 as initiative versus guilt. As preschool children mature physically and intellectually, they increasingly realize that they have the power to make things happen. They gain mastery over their bodies to accomplish more types of behavior, they take pride in their ability to solve problems, and they begin to understand that other people have different motivations and perceptions from their own.

WHAT YOU SHOULD KNOW ABOUT . . .

EVALUATING A CHILD'S BEHAVIOR

All children behave badly or even bizarrely from time to time. Parents and other care givers often find it difficult to decide if a child's behavior is so abnormal that professional help is needed. Psychologist Jane Kessler developed the following criteria that can be used in making that decision:

1. *Age discrepancy. Is the behavior common for the child's age, or is it behavior that should have been outgrown?*
2. *Frequency. Occasional abnormal behavior is common, as is abnormal behavior in times of physical illness or emotional stress. Frequent abnormal behavior without stress is cause for concern.*
3. *Number of symptoms. The more behavior difficulties, the more likelihood of trouble. However, a single acute problem, such as fear of school, could require professional help.*
4. *Degree of social disadvantage. A child who pulls his earlobes constantly has a less serious immediate problem than a child who constantly attacks other children.*
5. *Inner suffering. A child who obviously suffers shame or guilt from a behavior is in need of immediate help.*
6. *Intractable behavior. Children need help when all efforts to eliminate or modify difficult behavior fail.*
7. *General personality appraisal. If a child's total adjustment to family life and social life is poor, he needs help. If his overall adjustment is healthy, a particular problem is less serious.*

In Erikson's words, the child's energy is directed "toward the possible and the tangible, which permits the dreams of early childhood to be attached to the goals of an active adult life." This desire to achieve makes children eager to learn, to plan realistically, to accept guidance of parents and adults, and to work cooperatively with other children.

On the negative side, with the growing sense of power comes an increasing awareness of the limits on their behavior. Children begin to realize that they can act, or want to act, in ways that will make them feel guilty. Along with a child's ability to carry out a wide variety of behaviors comes the requirements of achieving self-control and of taking responsibility for one's actions. If children fail to control themselves, they can feel guilty.

Inevitably, the conflict between initiative and guilt produces negative emotions, which at times seem to dominate a child's behavior in the preschool period. Two consequences of this conflict are aggression and fear.

AGGRESSION

Aggression is an angry response to frustration. Toddlers and young preschoolers normally display aggression, usually in the form of temper tantrums, when they are frustrated by their own physical limitations (they can't screw the top back onto a jar) or by limitations on behavior imposed by their parents (they have to go to bed, take a bath, get dressed, etc.). After age 2 1/2 or 3, however, aggressive behavior increasingly involves disputes with playmates.

Much of this aggression involves conflicts over objects or privileges, such as who goes down a slide first. Anyone who watches preschoolers at play for even a few minutes will see one child grab a toy out of another child's hand or push another child away from a slide. This object-directed behavior is called *instrumental aggression*. Studies have shown that boys and girls equally display instrumental aggression.

Child psychologists generally agree that this behavior is both normal and developmentally necessary. Controlled aggressiveness in pursuit of a goal, such as succeeding in business or participating in a sport, is a desirable trait in older children and adults. Young children who display no instrumental aggressiveness may become adults who are too passive to succeed in adult life.

A second kind of aggressiveness, however, is not desirable. This behavior is called *hostile aggressiveness*, which is directed at persons, not objects. An example is a preschooler who hits another child after he's grabbed a toy, or who pushes another child off a slide or swing simply because he's angry or because he wants to exercise power. Older preschoolers may begin to exhibit verbal rather than physical hostile aggression by screaming at another child or calling another child nasty names.

One important task of a preschooler is to learn to control his anger and vent his emotions without resorting to hostile aggression. Few children or adults achieve perfect control, especially over verbal behavior. But children who consistently lack self-control and consistently engage in hostile aggression become bullies. Recent studies have shown that young bullies grow up to become aggressive teenagers and adults who suffer from severe personality and social adjustment problems.

These studies have identified parental behavior as a primary cause of bullying by children. Children of parents who frequently engage in hostile aggression strongly tend to imitate that behavior. Children of bullies become bullies, and children of child abusers or spouse beaters become abusers of their own children or spouses. While occasional physical punishment has been shown to be a deterrent to young children who don't display excessive aggression, it has been shown to increase the aggressive behavior of overly aggressive young children.

A number of techniques have been developed to teach children to control aggression. The first is ignoring aggressive behavior and strongly reinforcing cooperation, sharing, and other positive actions. The more aggressive the child, the more effective is praise as an alternative to punishment.

A second technique is increasing an aggressive child's awareness of the consequences of his behavior. Puppet shows, films, and books that emphasize the pain and sadness felt by victims have been shown to markedly reduce aggression.

A third technique is the use of humor. Laughter and aggression are incompatible emotions. Parents and other care givers can defuse a situation through humor, and children can be encouraged to meet aggression with humor.

FEAR AND ANXIETY

The preschool period is far more heavily marked by fear than any other period of development. The primary reason is the combination of a child's growing power to imagine during the time when his preoperational type of thinking doesn't allow him to adequately distinguish between what's rational and what's irrational. An infant or toddler might be frightened by the roar of a lion in the zoo, but the fear passes when the lion's out of sight. A preschooler has the ability to recall the image of the lion. At the same time, the same immature thinking that allows a preschooler to totally believe that Santa Claus comes down his chimney on Christmas Eve can lead him to totally believe that the lion can leave its cage in the zoo and come to his bedroom to attack him. In the same way, a preschooler who treats his teddy bear like a real person can also believe the vacuum cleaner is alive and ready to eat him up.

The common fears of preschoolers often frustrate and anger parents who don't fully understand the preoperational thinking of children that age. Because it's increasingly possible to reason with preschoolers about so many things as they grow older, parents may believe they can use logic to attack a specific fear. If a child is afraid of clowns, parents can arrange to have the child meet a man, then watch him put his costume and makeup on to prove to the child that a clown is just an ordinary person dressed up in a special way. In some cases, this technique may work; more often, it has absolutely no effect. The reason is that both logical and illogical beliefs about the same object can exist at the same time in the preschooler's mind.

The most important advice child psychologists give to parents is to accept the psychological validity of the fear and the fact that directly confronting the fear with logic probably won't work. Some objects that arouse fear are relatively unimportant in a child's life and can easily be avoided. For example, a child afraid of lions doesn't have to go to the zoo, and a child afraid of witches doesn't have to watch *The Wizard of Oz*. Left alone, most fears vanish by ages 5 and 6, when a child advances from preoperational thought to operational thought.

Other fears, such as fear of doctors, has to be addressed because every child has to go to the doctor. In addressing these fears, parents and other care givers must provide strong, consistent emotional support while assisting the child in gradually conquering the fear. Rehearsing fear-producing situations, such as playing doctor, can help. Observing others, such as watching the doctor examine a parent first, can also be of benefit. A third technique, called *counterconditioning*, involves associating a pleasant experience with the unpleasant experience, such as receiving a new toy as a gift when entering the doctor's office.

One final and important step parents can take is to limit a preschool child's exposure to objects and experiences that are likely to give rise to fears. Violent or frightening television shows, movies, and books top the list of potential hazards. So do scary toys, frightening amusement park rides, and events at which a child is surrounded by pushing crowds.

Moral Behavior in the Preschool Years

Encouraging a child to understand and accept a moral code of behavior is a goal of all parents and care givers. However, the ability to relate individual actions to an abstract code of right and wrong is only achieved over a very long period. Moral development doesn't begin until a child starts to associate with his peers, and its takes place in conjunction with cognitive, emotional, and social development.

The limited cognitive abilities of preschoolers and their strong egocentrism severely limit their understanding of what's moral and what's not. Jean Piaget has described the following moral characteristics of preschool children:

1. A preschool child is likely to judge any action in terms of its physical consequences, not the intentions behind it. He considers accidently breaking five glasses to be more serious than deliberately dropping one glass.
2. A young child sees actions as totally right or totally wrong, admitting no possibility that anyone else could have a different viewpoint.
3. A preschool child considers an action bad only if it means he'll be punished, rather than simply because it violates a rule or causes someone or something harm.

WHAT YOU SHOULD KNOW ABOUT . . .

CHILD ABUSE AND NEGLECT

The 1985 National Family Violence Survey sponsored by the National Institute of Mental Health showed that almost 2 million children a year—1 out of every 33 children under age 18—were very severely abused, and as many as 5,000 died as a result. One-third of these victims were infants under age 1 and another third were toddlers and preschoolers aged 1 to 6. Child abuse was the cause of 10% of all hospital emergency room visits by children.

The survey of children in two-parent homes showed that some kind of violence (including spanking) took place in 62% of homes. Severe violence took place in 10.7% of homes and very severe violence in 1.9% of homes.

The U.S. Department of Health and Human Services has estimated that 2.5 times as many children were the victims of serious parental neglect as were victims of child abuse. As many as 75% of these estimated 5 million neglected children were under age 6.

A number of studies have compiled some characteristics common to abused and neglected children. These characteristics are:

1. *They are special in some way.*
2. *They are products of a ''bad'' pregnancy or labor and delivery.*
3. *They were low birth weight or preterm babies and have medical problems or birth defects.*
4. *They cry and whine a great deal or not at all.*
5. *They may show signs of withdrawal or extreme attachment.*
6. *They are fearful of any adult approaching a crying child or fearful of an adult's authority.*
7. *They have behavioral or discipline problems.*
8. *They have school problems or learning problems, and they may commonly be left at day care or nursery school programs well before hours and may not be picked up until after hours.*
9. *They may be hyperactive or brain damaged.*
10. *They have a history of failure to thrive.*
11. *They are developmentally delayed.*
12. *They have burns, cuts, and bruises at different stages of healing.*
13. *They show poor hygiene.*
14. *They are inappropriately dressed for the weather.*
15. *They are malnourished or have feeding problems.*
16. *They show signs of fatigue.*
17. *They have a history of chronic infections, accidents, or poisonings.*
18. *They may have added to or caused financial problems.*

Studies have also identified some characteristics of parents who abuse or neglect their children. These include:

1. *They do not trust people.*
2. *They have no friends.*
3. *They do not join social or religious groups.*
4. *They have few, if any, support systems.*
5. *They are frightened of others.*
6. *They may or may not be possessive of their children.*
7. *They have marital problems.*
8. *They expect their children to perform as adults.*
9. *They want the child to meet their needs.*
10. *They have a philosophy of severe punishment.*
11. *They cope poorly in a crisis situation.*
12. *They carry out their harsh punishment in an impulsive manner.*
13. *They do not touch or stimulate their children.*
14. *They have a defective self-image.*
15. *They are reluctant to volunteer information about the child.*
16. *They delay medical care and refuse permission for diagnostic workups.*
17. *They are mobile, moving their residences and changing doctors and hospitals frequently.*
18. *They have disturbed family relationships or environmental stress.*
19. *They abuse alcohol or drugs.*

---

4. A preschool child doesn't understand the concept of reciprocity, of treating other people the way he'd like to be treated.
5. A young child's ideas of making up for doing something wrong are limited to severe punishment.
6. A preschool child is likely to look at accidents as punishments from some higher authority in retribution for some misdeed.

This limited understanding of morality means that parents and other care givers can have little effect on a child's behavior by attempting to describe an action such as lying as "bad." Slow progress can be made by helping a child see that actions have consequences that can be harmful. Strong positive reinforcement when a child does something right is also effective.

Practical Aspects of Parenting in the Preschool Years

THE COSTS OF RAISING CHILDREN FROM AGE TWO TO AGE FIVE

The annual cost of raising a single child drops about 14% after age 2, then continues to decline through the preschool years. Preschool children are less expensive because parents have already purchased the furniture for their room, they don't require very much special equipment, they stop wearing diapers, and they average significantly fewer doctor's visits per year.

According to economist Lawrence Olson, the annual cost of raising preschool children in 1985 was $5,323 for a 2-year-old, $4,747 for a 3-year-old, $4,437 for a 4-year-old, and $4,357 for a 5-year-old.

NURSERY SCHOOL AND PRESCHOOL PROGRAMS

During the last two decades, the percentage of 3-year-olds enrolled in a preschool program more than doubled, to 28.8%, and the percentage of 4-year-olds nearly doubled, to 49.1%. Experts project that these percentages will continue to increase dramatically over the next ten years.

One reason for this increase has been the increase in the number of working mothers. In 1985, nearly two-thirds of nursery school children had mothers in the labor force.

A second reason for greater enrollment is the decline in the average family size. With fewer siblings in the family and fewer children in many neighborhoods, parents turn to preschool programs so their children can meet other boys and girls.

The third reason for the explosive growth of preschool is the desire of many parents to give their children a head start on success in school through early exposure to learning materials and a learning environment.

The Benefits of Nursery School

The first benefit of nursery school is that exposure to a variety of other children of approximately the same age can influence social development. The peer group can provide a preschooler with status and identity, serve as a source of self-esteem, expose the child to other values and standards, provide training opportunities in social skills, and give experience in forming social bonds.

Second, a good preschool program stimulates development by providing activities that develop gross and fine motor skills, help in the acquisition of such concepts as counting and alphabet recognition, and promote creativity through arts and crafts.

Third, children who are given a choice of participating in well-designed activities under the supervision of a supportive and patient staff normally succeed at the task they select, boosting self-esteem and confidence that creates a positive attitude toward school.

Finally, nursery school can be great fun for a preschool child. Good nursery schools have play equipment and materials that are different from those at home, and preschool teachers are experienced at planning games, songs, and other activities designed to bring pleasure to young children.

The Disadvantages of Nursery School

It is common for young children to show some distress about separating form their parents during the first few days of nursery school. Distress that lasts longer and is more acute may be a sign that a child isn't ready for school. Some children develop socially and emotionally more slowly than others, just as some talk or walk earlier. Children who continue to react with great distress to attending a preschool program should not be forced to attend, because such forcing can cause lasting trauma. If parents and other care givers are worried by a child's slow social or emotional development, they should talk to their pediatrician, just as they would about slow physical, motor, or language development.

A poorly run nursery school program can also adversely affect a preschool child's development. By far the most critical part of any program is the quality of the teachers. Educational researchers have identified four basic styles of preschool teachers:

1. The authoritarian teacher is concerned with an orderly, quiet classroom and strict adherence to the rules. This teaching style can be damaging to preschoolers, who have not achieved the self-control necessary to sit quietly for long periods. Children punished by an authoritarian teacher can quickly develop a poor self-image. Even children who behave themselves under such conditions can develop a strong dislike of school.
2. The overpermissive teacher is emotionally responsive to preschoolers but often lets them run wild. In such conditions, preschool children can suffer physical injury. Equally damaging is that quieter children can easily be intimidated by the negative behavior of other children.
3. The inconsistent teacher alternates between being stern and being lax. Inconsistency produces confusion, in addition to the same problems produced by both authoritarian and overpermissive teachers.

4. The competent teacher maintains adequate control by using discipline appropriately, while at the same time encouraging achievement by gearing the program to the children's level of development.

A final disadvantage of nursery school or preschool is the danger of accidents and injury from unsafe facilities and inadequate supervision.

Making a Decision about Nursery School

Nursery school attendance has been shown to be beneficial for children from disadvantaged homes, but is not necessary for the normal development of other children. Parents who can't find or afford a good program are not harming their children or decreasing the chance that their children will perform well in elementary school.

The most important consideration in evaluating a nursery school is its effects on a child's attitude and self-image, not its curriculum. Generally, after a normal period of adjustment, a child attending a good nursery school or preschool program should look forward to going to school, should be positive about his relationship with his peers, and should return home happy and enthusiastic. Most of the benefits of a good nursery school are provided by competent teachers and teachers' aides. Experts recommend that parents visit a nursery school and observe classes to evaluate the quality of supervision and the suitability of the environment before they enroll their child.

CHILD SAFETY IN THE PRESCHOOL YEARS

Accidents are the leading causes of serious injury and death of preschool children. The rates of both accidental injury and death are higher in the preschool years than at any other stage of life. In an average year, one out of every three preschool boys and one of every four preschool girls requires hospital emergency room treatment for an accidental injury.

Accidental injuries are most common in the preschool years because young children are very active physically, but lack the cognitive ability to recognize and evaluate dangerous situations, activities, and equipment. Preschoolers require safe play areas and adequate adult supervision to avoid serious injury.

Seventy percent of all accidental deaths of preschool children result from motor vehicle accidents. Approximately half of the victims are child pedestrians who are struck by vehicles while dashing into or playing in the street. Experts believe that 60% of the motor vehicle-related deaths of preschoolers could have been prevented with sufficient adult supervision or placing the child in a car seat or other adequate restraint.

Drowning accounts for approximately 10% of preschool deaths. The incidence of drowning peaks between age 2 and age 3. Almost all drowning deaths could have been prevented by adequate adult supervision.

Fires cause 4% of accidental preschool deaths. One of every three preschool victims was either left alone or in the company of young siblings at the time of the fire.

Firearms cause 3% of preschool accidental deaths and poisoning causes 2%. Both are preventable with adequate precautions.

Of the approximately 5 million annual preschool injuries, an estimated 189,000 American children need hospital care for accidents suffered in playgrounds. Seventy-two percent of these injuries result from falls from playground equipment. The equipment involved in the injuries include:

Climbers	42%
Swings	23%
Slides	16%
Merry-go-rounds	8%
Seesaws	5%
Other	6%

There were 591,000 children treated at hospital emergency rooms in 1986 after injuries with playthings. Bicycles and tricycles accounted for 60% of these injuries, while other toys accounted for 16%.

GLOSSARY

ACCOMMODATION: The process by which a person modifies an action or concept to meet the demands of the environment

ADAPTATION: A reaction to new experiences through both accommodation and assimilation

ADAPTIVE BEHAVIOR: Behavior that helps a child adjust to the environment

AGGRESSION: Hostile behavior that is unprovoked

ANIMISM: Attributing the characteristics of life to inanimate objects

ANXIETY: An emotional state marked by feelings of apprehension and fear

APGAR SCORE: A method of measuring the condition of a newborn immediately after birth

APNEA: A medical term for short interruptions in a child's regular breathing pattern

ASSIMILATION: The process by which a child incorporates a new experience into his existing mental image of the environment

ASSOCIATIVE PLAY: Play in which children engage in the same activity, but without cooperating

ATTACHMENT: A strong affectionate relationship between people

BABBLING: A type of prespeech utterance in which an infant repeats consonant and vowel sounds

BEHAVIORISM: The school of psychology that believes learning is the most important influence on development

BEHAVIOR MODIFICATION: The use of operant conditioning to change behavior

BONDING: The formation of a strong, permanent attachment between parent and child

CENTRATION: The tendency to focus on one aspect of a situation or object, neglecting all other important aspects

CEPHALOCAUDAL PRINCIPLE: The principle that physical development proceeds from the head downward

CESAREAN SECTION: Delivery of a baby by means of a surgical incision in the walls of the abdomen and uterus

CHILD ABUSE: Harm inflicted on a child by the use of physical or psychological violence by an adult or older child

CHILD DEVELOPMENT: An academic discipline that studies the processes by which a human being grows and matures from birth to adulthood

CLASSICAL CONDITIONING: Learning process by which a neutral stimulus, such as the ringing of a bell, becomes associated with a meaningful stimulus, such as the presentation of food; eventually, the bell alone produces the same response as presentation of the food

COGNITIVE DEVELOPMENT: The process by which a child learns to think, remember, solve problems, and make decisions

CONSERVATION: The ability to understand that a change in appearance doesn't necessarily mean a change in the fundamental nature of an object

COOING: The earliest stage of verbal utterance, characterized by squeals and gurgles

COOPERATIVE PLAY: Play in which two children engage in the same activity in accordance with a mutually accepted set of rules or behaviors

DECENTER: The ability to consider all aspects of a situation or object

DEPTH PERCEPTION: The ability to accurately judge the distance between two objects, or between one's self and an object

DEVELOPMENTAL NORMS: The statistically average ages at which certain behaviors, characteristics, or abilities emerge, as determined by direct observation of a significant number of children

DISCIPLINE: Teaching a child accepted standards of behavior by setting limits and enforcing them

DISCRIMINATION: The ability to respond to some stimuli but not others

DISCONTINUITY THEORY: The belief that development takes place in an erratic series of stages rather than at a steady, predictable pace

DRAMATIC PLAY: Play that involves pretending, or use of the imagination

ECHOLALIA: A stage of preverbal utterance in which an infant imitates sounds made by others

EGOCENTRISM: Looking at the world only from one's own viewpoint; the inability to understand or appreciate the viewpoints of others

ENVIRONMENT: Every person, object, and force with which an individual comes in contact

EXPRESSIVE JARGON: Preverbal utterances of meaningless syllables expressed with the pauses, inflections, and sentencelike rhythms of real speech

GENDER CONSISTANCY: The understanding that gender is a permanent characteristic that cannot be changed by behavior or dress

GENE: The basic unit of heredity

GENETIC PREDISPOSITION: The inherited tendency to acquire a certain behavior or characteristic

GROSS MOTOR DEVELOPMENT: The acquisition of strength and control over the large muscles of the body that are involved in such activities as running, jumping, and climbing

HABITUATION: The steady decrease in response to a stimulus that comes through repeated exposure

HOLOPHRASE: A one-word sentence used to express a more complex thought; characteristic of early speech

HYPERACTIVITY: A type of behavior characterized by a short attention span, frenetic activity, impulsiveness, and emotional volatility

IMITATION: Learning behavior by watching others

INNATE: Any condition, characteristic, or behavior that is present at birth

INTELLIGENCE: Overall mental ability, including memory, problem solving, and decision making

INTELLIGENCE QUOTIENT (IQ): An index that measures performance on a standardized test of intelligence; an IQ of 100 is average

IRREVERSIBILITY: The inability to mentally reconstruct an event or sequence of behaviors in reverse order

LANGUAGE ACQUISITION: The process by which a child learns vocabulary and the grammatical rules of language

LATERALIZATION: The process by which one of the two hemispheres of the brain assumes control over a specific function, such as speech

LEARNING: The acquisition of knowledge, skills, and behaviors through experience

LOCOMOTIVE DEVELOPMENT: The acquisition of the ability to move from one place to another, by crawling, walking, etc.

LONG-TERM MEMORY: The ability to store information, then recall it after a long period

MATURATION: Acquisition of skills, characteristics, or behaviors as a result of aging, rather than experience

MENTAL AGE: An index of a child's performance on intelligence tests, in comparison to previously established norms

MORAL DEVELOPMENT: The acquisition of the rules that govern social relationships between individuals and between an individual and society as a whole

MORPHEMES: The smallest unit of words that contain meanings

NEGATIVE REINFORCEMENT: Discouragement of a behavior through the administration of a punishment

NEONATE: A newborn infant from birth to 4 weeks of age

OBJECT CONSISTENCY: The understanding that the physical characteristics of an object remain unchanged even when the object is viewed from a different angle or distance

OBJECT PERMANENCE: The understanding that an object exists even when it cannot be directly perceived

OBSERVATIONAL LEARNING: Acquiring knowledge, skills, or behaviors by watching others

ONLOOKER PLAY: Play in which one child watches one or more children play

OPERANT CONDITIONING: Learning that results from repeated reinforcement or punishment

PARALLEL PLAY: Play in which children play side by side but each engages in different activities

PEERS: Children of approximately the same age

PERCEPTION: The process of interpreting input from the senses

PERCEPTION BOUND: The immature tendency to make decisions only on the basis of what one perceives, ignoring experience and other factors

PROJECTION: The tendency to attribute one's own unacceptable thoughts or behaviors to others

PROSOCIAL BEHAVIOR: Behavior that promotes social interaction, such as helping, sharing, and cooperating

PROXIMODISTAL DEVELOPMENT: Development that takes place from the center of the body outward

RECEPTIVE LANGUAGE: A young child's nonverbal response to adult speech

REFLEX: An involuntary response of the body to a stimulus

REGRESSION: Retreat to an earlier developmental level

RESPONSE: Any behavior or psychological reaction produced by a stimulus

SCHEMA: A mental representation of an idea or event

SEMANTICS: The study of the meaning of words and sentences

SEPARATION ANXIETY: An apprehensive or fearful response by a child to separation from the habitual care giver

SEX ROLES: A certain set of behaviors expected of and considered appropriate for each sex

SHORT-TERM MEMORY: Type of memory in which stored information can only be recalled for a short period of time

SOCIALIZATION: The process by which a child learns the accepted values and behaviors of his society

SOLITARY PLAY: Playing alone

STIMULUS: Something that evokes a response

STRANGER ANXIETY: An apprehensive or fearful response to unfamiliar people

TELEGRAPHIC SPEECH: An abbreviated form of speech in which only the essential words are included, without modifiers, articles, etc.

TEMPERAMENT: An individual's unique response to situations and people

THEORY: A general principle that attempts to explain the relationships among a number of facts or conditions

INDEX